THE CREATIVE PROCESS
OF PSYCHOTHERAPY

NORTON PROFESSIONAL BOOKS

THE CREATIVE PROCESS OF PSYCHOTHERAPY

Albert Rothenberg, M.D.

DIRECTOR OF RESEARCH, AUSTEN RIGGS CENTER
CLINICAL PROFESSOR OF PSYCHIATRY, HARVARD UNIVERSITY
MEDICAL SCHOOL AT CAMBRIDGE HOSPITAL

W · W · Norton & Company · New York · London

Copyright © 1988, by Albert Rothenberg, M.D.

Published simultaneously in Canada by Penguin Books Canada Ltd., 2801 John Street, Markham, Ontario L3R 1B4.
Printed in the United States of America.

First Edition

Library of Congress Cataloging-in-Publication Data

Rothenberg, Albert, 1930–
  The creative process of psychotherapy.

  "A Norton professional book." – P. facing t.p.
  Includes index.
  1. Psychotherapy. I. Title. [DNLM: 1. Psychotherapy–methods. WM 420 R846c]
RC480.R668 1988   616.89′14   87-23964

ISBN   0-393-70046-1

W. W. Norton & Company, Inc., 500 Fifth Avenue, New York, N.Y. 10110

W. W. Norton & Company Ltd., 37 Great Russell Street, London WC1B 3NU

1 2 3 4 5 6 7 8 9 0

The picture is not thought out and determined beforehand, rather while it is being made it follows the mobility of thought. Finished, it changes further, according to the condition of him who looks at it. A picture lives its life like a living creature, undergoing the changes that daily life imposes upon us.

Pablo Picasso

I feel recently that I am seeing and experiencing things that I never paid any attention to before. I see new streets when I drive my car, and I actually have noticed some birds in a tree. When I came to work the other day, I became aware of parts of the hallway going in that I never realized were there. And people—I hear different things in what they say. Instead of walking out when I feel threatened, I decide to stay.

Patient in psychotherapy

Acknowledgments

Material contained in this book has appeared in other versions in the *Journal of the American Academy of Psychoanalysis* and in *Psychoanalysis and Contemporary Thought*. I gratefully acknowledge the interest, cooperation, and generous expenditure of time and effort of my research subjects—both named and anonymous—and the instructive therapeutic work of my patients—all anonymous. Also, my appreciation goes to the staff of the Austen Riggs Center for their cooperation, counsel, and high level of clinical performance with both inpatients and outpatients that served as a current background for materials and formulations presented here. Special gratitude is due to Dr. Daniel P. Schwartz, Medical Director, for his administrative support and for his own consistent example of highly creative therapeutic work.

For various types of contributions, I thank the Trustees of the Austen Riggs Center, Dr. Leo Goldberger, Susan Barrows, Dr. Alan and Eva Leveton, Dr. William B. Johnson, Jackie Cunningham, Kathleen Much, the staff of the Center for Advanced Study in the Behavioral Sciences, and members of the psychiatry departments at the University of Rochester, Columbia University, Dartmouth College, Northwestern University, as well as the American College of Psychoanalysts, who heard portions of this work in progress. Helen E. Linton, librarian of the Austen Riggs Center, provided invaluable bibliographic and reference help and Virginia Heaton expertly and diligently word processed this book into being. My wife, Dr. Julia J. Rothenberg, contributed her own exceptional clinical acumen, editorial and conceptual advice, and her constant and extraordinary love.

Partial support for this project was provided by the following: Gladys B. Ficke Fund; the Center for Advanced Study in the Behavioral Sciences, Dr.

Gardner Lindzey, Director; John D. and Catherine T. MacArthur Foundation.

*   *   *

The use of the masculine pronoun throughout this book, especially as a generic for both patients and therapists, is not intended to be sexist. The purpose is solely simplicity and smoothness of style and description. In its uniformity, it incidentally reverses a subtly sexist tendency in past works on psychotherapy that used the masculine pronoun for the therapist and the female one for the patient.

Contents

Introduction

Treatment of illness through psychotherapy is a demanding task. All of us who practice this procedure experience serious demands and frustrations, but interestingly, we also have the sense of engaging in an especially worthy endeavor. What is there about the experience that gives us such a feeling? Surely, we are not merely grandiose professionals who have gathered together to carry out practices that feed our own self-esteem. Surely, we are not guided by quasi-religious or mystical beliefs that we try to impart to our patients. On the contrary, feeling that we practice without belief or illusion to any large degree, most of us pride ourselves in appraising reality well and avoiding excessive value judgments. Yet, something especially worthwhile seems to be occurring. The patient tells us this, often in an exaggerated way, but even after those exaggerations are analyzed and discounted, the feeling remains. It is an anticipation of experiencing this special worthiness that often carries us through the sometimes wearisome and frustrating hours, days, and years of difficult therapies.

We cannot rest on any laurels, however. Neither the difficulty nor the sense of worthiness justifies taking full satisfaction in our treatments as either excellently done or resulting in completely realized amelioration or cure. Long before psychotherapy was challenged by biochemical and neurobiological knowledge and advances, as it is today, there was a need to improve practice. No therapy used today can claim to be fully developed, either in theory or practice, and none can claim widespread effectiveness. Although there are surely many explanations available for this state of affairs, such as inadequate knowledge of the psychosociobiological bases of human development and behavior, as claimed by experimentalists and theorists, or inadequate use of certain approaches to patients or clients, as claimed by followers of particular schools or orientations, I shall here claim yet another one. I believe there is no theory of psychotherapeutic practice, systematically drawing on current psychological knowledge of development and behavior, that clearly points to areas requiring improvement. In short, there is no general conception of treatment that requires a therapist to perform at the highest level of which he is capable.

In proposing here a conception of psychotherapy that taps a therapist's highest resources, I need first to address the paradox of a healing procedure based on scientific and objective precepts that incorporates strong moral and aesthetic values of personal dignity and freedom, respect for uniqueness and choice, and a certain emphasis on intuition and imagination. It appears that our best therapists have these paradoxical qualities; they are highly rigorous, consistent, and logical, and they also allow themselves free rein on their intuitiveness and imagination. They are scientific and rely on system-atic data and theory, and they are aesthetic in their appreciation of intensity, narrative, interpretation, and leaps of understanding. To some extent this paradox is the bane of our psychotherapeutic existences. Because we value the aesthetic and humane side of psychic experience, and because we value intuitive understanding, we are accused of lacking scientific understanding. Indeed, we are accused of lacking any science at all. That this accusation is patently false in that there need be no cancelling out of science in an aesthetic perspective, and that the aesthetic perspective is itself amenable to systematic scientific study, analysis, and understanding, is a major point of this book.

The reason for the paradox, as well as the answer to the puzzling question about the sense of special worthiness of psychotherapy, is that the process of therapy is a creative one. The creativity involved in the therapeu-tic experience is one of the factors that touches on aesthetics, scientific imagination, and matters of value and worth. In the material to follow, I shall attempt to show that psychotherapy shares many constituents with creative processes in other fields such as the arts and the sciences. The relationship is not merely a matter of analogues and analogies; rather, we find that the most effective psychotherapist uses particular creative opera-tions in treatment.

Not so fast, you say. Creativity is a very complicated and a difficult matter to talk about and study. Many people have opinions about it but little concrete evidence is brought forth. Also, definitions of creativity are often ignored in general conversations and even in professional literature and, when they are given, they frequently are not fully applicable. Issues of elitism and democracy enter in as well. Is creativity the province only of geniuses or is everyone potentially creative? Or, less extreme, is there a qualitative difference between high-level creativity and other types, or is it a matter of degree?

All of these concerns and questions are appropriate and meaningful, and my replies are both explicitly and implicitly given in connection with the approaches outlined in this book. First, however, the red thread that runs through the questions and my discussion of psychotherapy should be teased out and looked at. This is the fact that creativity is a highly esteemed matter in our culture and society. The topic generates many questions and strong opinions just because it is so perfused with positive value. Although the literal definitions of "create" and "creativity" consist only of "bringing something into being" and "the capacity or state of bringing something into being," respectively, the terms usually connote far more in usage. Almost always we employ the terms in an honorific sense. The entity brought into being is either intrinsically valuable or useful in some distinct way.

In addition, when the terms are applied in the arts and sciences and other fields involving specially valued activities, they usually involve the idea of bringing into being something new. Simply making something that has been made before, such as a part for an automobile, is not considered creating, although the term may sometimes be used that way in ordinary conversation. Now, if we take the idea of the "new" or of "newness" seriously, we must consider whether there is some sort of break or discontinuity with the past in the course of a creative process. Something really new must be radically different from anything that existed before. Although there are many elements that imitate and repeat the past in a created artwork or a creative discovery or theory in science, there would need to be some break with the past if these contained something truly new and unfamiliar.

Creativity and the creative process, in the definition I shall follow here, are the state, capacities, and conditions of bringing forth entities or events that are *both* new and valuable. Given such a definition of the phenomenon, how could a scientist really ever hope to bring forth valid evidence about it, as I have suggested one could? Value is surely difficult for science to deal with because it is so variable and imbued with subjective judgment. On top of that, discontinuity in natural events, suggested by the aspect of newness, is a very difficult problem because the scientific approach characteristically involves tracing out continuous sequences and looking for correlated events, interlocking causes, or other invariant connections between past, present, and future.

From the beginning, I have geared my research on the creative process toward taking these serious problems into consideration. Rather than using standard psychological tests, life history interviews, or a general approach to a creative person's life work, I first adopted an exploratory approach. If new processes and phenomena were to be investigated, I would therefore try to document them as they first appeared and subsequently unfolded. In order to ensure as much as possible that the particular sequence I was studying would result in products of value, I would explore the unfolding phenomena with people who had previously had a high degree of creative success. Also, in order to find out whether creative capacities existed in everyone, I would proceed to study creativity in persons who were by general consensus considered to be creative and then see if there were qualitative and quantitative differences. I would study high-level creativity to start.

To do this, I developed an interview approach focused on work in progress. Starting the inquiry with the creative work and tracing psychological processes related to the production of that work increased the likelihood that any findings would be directly related to the creative process. I chose initially to carry out the research with literary creative persons because I knew literature fairly well and also because I suspected that factors in verbal creativity might be directly applicable to the verbal interaction of psychotherapy.

In addition to research with contemporary subjects, I attempted to take into consideration the important criterion that creative accomplishments are assessed over time; they must meet the so-called "test of time." Through a special technique of studying manuscript revisions of writers of the past, such as Eugene O'Neill and Maxwell Anderson, and developing and assessing predictions with independently gathered life history data, a retrospective study of literary creative processes was achieved. For example, after manuscript studies were completed, O'Neill's surviving widow, Carlotta Monterrey O'Neill, and Anderson's eldest son, Quentin Anderson, were interviewed and hypotheses were independently assessed. Later, as findings began to develop, I applied both similar and different types of research methodology to creativity in visual art and science. In addition to interviews, an extended series of experimental studies with creative and noncreative subjects from several different fields was carried out by myself and colleagues.

Side by side with these investigations I have continued to practice psychotherapy and to observe the therapeutic work of my colleagues and supervisees. Considering relationships between specific research findings and the practice and theory of psychotherapy has borne fruit. It has helped account for the sense of worthiness of the therapeutic endeavor and, in reciprocal fashion, enriched my understanding of creative processes of all types. The conclusions and the extensions of those conclusions discussed in the pages to follow were the result.

THE CREATIVE PROCESS
OF PSYCHOTHERAPY

CHAPTER I

The Creative Process of Psychotherapy

The propositions I shall present derive from findings about psychological processes involved in creativity in the arts and in science. These findings consist primarily of special types of cognitive, motivational, and affective processes operating at all phases of the creative process. Discovered initially through intensive and extensive research interviews with highly creative research subjects, not patients in therapy, they have been further demonstrated through objective psychological and quantitative analyses of creative works in progress, and through experiments involving creative persons and controls.[1] Research subjects have consisted of Nobel Prize laureates in science and literature, awardees of distinctions such as the Pulitzer Prize, National and American Book Awards, Bowdoin Poetry Prize, and other literary prizes, membership in United States and British institutes and academies of arts and sciences, or science alone, as well as neophyte and potentially creative persons from a wide age range.

Initially, this research consisted of a series of intensive interviews with highly outstanding American poets, novelists, and playwrights during a period of their lives when they were actively engaged in some particular creative work. Located throughout the continental United States, these persons were offered pay for participation in the project and they agreed to submit to me their ongoing manuscript work in progress prior to our sessions. We met regularly on a weekly or biweekly basis for periods of more than two years in many cases (from the inception to the time of publication of the work), and our sessions focused directly on work in progress. Starting with the manuscript material, we discussed the following:

nature and source of revisions, themes, fantasies, inspirations; dreams and life experience connected with the work; affects, thought processes, and conflicts occurring during composition and in the interim periods. Although current psychological processes were in the forefront of the research interview, childhood background, previous writings, and other past information also became pertinent. We met regularly, whether or not manuscript material was produced, and I assured the subjects of anonymity and confidentiality.[2] A similar but modified research design was also applied later to creative persons in the visual arts and in science. More than 75 such subjects have been interviewed for a total of more than 1800 hours.

The experimental studies were based on hypotheses developed during the interview studies and involved presentation of specially constructed visual stimuli and the administration of word association tasks. Subjects ranging from highly talented college students to Nobel laureates in science were tested or exposed to experimental manipulations, and intergroup and intragroup control comparisons were made. More than 1,000 persons have been subjects in these experiments, and results have confirmed specific hypotheses and supported interview findings that I shall present.

In applying these findings to the theory and practice of psychotherapy, I shall be directly concerned neither with the therapeutic value of creative activities nor with the psychotherapy of highly creative people, although most of what follows should have some pertinence to both. My purpose is the direct application of specific creativity findings to psychotherapy: How can an understanding of the kinds of thinking involved in the creation of art and literature, and in the attainment of outstanding discoveries in science, apply directly to the treatment of mental illness?

To propose some answers to this question, I shall first adopt the broadest possible perspective on the general issue of mental illness. I do this especially because we are today beset with much pressure from those who insist that we should only be tracing physiological factors in mental illness and only treating such illness to the extent that it is physiological. There is a hue and cry that treatment should "get back" to medicine, and this means to "get back" to the biochemical and the clearly observable. It behooves us, therefore, to consider whether there is a specific common ground between psychological and physiological factors in illness of all kinds.

Let us assess the fundamental issue of normality. As we well know, the definition of psychological normality is very difficult. With so-called physiological normality and illness the definition seems much simpler and more clear-cut. When one contracts pneumonia with cough, sputum, and fever, neither one's organs nor oneself is functioning. At that point, one is not normal. To be normal, it is necessary to return to the way one was before the pneumonia. The deficiency must be corrected and then one will be "like everyone else"—lungs and person will function like the average or like the majority of persons and organs do. But with mental health and illness we will not accept this notion of the average or the majority as normal. Even in this country, which so strongly emphasizes democracy and equality, I believe that no one—neither patients nor therapists—would say that mental health is equivalent to being average or being the same as everyone else. Furthermore, returning to the average, or even to a previous state, may realistically not be sufficient for ameliorating mental illness. Once one has such an illness, almost invariably there are continued problems.

This also applies in a lesser way to physiological illness. After having pneumonia, one is never—even after having stayed in bed, received penicillin or some other medication, and eventually recovered—the way one was before. The diseased lung area is permanently scarred. Such a scar is rather minuscule, but it is nevertheless a residuum for life. Everyone is permanently affected by every disease he has. With the scar on the lung, of course, there is a deficiency, but it will not lead to recurrence of pneumonia unless there is further direct exposure to an infectious organism.

Psychologically, however, the problem of deficiency is both more insidious and more extensive, because patients (N.B., all human beings) are continually exposed to psychological dangers or threats comparable to invading organisms. In attempting to help someone return to functioning, much more is involved than for the doctor to administer penicillin. With the scar of mental illness, the person needs to be able to adapt *better* to his environment than before, and often to adapt better to his environment than others who have not been scarred. Growth is necessary for effective improvement.

Even if therapists did not often see things this way, patients would not allow them to think differently. Not only is it difficult with a particular patient to clarify the meaning of the therapeutic goal of helping him "function," but the patient usually rejects such a term or such a goal out of hand. Nor do patients accept the aims of "coping" or "adjusting," or even "adapting," very readily. They want to be better than they were, or better than others, and thereby able to deal with the constantly problematic environment human beings live in. In other words, both patients and therapists are oriented to, and engaged in, facilitating *creation*. Both are focused on the patient's creation of aspects of his personality, and both are engaged in an ongoing mutual creative process that involves the patient's personality attributes and personality structure.[3]

By creation of personality attributes and structure, I mean something directly analogous to creation in the prototypical areas of the arts and sciences. As in the latter areas, there is also in psychotherapy the production of both the new and the valuable. The patient develops better personality attributes and structure—these are valuable both to the patient and to society at large. Moreover, these personality features are new to the patient because they result in part from a break with the past. Because they are unique to that individual, as all actively developed attributes intrinsically are, they are new to the world as well.

Psychotherapy therefore is intrinsically a mutual process of facilitating creation of aspects of the patient's personality, and the better the therapy the greater the degree of mutual creation. As therapists we focus on the past, or on the present and future, because the past or elements from it have become restrictive for the patient. To the extent that the patient becomes free from the past, he is in a position to make new choices actively and to adopt new alternatives. These choices arise from the patient's conscious and unconscious, cognitive and affective, decisions about what type of person he is and what type of person he wants to be. As clear-cut aspects of the creative process, such choices are based in part on a sense or a knowledge of the effects of the past and thus are free of the restrictions of the past; they are particularly free of the repetition compulsion. But there is also a continuity with the past; the patient makes choices partly on the basis of what he knows or senses to be the determined and fixed aspects of himself. He accepts factors in his past which cannot, or need not, be changed. When a radically innovative artist such as Paul Cezanne creates a new mode in painting, this is not totally divorced from anything that was ever done before. We appreciate the accomplishment of Cezanne partly because his work has links and continuity with that of past artists, especially the Impressionists.

Often what the patient chooses may not coincide with the therapist's own personal preferences. Nevertheless, at the points when such choices are made, it is incumbent on the therapist to be facilitative or, at least, not to interfere. Such points are not always easy to identify; they are manifest when the patient indicates thoughts and feelings involving freedom from past restrictions and determinants and an active pursuit of self-directed and self-defining goals. When these emerge, the good therapist knows that he must listen in a way that allows them to develop and evolve. In a similar way, creative artists sometimes interact in a facilitative or a non-interfering way with developing forms and structures in their materials.

In order to collaborate in the mutual creative process, the therapist uses a wide variety of technical procedures and approaches. Clarification, interpretation, confrontation, education, exhortation, and non-intervention all play a role. Furthermore, as psychotherapy must be based on science, the therapist must derive his technical approaches from a systematic body of knowledge and theory. He translates his assumptions into hypotheses that he tests and assesses to some degree in an ongoing way through his work with patients. While a freeing-up from the past is one aspect of psychotherapy that facilitates creation, particular additional factors must be involved.

An understanding of particular psychological factors involved in the creative process enables the therapist to apply and assess hypotheses about creativity directly in his therapeutic work. Also, it is desirable for the therapist himself to function creatively in order to initiate and facilitate the patient's engagement in the creative work. Beyond direct creative effects, modeling is necessary. Although therapists correctly discourage a patient's attempt to become just like, or a carbon copy, of themselves, some degree of modeling seems to be an inevitable and positive component of the therapeutic process.[4] Given such inevitable modeling, could a therapist expect the patient to undergo the enormous risk of changing himself and of actually engaging in creation if the therapist himself is unwilling to take any risks? To move with the patient toward the valuable and the new, the therapist should take risks, think flexibly, and engage in the highest degree of creativity of which he is capable. I specifically propose that he become familiar with, or enlarge on, and employ particular psychological modes and approaches used in creative processes.

HOMOSPATIAL PROCESS

One of these modes, discovered in the art and science researches, is the homospatial process (Greek: *homoios* = same). This process consists of *actively conceiving two or more discrete entities occupying the same space, a conception leading to the articulation of new identities*.[5] In the course of creating literary characters, metaphors, complete works of art, or scientific theories, creative persons actively conceive images and representations of multiple entities as superimposed within the same spatial location. These sharply distinct and independent elements may be represented as discrete colors, sounds, etc., organized objects such as knives and human faces, or more complex organizations such as entire landscape scenes, or else a series of sensory patterns or written words together with their concrete or abstract meanings. This conception is a figurative and abstract one in the sense that it represents nothing that has ever existed in reality; it is one of the bases for constructive and creative imagination. One of the tenets known from universal sensory experience is that two objects or two discrete entities can *never* occupy the same space. Nor can more than two. The creative person, however, brings *multiple* entities together in a mental conception for the purpose of producing new and valuable ideas, images, sound patterns, and metaphors.

Because of the difficulty in maintaining multiple elements in the same spatial location, the homospatial conception is frequently a rapid, fleeting, and transitory mental experience. Although this form of cognition often involves the visual sensory modality, and like all constructive imagination is probably easiest to describe in visual terms, the superimposed entities may be derived from any one of the sensory modalities. There may be entities and sensations of the gustatory, olfactory, auditory, kinesthetic, or tactile type.

The homospatial process is a special type of secondary process cognition; it is neither primary process thinking or a form of "regression in the service of the ego."[6] Nor is it a form of condensation or displacement, despite the sharing of superficial similarities such as the breaking of spatial restrictions. It is a specific ego function that serves to produce creative and adaptive results.

Unlike primary process condensation, the homospatial process involves no spatial substitutions or compromise formations, but sensory entities are consciously and intentionally conceived as occupying an identical spatial location. This produces a hazy and unstable mental percept rather than the vivid images characteristically due to primary process, because consciously superimposed discrete spatial elements cannot be held in exactly the same place. From this unstable image, a new identity then is articulated in the form of a metaphor or other type of aesthetic or scientific unity. Also, whereas in primary process condensation aspects of various entities are *combined* in the same spatial area in order to represent all of those entities at once, the homospatial process involves no combinations but rather whole images *interacting and competing* for the same location. For example, a patient's dream about a man named Lipstein is reported by Grinstein[7] and shown to be a clear-cut instance of a condensation of the names Grinstein and Lipschutz. Rather than such a compromise formation in a mental image which necessarily involves change or transformation of one or both of the elements entering into the compromise, the homospatial process operating with these same name elements would instead involve mental images of the full names Grinstein and Lipschutz as neither combined nor modified nor adjusted but visualized unchanged within exactly the same mentally depicted space.

Although the homospatial process involves sensory images and the alteration of ordinary perceptual experience, it is a conscious, deliberate, and reality-oriented mode of cognition. Ordinary perceptual experience is consciously manipulated and mentally transcended in order to create new and valuable entities. The homospatial process is a type of logic-transcending operation that I have called a "translogical process."[8] Such a process deals with reality by improving upon it. As reality-oriented, reality-transcending, and deliberate, it is a part of the secondary process mode.

Examples of this process that I have previously described are a poet research subject's superimposition of the mental image of a horse together with the mental image of a man. This complex concatenation of images led to a central creation in a poem concerning the alienation of modern man. Constructed as a metaphorical description and poetic "image," this central creation presented the horse and rider as virtually fused, as follows:

> Meadows received us, heady with unseen lilac.
> Brief, polyphonic lives abounded everywhere.
> With one accord we circled the small lake.[9]

Also, playwright Arthur Miller told me, in the course of a research interview, that his initial conception of the play "Death of a Salesman" consisted of superimposed mental images of a man occupying the same space as the inside of his own head. Novelist Robert Penn Warren indicated that he created the character Jack Burden in his famous novel *All the King's Men* from a mental superimposition of his self-image or self-representation upon the mental images or representations of a young man he had known. A Nobel laureate microbiologist reported that he visualized himself superimposed upon an atom in an enzyme molecule in the process of constructing a new scientific theory. From another source than my own researches, Pyle has reported that the scientist Fuller Albright developed innovative and useful formulations of cellular mechanisms "by thinking of himself as a cell."[10]

Experimental assessment of the creative effect of the homospatial process has been carried out by means of an externalized concrete representation of the mental conception consisting of transilluminated superimposed slide images.[11] In one experiment the function of the process in literary creativity was assessed. Ten pairs of slide images, specially constructed to represent literary themes of love, animals, war, aging, etc., were projected superimposed and side-by-side respectively to an experimental and matched control group of creative writers. An example of superimposition of one of the image pairs, consisting of nuns in front of St. Peter's and racing jockeys, is shown in Figure 1. Subjects in both groups were instructed to produce short literary metaphors inspired by each of the projected images. Results were that metaphors produced in response to the superimposed images, representing externalizations of the homospatial conception, were "blindly" rated significantly more highly creative by independent writer judges than the metaphors produced in response to the side-by-side images. By shortening time of exposure of the projected images and encouraging mental imaging in another identically designed experiment with other creative writer groups, results were produced that supported the conclusion that creative effects were due to *mental superimposition* of imagery.

In order to trace connections between the visually stimulated homospatial conception and a visual creative result, and to replicate the findings in artistic creativity, another experiment was carried out with visual artists. Subjects were asked to create pastel drawings in response to either superimposed or side-by-side slide images under the same experimental conditions

FIGURE 1: An example of a superimposed (homospatial) stimulus. The slide photograph of the nuns at bottom left is projected on a screen together with the slide photograph of the jockeys at bottom right to produce the superimposed effect at the top [originals in color].

as in the literary experiment. Independent artist and art critic judges rated the products and the superimposed image presentation resulted in significantly more highly creative drawings. Also, specific features of line, color, etc., of the drawings themselves gave evidence that they were produced from superimposed mental representations.

Another experiment was carried out with highly talented, award-winning artists to assess whether the results of all the previous experiments could have been due to stimulus presentation effects. Single images were constructed to represent composite foreground-background displays of the same slide pairs used in transilluminated superimposition. This experiment also showed significantly higher rated created products in response to the superimposed images. All the experiments together indicate a distinct connection between consciously constructed superimposed images representing the homospatial conception and the production of creative effects.

JANUSIAN PROCESS

The term I have used for another creative function derives from the qualities of the Roman god, Janus. This god, a very important one in the Roman list, had faces that looked in diametrically opposite directions simultaneously. As the god of entryways and doorways, he was able to look both inside and outside at once. Very likely this function became symbolically elaborated because he was also the god of beginnings who looked both backwards and forwards—commemorated by the calendar use of his name in the month January—and in several myths he was considered the creator of the world. Although he is often depicted as having two faces (*Janus bifrons*), Roman doorways were multifaceted, having four or even six entryways, and in Roman literature he is described variously as having two, four, or six faces, all looking in opposite directions.[12] On the basis of this feature, and his mythological importance, I have used his name for another empirical finding, the janusian process.

The janusian process consists of *actively conceiving two or more opposites or antitheses simultaneously*. During the course of the creative process, opposite or antithetical ideas, concepts, or propositions are deliberately and consciously conceptualized side-by-side and/or as coexisting *simultaneously*. Although seemingly illogical and self-contradictory, these formulations are constructed in clearly logical and rational states of mind in order to produce creative effects. They occur as early conceptions in the development of artworks and scientific theories and at critical junctures at middle and later

stages as well. Because they serve generative functions during both formative and critical stages of the creative process, these conceptions usually
undergo transformation and modification and are seldom directly discerni-
ble in final created products. They are formulated by the creative thinker as
central ideas for a plot, character, artistic composition, or as solutions in
working out practical and scientific tasks.

Simultaneity of the multiple opposites or antitheses is a cardinal feature.
Opposite or antithetical ideas, beliefs, concepts, or propositions are formulated as simultaneously operating, valid, or true. Firmly held propositions,
for example, about the laws of nature, the functioning of individuals and
groups, and the aesthetic properties of visual and sound patterns are conceived as simultaneously true and not-true. Or, opposite or antithetical
propositions are entertained as concomitantly operative. A person running
is both in motion and not in motion at the same time, a chemical is both
boiling and freezing, or kindness and sadism operate simultaneously. Previously held beliefs or laws are still considered valid but opposite or antithetical beliefs and laws are formulated as equally operative or valid as well.

These formulations within the janusian process are waystations to creative effects and outcomes. They interact and join with other cognitive and
affective developments to produce new and valuable products. One of these
developments may be a later interaction with unifying homospatial process
effects. Others may be the use of analogic, dialectic, inductive, and deductive reasoning to develop theories, inventions, and artworks. The janusian
process usually begins with the recognition and choice of salient opposites
and antitheses in a scientific, cultural, or aesthetic field, progresses to the
formulation of these factors operating simultaneously, and then to elaborated creations. For example, in an interview with one of my poet research
subjects carried out shortly after he had begun the earlier mentioned poem
concerning the alienation of modern man, he described a germinating idea
involving the formulation that a horse was simultaneously both a beast and
not-a-beast, and also both human and not-human. This formulation developed from his chance encounter some time earlier with a horse in Arizona's
Monument Valley which evoked thoughts regarding separation and opposition between human and animal species. Over the following several weeks,
he engaged in various types of thinking—including the construction of
other homospatial and janusian formulations—and constructed a five stanza
poem in which the initial idea was transformed and elaborated. The final
lines of the poem referred to that initial idea in the following way:

> About the ancient bond between her [the horse] kind and mine
> Little more to speak of can be done.[13]

Numerous other research subjects have also described central formulations and breakthroughs for novels, plays, and scientific discoveries that manifested simultaneous antithesis or opposition. Playwright Arthur Miller told me that his initial idea for the play "Incident at Vichy" consisted of conceiving both the beauty and growth of modern Germany and Hitler's destructiveness simultaneously. In science, Nobel laureate Edwin McMillan's formulation of "critical phase stability" leading to his development of the synchrocyclotron (later called the synchrotron) was derived from a sudden realization involving simultaneous opposition. The synchrotron is a high energy particle accelerator that has allowed for the discovery of a number of new particles and other nuclear effects. McMillan described the sequence of events to me in the following verbatim transcription:

It was in the month of July. I think it was the month of July. I didn't put down the date—I should record these things. It was night. I was lying awake in bed and thinking of a way of getting high energy and I was thinking of the cyclotron and the particle going around and encountering the accelerator field—the right phase each time around. And I thought of what will happen if the resonance is wrong, if the period is wrong, what will happen? And I sort of analyzed in my mind that it's going around and it's being accelerated, and it's getting heavier; therefore, it's taking more time to get around, and it will fall out of step. *Then it gets behind and it gets the opposite sense. It gets pushed back again, so it will oscillate. It's going to oscillate back and forth, be going at too high and too low energy*. Once I realized that, then the rest was easy.[14]

If the timing is wrong, it's not going to fall completely out of step but it will overshoot and come back. Phase stability, I call it phase stability. The very next day I called it phase stability. Phase is the relation—time relation—of what you're worried about. Stability implies that it clings to a certain value. It may oscillate about, but it clings to a certain fixed value.

Here, McMillan described the sudden formulation of a critical concept that led to the construction of the synchrotron. He conceived the simultaneously opposite states of too high and too low energy. Realizing that out-of-step particles would fall back in the accelerator field, he grasped the idea that these particles would be forced to accelerate. Consequently, they would oscillate and be both too high and too low in energy with respect to the overall accelerator field. They would be lower in energy because they were heavier and out of phase and would be also higher in energy because they would overshoot. Consequently, they would be stable overall with respect to the field. As McMillan told me in further elaboration: "Once you have an oscillation, you have the element of stability. The things will stay put. They will wiggle around but they won't get away from you. Then all you have to do is to vary your frequency, or vary the magnetic field, either one or both, slowly, and you can push this thing anywhere you want. That all happened one night and the next day I started to write down the equations for that and proved that it would work."

Other research subjects in both art and science have also described such janusian formulations. Outside of data from my direct investigations with living creative persons, I have in addition presented detailed documentary evidence indicating that both Albert Einstein and Niels Bohr used a janusian process in the development of the general theory of relativity and the theory of complementarity, respectively.[15] For Einstein, the key formulation providing the "physical basis" of the general theory—what he called "the happiest thought of my life"—consisted of the idea that a person falling from the roof of a house was both in motion and in rest at the same time. For Niels Bohr, his initial formulation of complementarity—the theoretical construct on which quantum physics is based—was that light and electrons possessed antithetical wave and particle features simultaneously.

A tendency or capacity for the use of the janusian process, manifested by rapid opposite responding on word association tasks, has also been identified experimentally. Standard Kent-Rosanoff word association tests were individually administered to rated-as-creative[16] college students and business executives and to Nobel laureates in science. Control groups consisted of matched but rated-less-creative students and business executives, and high IQ psychiatric patients. Test instructions were to give the first word that came to mind in response to a standardized list of word stimuli; both speed and content of response were electronically recorded. The experimenters made special attempts to reduce any anxiety related to testing in order to ensure spontaneous and valid associational responses. After factoring out any tendency to give common and popular types of responses, results indicated a significantly higher number of rapid opposite responses given by creative subjects than by subjects in any of the control groups.[17] Speed of opposite responding among creative subjects in these experiments was extremely rapid, averaging 1.1 to 1.2 seconds from the time the experimenter spoke the stimulus word, suggesting the formulation of simultaneous, or virtually simultaneous, opposite associations.

In the chapters to follow, I shall discuss the specific ways these two processes, homospatial and janusian, are used to facilitate the mutual creative process of psychotherapy. To some degree, they are part of every creative therapist's function and skill, and to some degree, they must be further developed. I shall explore metaphor as therapeutic intervention, empathy, grasp of conflict, paradoxical and ironic interventions, and error in the overall context of treatment, and describe the ongoing and overall creative function of the process of articulation. In the final chapter I shall discuss the patient's active creative role and the reasons for the therapeutic effect.

Before embarking on this detailed exposition of the creative process of psychotherapy, I shall turn to a broader aspect of the therapist's creative functioning and one that serves as a background for some of the specific operations. In describing this next factor, the focus on form in creative activities, I shall take an opportunity to set up a slight mystery at the start.

CHAPTER II

Form and Function in Psychotherapy

The following verbatim interchange[1] occurred at the end of a female patient's fifth psychotherapy session (P = patient; Th = therapist):

P: Well I . . well I know for one thing that I, at least as I am now, unless something would just completely go off, that I . . could *never* take my own life. Goodness knows, I . . I'd . . I am just not made that way.

TH: Mm-hmm.

P: And that's the pity of it, 'cause I'm sure I'd have done it fifty times by now.

TH: Really!

P: Not . . I . . I can't ever think . . specifically in terms of . . suicide. I can just feel awful sorry for myself and wish I were dead. But—

TH: Does that mean that during this past week or two you have, on occasion, had feelings that were so painful that it seemed to you—

P: Yeah, I just . . as I lay awake . . [at] night and couldn't . . just couldn't see *any* direction out of it, and . . then I wished that there would be some way that I could go to sleep and never wake up in the morning.

TH: Oh yeah.

P: But it didn't occur to me to go out and turn the gas on.

TH: Mm-hmm.

P: I mean . . if I ever am faced with a realistic possibility like that, then I . . .

16

TH: Yeah.

P: . . . know what the decision is.

TH: I don't think you should be alarmed.[2]

Hearing this from a patient we, however, might well be alarmed. It is likely, of course, that the therapist is really also alarmed and that his quick reassurance is probably directed both at himself and the patient as he listens to her manifestly denied but nevertheless threatening references to suicidal intent. Should he, or we, be seriously alarmed at hearing such content of dialogue in a therapy session? After all, suicide is a serious risk of mental and emotional illness and we must—although committed to understanding the meaning of a patient's communications—be ready to act to prevent suicide and the end of a patient's life and therapy.

To answer the question about whether to be alarmed, all but the most impulsive and risk-taking therapist would, I assume, want to know more. Certainly that seems a reasonable request, but my next question then is: What type of information would be most helpful? Would it be necessary to know the patient's history, diagnosis, and the kind of material that would help to construct a detailed psychodynamic formulation of her difficulties? Of course, all that would be helpful, would be used in treatment, and might directly answer the initial question. But I doubt it. Primarily, such material would add more *content* to the information we already have and this content could not clarify the circumstances under which the above interchange occurred. It would not, in other words, give information about the context in which the patient's remarks were made and would not therefore enable us to follow the *form or structure* of the therapy session. A focus on the form would, I believe, give a better answer to the question than content information alone. For example, a key to my answer may be partially derived from formal information I have already provided that the interchange occurred at the end of a therapy session. More information about the session itself, therefore, will be necessary. Before providing it, however, I want to clarify what I mean by a focus on form or structure (I shall use these two terms interchangeably throughout).

Form or structure in psychotherapy is the same as in any creative activity.[3] Form consists of the shape or organization of something rather than of the material of which it is composed.[4] It includes the patient's tone of voice, posture, and facial expressions and, more important, the patterns, sequences, and organization of communications and interactions. It consists of the manner and method of production—the container, so to speak, rather than the contained. In artistic fields, form or structure consists of patterns, sequences, and organization in the same way. In poetry, there are formal composition types such as lyrics, ballads, sonnets, epics, as well as formal general features such as stanza, rhythm, rhyme, and tropes. In visual art, there are also formal composition types such as abstract and realistic, and formal general features such as color, pattern, and composition. With regard to music, formal features are almost too numerous to list. Indeed, for this reason, music is sometimes considered to be virtually a purely formal type of art. "All art constantly aspires towards the condition of music," said Walter Pater[5] and by this he meant that art aspires to be primarily, or completely, a matter of form. Scientific theories and discoveries also have formal properties that I shall go into later.

Although Pater's statement is probably overblown, at least as far as aesthetic appreciation is concerned, a focus on form is a significant aspect of the creative process in all fields. This focus on form includes both janusian and homospatial processes, which are formally oriented, and it has other characteristics as well. In the course of a creative activity, a mental focus on the formal features of the material—be it words and sentences, tones and phrases, paints, clay and physical objects, or mathematical formulae and atomic behavior—is a creative psychological operation that helps determine both content and form of the created product. It is an aesthetic maxim—and a correct one, I believe—that form and content are highly interrelated in a final created product, each determining and influencing the other. This is also the case in a broad manner throughout the creative process, but there a focus on form often takes primacy and functions to determine and generate new content along the way.

To illustrate this primacy of focus on form, I shall describe a sequence from the poetic creative process of Richard Wilbur. This concerned the creation of his poem entitled "Running."[6] The data were derived from a series of interviews and procedures carried out with Mr. Wilbur during the several week period that he wrote it.

This poem was composed in three parts as follows: (1) 1933 (North Caldwell, N.J.); (2) Patriot's Day (Wellesley, Mass.); (3) Dodwells Hill Road (Cummington, Mass.). In the first part, the poem describes a young boy's happy experience of running on a farm; the second part depicts this boy grown up and watching the annual Boston marathon race together with his son; the third and last part focuses on him as a maturing narrator attempting to run with the impediments of aging and "passing on" his happy childhood memories to a new generation of boys. The poem was based on Wilbur's own boyhood experiences on his family farm in New Jersey and his adult experience at his house in Massachusetts.

His initial idea consisted of the phrase, "at rest within his run," a simultaneous antithesis and janusian formulation. This was later used as a phrase in the final poem. Through both information collected in the intensive series of interviews and a systematic testing procedure yielding the author's direct associations to words and phrases both deleted and added to the poem in the course of writing,[7] I had been able to determine that one of the unconscious conflicts connected with the poem was Mr. Wilbur's experience of being razzed in a school locker room as a boy because of having no hair on his legs.

After his initial idea, the first lines for the poem he wrote were the following:

> Past Rickard's house, past Goodman's house I ran
> Down the dirt drive and where
> The sloping curve began
> Went breakneck on and ran into the air,
>
> Seeing the ground beneath me gold and blurred
> Which with two lopes I spurred
> Then with a perfect third
> Spanked

The poet wrote this fragment all at one sitting, then stopped and returned to it later. In this portion, there is already an exquisite focus on the sound and rhythm of words and phrases, such as the rhymes between "ran" and "began," "where" and "air," "blurred," "spurred," and "third"; the alliteration of "Seeing," "spurred," and "Spanked"; the assonance of "sloping" and "loped"; the development of cadence and repetition. There is little here, however, that connects with the poet being teased about the hair on his legs and, in essence, his manhood. It was in his next writing session that his focus on the formal feature of rhyme helped to generate an important piece of content in the poem related to that conflict. Focused on improving the sound features of the beginning, he worked on adding a new first line. He therefore needed another rhyming word to lead up to the rhymes he had initially constructed for the first stanza—the end words "where" and "air"— and tried "aware" as follows:

> Thinking of happiness, once more I race
> Down the cart-road past Rickard's house, aware

This rhyme construction, although it was not used in the final poem, started the poet on a new idea, "Thinking of happiness," that he explicitly used in the poem. He moved it to the last line of the first section as the following: ". . . and with delighted strain/Sprinted across the flat/By the bull-pen, and up the lane./Thinking of happiness, I think of that." The idea of "Thinking of happiness" became an explicit theme of the entire poem emphasizing the gratification of his achieved mastery in running. This celebration of his achievement was a psychological compensation for damaging effects of the boyhood teasing.

The final version of the first part of the poem was as follows:

> What were we playing? Was it prisoner's base?
> I ran with whacking Keds
> Down the cart-road past Rickard's place,
> And where it dropped beside the tractor-sheds
>
> Leapt out into the air above a blurred
> Terrain, through jolted light,
> Took two hard lopes, and at the third
> Spanked off a hummock-side exactly right,
>
> And made the turn, and with delighted strain
> Sprinted across the flat
> By the bull-pen, and up the lane.
> Thinking of happiness, I think of that.

Such use of rhyme, alliteration—note the introduction of the "k" sounds in "whacking Keds," which were suggested by the name "Rickard" and placed in the line before—and other formal devices to suggest and generate aesthetic and emotional content is characteristic of the poetic creative process. Rather than starting with clearly defined ideas, emotions, or meanings and fitting them into a poetic structure consisting of sound associations, rhythms, and images, poets focus on the latter in order to clarify, suggest, and determine the former to some degree. This has been shown over and over again to me by constant shifts in sequence during the creative process and the construction of parts in sometimes radically different order than presented in the final product. An early rhyming phrase in a sequence is often conceived after a later one is composed, use of a particular meter and rhythm in a line leads to extensive modification of earlier portions of the poem, and phrases and images are constantly shifted around. This shifting of sequences is not simply a matter of the poet's changing his mind or deciding on a different way of presenting the material for greater clarity, as in expository writing; it is a focus on sequence both for aesthetic reasons and for its own sake. It is a focus on sequence because of the meanings and ideas sequence introduces and suggests.

The focus on form operates during the creative process in music, visual arts, other forms of literature, performing arts, as well as in science and other fields of creative activity, as I shall illustrate later in this chapter. Now, let us return to the verbatim material of the psychotherapy session quoted at the beginning of this chapter and see how this focus on form can help to answer the question I raised. Some further contextual information will be necessary, as follows: The 25-year-old patient came to therapy because of difficulties in obtaining sexual satisfaction with her husband. He was a full-time law student and they had been married for two years. Initially, she and her husband (Bill in the following) had sought help from their pastor, but after several interviews both were referred by the pastor to individual psychotherapists. Up to the point of the excerpted fifth weekly session I presented, the patient had complained mildly of the therapist's nondirectiveness and talked of her difficulties in achieving orgasm in intercourse. She also began to reveal some dissatisfaction with her husband.

With respect to the formal factor of sequence, a psychotherapy session can be broadly divided into beginning, middle, and end. The material I presented above occurred, as I said, at the end of the session, and was the culmination of a series of interactions between the patient and therapist. Such a presentation at the end of a session could possibly represent a revelation of suicidal preoccupations that the patient has held back until the end, or it could be a response to something the therapist has introduced earlier. Often, however, the presentation of anxiety-provoking material of any kind at the end of a session derives from a patient's concerns about endings of any sort and difficulties with any kind of separation. At the other pole of the sequence, material presented by the patient at the beginning of the session—anxiety-provoking or not—tends to reflect issues related to taking initiative. Also, it always reflects the patient's initial preconscious concerns. These concerns are derived both from experiences during the interim between sessions and from feelings and thoughts about the immediately preceding session with the therapist. Therefore, let us look at the differently toned interchange at the very beginning of this session to see what light it can shed about the end:

P: I think I'll have to buy some Air-Wick and put it in the corridor outside your office. Have you noticed that odor?

TH: Smells bad, does it?

P: Ooohh—understatement. Each week I keep trying to see how long I can hold my breath going along there. And I can never quite get through it.

TH: Mmm.

P: But, very nasty atmosphere. I have wished this week, as I did last, that the interviews were at a different time in the week, because it seems like such stress and strain comes in between. And then by the time I get here I'm kinda calm and collected again. It doesn't seem useless, but it's in these more trying periods I've wished that I could get things out of my system then.

TH: How would it be different if it were at a different time?[8]

The interaction at the very beginning of the session and in the few minutes following, brief as it is, gives some possible clue to the way the session might unfold and to the meaning of the patient's veiled suicidal threat at the end. Although we can assume that there most assuredly was an odor in the hall, the fact that the patient brings that up at the very beginning out of a possible universe of discourse has meaning. From the therapist's reaction, it is clear that she is neither hallucinating nor inebriated and, most pertinent to the form, *she has not brought this up in any of the four previous sessions.* Most probably, she is experiencing preconscious or conscious negative feelings toward the therapist or the therapy and her immediate reference to the bad smell indicates the idea: "This therapy [you] stinks."

If this is so, why does the patient feel this way? The next clue is that, after referring to the odor, she states that she would like to have her sessions at a different time. Notably, she does not say that she would like the sessions to be at a particular other day and hour, but at times when she is upset. The therapist, in other words, is not with her at a point when she feels upset. The suggestion is that he is not with her enough, and by extension, therefore, that she would like him to be with her all the time. Why might this be an issue for her and what does it have to do with her negative feelings toward the therapy? Why is it an issue at this particular time? The next sequence of interaction provides further clues and a probable answer to these questions:

P: I don't know whether it's just that it's bound to coincide like that, that during the week after an interview, things'll happen, or whether it's just happened that way so far, but . . .

TH: Hmm.

P: . . . seems like both times I get here when I'm, oh, over most of it. And it's kind of a false security . . .

TH: Mm—hmm.

P: . . .'cause I thought I'd hit the lowest depths last week. But I—

TH: But there are still lower ones, hunh?

P: —guess I haven't. Yeah, a few other untried places.

TH: What happened this week?

P: I'm afraid now there're going to be quite a few. It's . . oh, just . . .

TH: You mean you have a feeling that it's going to get *worse?*

P: Well, I just don't know. I think that it gets worse so that it seems to involve Bill more. And as he gets into his, then we both seem to be in it together. And while we knew there'd be bad moments, just the fact that they are seeming to coincide isn't good. And yet I think it's probably natural. And if we can just get through 'em, it . . . [long pause] I think he is probably going to cancel the rest of his therapy . . partly because of time and partly because he thinks it's too disturbing now.

TH: Hmmm.

P: And I can see part of it, but . . .

TH: How many did he have?

P: He just had one.

TH: That's enough.[9]

The patient says that her husband is planning not to continue with his own therapy. Listening for a pattern in this sequence—recognizing that there will be connections among thematic elements at the beginning of a therapy session—should lead the therapist to pay particular attention to what the patient has just said. The husband deciding not to continue with his therapy is a factor that can explain the two earlier themes. The patient has first complained about the therapy ("odor"), and then about the fact that she doesn't see the therapist enough. Or, at least not at the right times. The immediate reason for these feelings may very well be the husband's behavior. He feels free to drop out of therapy, but she somehow wants, or is expected to, continue. She finds, in fact, that she needs to see the therapist more. She must feel a good deal of resentment about both her husband's behavior and the constraining effect of her own felt need at that point. Of pertinence with respect to the question of later suicidal potential, she speaks at this early point in the session of being at the "lowest depths" but, in response to the therapist's searching question, she makes no allusions at all to suicide and even suggests that she hasn't experienced the full depth or all the features, i.e., "a few untried places," of depression.

Unfortunately, the therapist does not recognize the form or pattern of these themes at this point and in the next portion of the session he goes on to ask primarily about concrete details pertaining to the husband's therapist. She volunteers that her husband has used the excuse of facing bar exams and being afraid of any "emotional letdown" as the reason for not pursuing therapy. In response, the therapist asks rather mildly about her feelings by questioning whether she is disappointed. Her first reaction is mild as well; she says, "In a way, yes." Then, in describing the disturbances between herself and her husband, she says: "It seems like I have to about go off my nut before he actually figures out that something disturbs me." Although the patient is explicitly describing her husband, her remark at that point might well pertain to the therapist's mild or minimal recognition of her distress.

During the remainder of the session, and in response to the therapist's clarifying questions and urging, the patient goes on to describe the particular conflicts that occurred between her husband and herself during the previous week: He didn't give full attention to her birthday, he made her feel guilty about expressing her feelings and characteristically wouldn't express his own, and he spent a lot of time on a variety of activities but very little on studying for his bar exam. At one point halfway through, after the therapist tries to explore her feelings about divorce, she shifts to the therapy and indicates that she experiences emotional stress and strain, as follows:

> P: And I think that possibly there might be, just in going on with these, that it's going to be a very difficult end of the year. And, I'm—
>
> TH: I didn't quite understand, have you asked yourself whether you should stop too . . . the therapy?
>
> P: No, not really seriously considering it, 'cause I feel like now I'm just in the middle of it, that it'd—you can't go either direction. I mean I can't back up by myself.
>
> TH: Mm-hmm.
>
> P: And that if I can just hang on. And I have gotten so much out of it, particularly the last couple of times, stuff that broadened. . . . I'm very grateful that you were nondirective 'cause if you told me some of this stuff, naturally I can build up my defenses so fast. But I have some of it, when it sinks in under my own thought processes.
>
> TH: Can you point to anything that you mean especially that seemed—
>
> P: Well, just the general fact that I thought I saw myself and knew myself, but I didn't. I mean we analyze so much ourselves and I thought I could pretty well size up the kind of person I was, and

everything. But I don't think I was able to do that; I'm beginning
to get a little idea, but that's a ghastly experience—

TH: I just wondered, that's a ghastly . . hunh?

P: Getting to see yourself as others see you is kinda demoralizing.

TH: Really! What—

P: Some of it.

TH: What have you seen that you don't like the looks of?[10]

Focusing on form and structure in this excerpt supports the contention
that the patient has been resentful about her husband's stopping therapy
throughout. The patient's positive statements about her therapy follow
immediately after the therapist's recognition that she herself has had
thoughts about stopping. Just as with the earlier negative statements, the
positive statement here should not be taken literally and as a matter of
content alone. Although she may very well have positive feelings about the
therapy, the sequence indicates an immediate feeling of relief generated by
the therapist's preceding question. His open recognition that she might
have considered stopping therapy must have helped her to feel less trapped
and also less guilty about any negative feelings toward him and the therapy.
That this feeling and not an enthusiasm for the therapy is predominant is
further evidenced by her lighting on the one factor that she constantly
complained about previously, the therapist's nondirectiveness. It seems unlikely that she would have changed her mind about those complaints so
quickly, especially since the therapist has just done the contrary and been
somewhat active and directive in his question. Also, it would appear that
the therapist himself is appropriately unconvinced, since he asks her for
details about what she has gained. At this point, he seems focused on the
form and sequence of the interaction and has better understanding.

Although the therapist here has apparently reversed some of the problematic effects of his missing the meaning in earlier sequences, the persistence of the theme into the middle portion of the session and the fact that
he has not yet acknowledged (or recognized?) the theme of her active
resentment about her husband's stopping has pertinence to the suicidal
threat appearing at the end. In the remainder of the session, the patient
talks primarily about how her husband is not sufficiently concerned with
her feelings or needs. At one point, she and the therapist touch again on the
husband's stopping therapy, but the therapist only tells her there is not
much she can do about it.

Then, pursuing the matter of the husband's insensitivity and lack of
emotional responsiveness toward the end of the session, the therapist, who

is still focused primarily on the content, suggests there may be a connection to the patient's dissatisfaction with sexual intercourse. This produces the following material and interchange, which immediately precedes and leads up to the section containing the suicide threat I quoted at the beginning of the chapter:

P: And we haven't had intercourse since . . well, I guess a week ago Sunday, or some time like that. And it . . w . . the idea of it still just is . . completely repulsive to *me*.

TH: Mm-hmm. . . . I guess we have to recognize that your having come into treatment *has* in some sense stirred these things up.

P: Yeah.

TH: I mean before you said you just weren't interested, and now—

P: Yeah.

TH: —it's actually a little repulsive. But I don't think that should alarm you.

P: I have a feeling that it just may go to the very depths . . before we got out of it, but I want to know how far I am from the bottom.

TH: Yeah.

P: Is there any way of telling how long this goes on?

TH: No. No, I don't think so.

P: I feel in some small way as though there's *some* progress, but—

TH: I certainly sympathize with your feeling that it might be better if you could have more frequent interviews. Unfortunately, we can't.

P: Yeah, well, actually I couldn't either, from a time standpoint.

TH: I see.

P: I think—well, I don't know. I used to think that, when these things would bother me if I were home an afternoon, like I usually am on Friday, I could sorta get them out of my system by myself.

TH: Oh, yeah.

P: But I never could, and I just got into a—

TH: Just fretted and stewed about it, yeah.

P: —depressed, morbid kind of thinking, which I don't think was healthful.

TH: Yeah, but I think our attitude should be that we'll accomplish what we can—in the time we have, hmmm?

P: I was so concerned about the depression—and I had been about his, too—never knowing how far a person can go on, how much of it you can take before you do just crack. And I still don't know, but I—

TH: I don't think you should be concerned about your basic stability.

P: I *have* been very concerned about it.

TH: About *yours?*

P: Yes.

TH: [softly] What do you mean?

P: Well, I just—

TH: You've been scared?

P: Yeah, I've really been awfully scared.

TH: What do you think by that?[11]

The patient's answer to this awkwardly phrased question is at the beginning of this chapter. Here, then, is the specific sequence leading up to the patient's veiled threats of suicide. After bringing up her basic feelings about sexual intercourse with her husband, the therapist both minimizes their intensity (she: "completely repulsive"; he: "a little repulsive") and frightens her about the therapy by saying that treatment has *stirred up* her distressful feelings of repulsion. As she then increases the intensity of her distress and complaint, he shifts to the time issue she brought up at the beginning of the session. In his change of wording to "more frequent interviews" he has apparently come to realize that she actually wanted more time with him. It seems to be too late, however. Instead of having consistently followed the form and structure of the patient's utterances, and instead of recognizing underlying feelings and thereby accepting them as they arise, the issue has changed. In bringing up more frequent interviews at this point, the therapist is responding to the patient's threat and aggression. She is now demanding help and response from him just as she probably does with her withholding husband. His guilty apology that he cannot see her more often is rejected by her with a competitive reference to her own time commitments, and then followed by continued magnification of the intensity and seriousness of her distress.

We are now in a position to answer the question about whether her allusions to suicide should alarm us. The therapist has at no point recognized the patient's feelings of jealousy and competition with her husband, although the sequences suggested them throughout the session. These feelings, we may assume, are directly or indirectly connected with her repulsion for sexual intercourse with him. In light of this lack of recognition, and also of any recognition of connections between her hostility to her husband and hostility to the therapist, we can answer with a fair degree of confidence. The patient alludes to suicide at the end of the session in order—consciously or preconsciously—to get a rise out of the therapist. His intended reassurances both about her feelings of revulsion about intercourse and about feeling alarmed are experienced by her as a need to apply further emotional pressure.

Her very final comment of the session, after the therapist's statement given at the beginning of this chapter that she shouldn't be alarmed, is "Thanks, I consider you an authority." To which he, catching the hostility in this remark, says: "A hot potato! I'll see you next week." We can say that this patient is motivated to disturb the therapist but is very likely not at the actual verge of committing suicide at this point.[12] We can also say that, by missing the significant meanings contained in the form and sequence of this session, such as difficulties with dependency, jealousy, and hostility, the therapist was not helpful enough to the patient. Her suicidal threat was also her indication that she hadn't been helped.

It might now be argued that what I am calling a focus on form and structure is none other than awareness of transference, concern with process material, or a method of stressing the here and now. Why, the argument might go, is it so important to recognize sequence specifically or even to comment on it right away? Can't the therapist pick up such factors as the patient's hostility in other ways? After all, he did ask about her disappointment, about stopping therapy, and recognized her hostility to him at the very end of the hour. The first answer to this argument is that it is possible to get at hostility in other ways, but the lack of attention to sequence results in the missing of feelings *when they arise and are felt by the patient*. This patient was concerned about her feelings of hostility from the start and she felt that it was unacceptable to express them. The therapist's lack of recognition and response at the time she felt hostile must have made her feel that these feelings were as unacceptable to him as they were to herself and others. As for eventually recognizing the hostility at the end of that hour or in subsequent ones, that surely is a creditable and effective possibility, but it runs the risk of coming too late. The second answer is more extensive and it concerns the nature of the psychotherapeutic enterprise.

FORM AND STRUCTURE AS A BASIS OF TREATMENT

Focus on form and structure is important because it derives from the character of psychotherapeutic treatment. Inclusive of factors of transference, stress on the here and now, and attention to process, but more encompassing than any of these, form and structure are foundations from which many treatment effects derive. First and foremost, most types of psychotherapy consist of a structural agreement between at least two persons, one of whom is a patient needing help and the other a therapist skilled in helping. These persons mutually agree to spend a designated time together for the purpose of alleviating the difficulties of one of them, the patient. Because the time agreed upon is designated as to duration and periodicity it has specific structure and form.

Designation of this structure (I shall drop the term "form" for the moment because it tends to suggest "formal psychotherapy") as the sole vehicle for treatment is itself a major factor in the therapeutic effect. That is to say that deciding that regular meetings of particular duration and frequency will take place and that the therapist will do nothing else with respect to the patient, i.e., *will take no action in the patient's real world*, and carrying out this decision to the letter, will have far-reaching therapeutic consequences. Setting up such a structure provides the patient with a trial domain in which he can reproduce and work out interpersonal difficulties or else, as Arlow states it, come to realize that interpersonal difficulties are intrapsychic.[13] A patient can display to the therapist and to himself the full range of problematic thoughts and actions and both can assess the reality of their effects.[14] When change seems necessary, the patient can try out new ways of thinking and behaving without fear of lasting consequences. The therapist is neither parent nor sibling, nor employer, lover, wife, husband, child, nor anyone else who can effect real consequences in the patient's life. Through the therapist's behavior within the structure he constantly makes clear to the patient that he will have no such effect even though the patient— because of difficulties, emotional scars, and dependency—may constantly want and try to get the therapist to do so.

A primary feature of the therapist's action is to show the patient this critical paradox of the therapeutic situation. Although patient and therapist have contracted only for a defined structure, with the patient's benefit as the primary goal, the patient repeatedly tries (usually unconsciously) to subvert that very structure. A patient does this by attempting to get love and commitment from the therapist, by trying to get him to intervene in the patient's difficulties with other people, and by otherwise attempting to get him to solve his problems rather than doing that himself. Also, the patient comes late to therapy, misses therapy sessions, calls the therapist outside of designated times, and otherwise tests the therapist's commitment to the principle and agreement about structure. Almost invariably, a patient tests whether a therapist accepts or rejects his explicit and implicit thoughts or behavior on the basis of alterations in structure. Telling interesting and important stories and bringing up disturbing feelings just as a session is about to close are instances of such testing. If a therapist resists and does not extend the length of those sessions, he maintains the therapy as a trial domain where the patient's behavior, whether negative or positive, has no concrete or real consequences.

Attempts by the patient to alter the structural agreement are matters to be looked at and understood because the agreement was designed primarily to help the patient. Understanding deviations, therefore, aids in clarifying ubiquitous self-defeating tendencies. When the therapist is responsible for altering the structure by actions ranging from necessary ones, such as going on vacation or falling ill, to problematic ones, such as coming late for appointments, falling asleep in sessions, or actively intervening in a patient's life, he influences the experience of a trial domain. Although it is best for the therapist to introduce as little alteration as possible, when necessary interruptions occur, it is important for the therapist and patient together to consider their impact on the therapy. Patients properly have feelings about such interruptions and may often experience them, realistically or unrealistically, as produced by their own behavior.

There are exceptions and limits to the principle of a structured trial domain. Both soon and late, there are consequences in the real world, but these are produced by the patient's behavioral changes and not the direct action or intervention on the patient's behalf by the therapist.[15] Also, inflexibility of structure can become so artificial that it has no impact or meaning. Nonetheless, as a result of experiences within the therapeutic structure, the patient alters his perception of himself and others and hopefully brings about positive real consequences.

As for the nature of the structure decided upon, 50- or 45-minute sessions have, of course, been traditionally used in individual psychotherapy. Although there is nothing magical about that duration of time, experience has shown it to be workable for exploratory therapy. Other time periods may surely be used, but it is important to note that different forms and structures, as well as different types of sequences, result from 30-, or from 15-minute, sessions and from session frequencies of one, or two, or three, or four times weekly.

Development of transference, the appearance of insight, the expression and acceptance of feelings, and understanding of the effects of the past on the present, all depend on and in some degree arise from the structural nature of psychotherapy. Transference develops and is recognized in part because of the lack of real consequences and the reliability of the structure. Patient insight into transference and the effects of the past on the present derives from awareness of the discrepancies between wishes or expectations and the nature of the structural contract. Also, acceptance and expression of feelings are promoted by the structure's essential neutrality. In those therapies in which structure is not specifically contracted or fixed, exploration and working-through are seldom possible or desired because a trial domain of interpersonal behavior is not established. In these therapies, transference often is unexplored and, sometimes, is unexplorable because too many spillovers into real consequences occur. The therapist provides variable lengths of time, gives directives and advice, and otherwise does not delimit the therapeutic structure. However, even in these, there are some implicit limits on time and therapist involvement that constitute variable degrees of structure. Interpretation, insight, and some important working-through frequently occurs.

Because of the structural nature of psychotherapy, the unfolding structure or form of each therapy session requires special focus and attention. The sequence and pattern of communications within the session provide an understanding of the patient's interpersonal responses and intrapsychic preconscious and unconscious meanings. Also, sequences and patterns between therapy sessions, such as when a therapist makes a mistake at the end of one session and the patient begins the next session vaguely angry and complaining, require attention and possible interpretive intervention. Broader patterns involving the beginning, middle, and end phases of therapy are reflective of the patient's characteristic ways of experiencing the phenomena of encounter, growth, and separation, respectively. When the therapist intervenes on the basis of his understanding of such structural factors or, going further, when he points out such sequences and patterns to the patient together with an interpretation, he is focusing on structure or form to generate meaning in a therapeutic creative process.

A young female patient whose therapist was about to go on vacation, for example, began a therapy session talking about her anger and fury at a florist who had been taking care of her plants. She herself had been away from home and the florist had put her plants in a greenhouse, used a pesticide, and they died. While listening to her continuing vituperation, the therapist thought there might be some connection with angry feelings about his upcoming vacation but little she said suggested any direct relationship. He felt baffled by her furious diatribes but, picking up on the plant care issue, he simply commented that she seemed concerned about caring "today." Without a moment's hesitation, the patient then became angry at him. She said that he was wrong and she was only reporting on the events in her life since the last therapy session.

Then, she shifted to describe a recent discussion she had had with a male friend and reported his comments in detail. At one point in the discussion, she said, she became very annoyed at him because he was just "making conversation." Noting that the patient shifted to talk about this young man immediately after his comment, the therapist surmised a connection with this complaint. He commented that she seemed to feel that he too had just been making conversation earlier but he knew she really *was* concerned about caring and being cared for. In response, the patient became thoughtful and then began to talk about her angry feelings about the therapist's lack of care and impending vacation. The focus on the sequence of the patient's productions had therefore provided understanding which, when conveyed to the patient, allowed her to talk about her problematic concerns in a mutually collaborative creative process.

In another instance, an adolescent male patient spent the early portion of a session on a series of complaints: not being able to sleep; feeling he had to come to therapy that day; having to sit in the therapist's office. Thinking there was something more to what was going on, the therapist said that he understood that the patient felt like complaining but didn't know what he was really complaining about that day. At that, the patient became angry at the therapist and denied that he was complaining at all. Moreover, he had been told that he complained too much all his life and he couldn't take any more of that. He shifted to talk about another topic and his anger dissipated by the end of the session. However, he missed the next appointment.

When he returned for the following scheduled time, he began by stating that he had missed the previous session because he had slept late. Listening for some moments to the patient's elaborations of the excuse, the therapist then asked if he had continued to be bothered about the topic of complaining in the earlier session. At first denying any connection between the previous session and his sleeping late, he later returned to the topic and spoke of a feeling that he should never complain at all. Also, he talked of all the difficulties that complaining had brought him in his life. At one point in the account, he made a fleeting reference to his mother, and the therapist asked whether the feeling about complaining was connected with her. For a brief moment, the patient hesitated and then said that he guessed he could have said "yes" to that question right away. Noting the hesitation in reply to his question, the therapist asked whether the reason the patient paused was that he was afraid that saying "yes" would be *a complaint against his mother*. To this, the patient immediately replied "maybe" but in later sessions he returned to this intervention and acknowledged its validity and importance.

In this example, the therapist focused on the meaning of sequences both between sessions and within the session itself. Although his exploratory focus on the intersession sequence of missing an appointment after being angry at the therapist may seem somewhat routine to an experienced practitioner, it nevertheless is one of the potentially creative actions of everyday psychotherapy. More complex intersession sequences, such as when a patient comes into a session sad or anxious or angry because of something touched on but not discussed in the session immediately previous, are a greater therapeutic and creative challenge.

With regard to the sequence within the session, the therapist realized that the patient's hesitation in response to his question had a specific meaning for the topic itself. The patient could not at first answer the therapist's question about the connection between fear of complaining and the patient's mother because the answer itself would comprise a forbidden complaint. In this way, the therapist's focus on the form and structure revealed a preconscious concern, generated further content, and helped the patient experience both his feelings and his anxiety about them in the here-and-now trial domain of therapy. Later, in Chapter VII, I shall provide another illustration of a therapist's focus on form and structure within a therapy session in my discussion of the form-related factor of articulation.

FOCUS ON FORM AND STRUCTURE
IN CREATIVE PROCESSES

In the carrying out of psychotherapy, the focus on form and structure is, of course, continuous and far more extensive than provided by the foregoing short examples. In other creative activities, this focus is also extensive and serves to generate meaning and content throughout the creative process. As I stated earlier, a focus on form and structure operates in a wide range of creative activities and therefore has numerous types of manifestations. With respect to other types of literature beside poetry, novelist John Hersey told me that there came a point in the writing of every novel when he had "a distinct sense of its shape." When I asked him then whether he could draw the shape of the particular novel in progress we were talking about, he said that he thought that he could do so. With a pencil, he traced a series of vertical lines producing an undulating shape. I thought right away that these lines described an emotional pattern, and I suggested that. Agreeing, he said he thought the shape corresponded to a flow of tension and release but also there was a matter of expansion and contraction of scope and significance. In some portions of the novel, wide geographical areas were included, more people appeared, and events were built on and compounded. Alternately, there was restriction of locales, of people, and of plot. His sense of the shape guided the production of content. Noticing that the separated lines in the overall shape he drew also looked like rhythmic beats, I asked him whether there was also an auditory quality to the shape he described. He thought that this might be so because he often found himself mouthing sentences as he worked. There might be a cumulative sound effect.

Playwright Arthur Miller spoke of visualizing a specific geometric pattern in the early phase of writing a play. This conception gave him what he specifically called the "structure" of the play. Elaborating on this, he told me that structure was the first problem he always had to solve in the writing of plays. Other playwright research subjects spoke of similar types of general patterns as critical guiding factors at both early and continuing phases of the writing of a play.

To return to poetry, "Beat" poet Michael McClure told me he deliberately used a rhyming sequence in order to help him to recapture forgotten childhood memories. A final poem, in clear-cut "Beat" style, became a series of childhood memories framed by rhyme. On the other end of the stylistic spectrum, poet and novelist Robert Penn Warren described a focus on the sounds of words and phrases as a key generative factor in composing poetry. Pointing to the back of his throat as the locus of the sound he made and heard, he overenunciated various possibilities of poetic lines. As I clarified this process with him, he told me that it was the muscular play of his mouth and throat that had a good deal to do with his feeling for the sound. There was a sense of movement in the sound that represented an emotion to be conveyed. Words and phrases suggested by the movement were coordinated with meaning and used in a particular poem. So important and generative was this focus on sound and formal properties of words and phrases that Warren practiced it by reading poems of other poets and trying different types of locutions for particular lines. With trial word changes, he changed rhythms and sounds and thereby studied how the other poet had achieved his effects.

With regard to primacy of form in other creative fields, Mies's landmark study of Beethoven's creative process, based on a careful and extensive analysis of composition notebooks, indicates the generative function of Beethoven's focus on pattern and sequence. Mies concluded: "I consider that in the work of the great masters . . . nothing short of the right form will release the desired content."[16] Analysis of musical composition by other musicologists such as Meyer and Epperson[17] and by composer Leonard Bernstein[18] support this conclusion, although they would substitute the terms "meaning" or "musical symbol" for Mies's term "content." Together with sequence, formal factors of repetition, inversion, transformation, symmetry, and asymmetry are generative foci throughout the musical composition process.[19]

In visual art, focus on pattern and form is clearly evident in the artworks of the twentieth century. In abstract art particularly, forms are presented or manipulated in geometric and "pure" shapes and relationships in order to generate content and meaning.[20] Prior to the modern emphasis, however, artists have always looked at shapes and tones projected onto imaginary planes in order to develop subject matter. For example, Leonardo da Vinci described the process as follows: "When you look at a wall spotted with stains, or with a mixture of stones, if you have to devise some scene, you may discover a resemblance to various landscapes, beautified with mountains, rivers, rocks, trees, plains, wide valleys, and hills in varied arrangement; or again you may see battles and figures in action; or strange faces and costumes, and an endless variety of objects. . . . "[21]

In science, form and structure also are generative in creative thinking. Scientists engaged in theory building and construction speak constantly of the guiding principle of elegance. This principle is not important simply for aesthetic pleasure but because of its usefulness in producing empirically appropriate formulations. For these scientists, elegance or formal simplicity is used as a major criterion for acceptance or rejection of various types of explanations and formulations. Allan Cormack, Nobel Prize discoverer of the CAT scan X-ray procedure, described the operation of this factor to me in the following verbatim comment:

Once you start being abstract and removing all kinds of things from reality—that is to say, if you do in the abstract what I do in mathematics—the abstractions are just as beautiful [as in art] and I find them more satisfactory. . . . It's this business of economy of means. . . . I think there's a great deal of satisfaction in seeing ideas put together or related. And there is a structural thing there just as much as in sculpture or painting or anything of that sort—form and economy of means. . . . Very often in biology you say, "If such-and-such went that way, will this go that way?" Very often the reason you ask why is because you found the previous thing to be attractive somehow.[22]

And the creative mathematician Poincaré documented the guiding function of this factor in the following way:

Now, what are the mathematical entities to which we attribute this character of beauty and elegance, which are capable of developing in us a kind of esthetic emotion? Those whose elements are harmoniously arranged so that the mind can, without effort, take in the whole without neglecting the details. This harmony is at once a satisfaction to our esthetic requirements, and an assistance to the mind which it supports and guides. At the same time, by setting before our eyes a well-ordered whole, it gives a presentiment of a mathematical law.[23]

As Holton and others have shown, the formal factor of symmetry also plays an important role in creative theorizing and the construction of experiments.[24] Einstein, for instance, criticized the theoretical "asymmetry" of the Maxwell theory he was supplanting in the very first line of his first (1905) paper on relativity theory, and his overall theory of relativity has been characterized as a theory of symmetry.[25] Pierre Curie, scientific theorist and co-discoverer of radium, asserted that: "When certain causes produce certain effects, the elements of symmetry of causes must be found in effects produced."[26] Regardless of whether this assertion is valid or, as Chalmers has tried to show,[27] useful, the comment indicates the importance of symmetry in guiding Curie's own thought.

Such thinking has, in fact, proved dramatically useful in modern particle physics. To cite a recent example, McMorris states, "It is . . . striking that in particle physics the aesthetic element of symmetry was employed to predict some as yet unobserved member, the Ω^- [omega hyperon, negatively charged] and η^0 [eta meson, neutrally charged], which were subsequently discovered. The whole exercise involved an appeal, not only to the elaborate SU(3) symmetry theory, but to unsophisticated symmetry of actual, regular geometrical arrangements."[28]

Detailed and specific structural patterns also guide and generate substance of scientific thought. Gruber has carefully documented the important function of the image of the "tree of nature" in Charles Darwin's development of the theory of evolution.[29] Throughout his notebooks, Darwin over and over drew a picture of a branching tree, making extensive notes and affixing labels to its various parts. Many points in the theory of evolution grew out of this structure, as Gruber enumerates in the following: "the fortuitousness of life, the irregularity of the panorama of nature, the explosiveness of growth and the necessity to bridle it so as to keep the number of species constant. . . . And, most important, the fundamental duality that at any time some must live and others die."[30]

Focus on form and structure, though ubiquitous in creative processes, is an approach to producing creative effects; it is not a sufficient cause. Form and content must be made to interrelate with, and complement, each other and an exclusive preoccupation with form would not accomplish that goal. Furthermore, none of my discussion here should be construed to suggest that content is of little importance in creative work or that creative persons are not vitally concerned with conveying substance. The substance or statement of a work of art is a critical feature of its value and the substance of a scientific creation is vital to its meaning and effective use. In psychotherapy, the content both of inner experience—including fantasies, thoughts, affects, motivations—and of interpersonal relationships must be understood, accepted, or modified to produce a therapeutic effect. In all types of creative activities, however, a focus on form and structure serves to reveal unseen and often previously unknown connections between elements of content. At the same time, this focus serves to produce connections where none were present, or at least apparent, before. Excessive focus on form and structure can occur and can produce sterile and uncreative effects in any endeavor. Sometimes, in psychotherapy, an excessive focus on form and structure can produce premature connecting and thereby obscure preconscious and unconscious meanings or even enhance patient defensiveness. It can serve defensive purposes for the therapist as well. By and large, however, the psychotherapist focuses on form in order to understand underlying meanings and facilitate the creative process, just as other creative persons do.

CHAPTER III

The Homospatial Process and Metaphorical Intervention

Creation of effective metaphors is one of the prime functions of the homospatial process. Multiple discrete entities are brought together into the same mentally represented space and the resulting conception is articulated into metaphorical phrases, e.g., "the road was a ribbon of moonlight," or more extensive metaphors, e.g., the central image of a poem, or the character Hamlet in Shakespeare's play. The multiple discrete entities in the mental conception may consist of sensory elements from either the same or different modalities. Resulting metaphors may be of the verbal type found in poetry and other forms of literature or they may be visual metaphors found in painting, sculpture, architecture, or dance. Auditory or sound types of metaphors are created as expressive factors in music and creative scientists develop conceptual types of metaphors to serve in the building of theories and models. An illustration of a visual metaphor is given by Aldrich[1] in his analysis of a painting by Oskar Kokoschka. In this painting, he points out, roofs of houses and mountains are juxtaposed in such a way as to form a whole and interact visually with one another. In this way, Kokoschka produced a visual metaphor in which the depicted mountain was "domesticated" and the house aggrandized. Examples of conceptual metaphors are "black holes in space," "big bang," "big crunch," colored and flavored quarks, which have generated so much theory and data in physics. Auditory metaphors consist of what Leonard Bernstein described as a transformation into an equivalence[2]; this involves an interaction relationship among independent and discrete elements and patterns.

To show how this process operates, I have previously described the creation of the poetic metaphor: "the branches were handles of stars."[3] Despite usual and time-honored intuitive impressions of how such metaphors have been created, I pointed out that this particular phrase resulted neither from a walk in the country at night, nor from analogic thinking, nor from noticing or imagining a close proximity between the tips of tree branches and distant stars. Nor was there some type of associative or bisociative (viz. Koestler[4]) combining of the words "branches," "handles," and "stars." The creation of that metaphor resulted from a mental superimposition of the words "branches" and "handles" and the images connected with them. Attracted by the formal sound qualities of the center portion of the words "branches" and "handles," and by their meanings, the creator *intentionally* represented them mentally as occupying the same space. While focused on this hazy image, he thought of stars as the particular idea or word with visual and auditory qualities that would connect branches and handles into an effective metaphor.

Another type of metaphor, "the tarantula rays of the lamp spread across the conference room," also involved superimposition and the mental representation of multiple discrete entities as occupying the same space. In this case, the creator was thinking about a vacation in the tropics and, among the various related words and thoughts, he became interested in the sound connection—the central "a" assonance—between the words "tarantula" and "lamp." He actively superimposed images of the spider and a light source together, along with the visual and aural images of the words themselves, because he felt they *ought* to be together. Light radiating out from the central source was immediately suggested by the mentally visualized spider legs in the superimposed images, and he thought of the phrase "tarantula rays of the lamp." In addition to evoking an ominous and interesting visual percept, the word "rays" had an assonantal relationship with both "tarantula" and "lamp."

After constructing this metaphorical phrase, he decided to elaborate with a suggestively meaningful context and conceived of "conference room." Once the entire construction was created, he thought of overtones such as the wars in the tropics, evocative contrasts between the slow crawl of a tarantula and the speed of light, and an awesome type of beauty, and he was pleased. This metaphor, it should be noted, has an adjective modifier together with a noun structure rather than what linguists call a "nominative" one, i.e., noun linked to noun by a copulative verb, as in "the branches were handles of stars." Both were created through the homospatial process. As another type of example, the metaphor "the heat sits in the window, unreeling its lines, baited for change" was created under experimental conditions designed to facilitate homospatial conceptions. This metaphor was produced by a writer research subject after exposure to a superimposed slide image of a sailboat together with a tenement house.

Creation of effective metaphors of this type and their use in treatment is the first application of the homospatial process in the creative process of psychotherapy. I suggest that the therapist be alert to those elements in the patient's behavior and underlying psychodynamics that lend themselves to the active construction of meaningful and descriptive metaphors. Such metaphors can be used directly as therapeutic clarifications, interpretations, and facilitators. To clarify and describe how this is so will require a definition and some exposition of the nature of metaphor.

Much has been written in recent years by linguists, philosophers, literary critics, psychoanalysts, and other types of psychologists and psychiatrists about the nature of metaphors.[5] Many writers start from Aristotle's definition of a metaphor as consisting of words denoting a transfer of a property from one element onto another to which it is not ordinarily connected. Other writers define it as the comparing or bringing together of similarities in dissimilar entities. Linguists specifically talk about metaphor as a deviant form of communication which cannot, in context, be understood literally. Philosophers and literary critics use some of these definitions but they are also especially interested in the way that poetic metaphors tend to bring together the concrete and the abstract. This latter factor especially applies to the function of metaphor in therapy.

The bringing together of the concrete and abstract can be included in a definition I shall use of poetic or created metaphors as consisting of nonliteral expressions that integrate two or more levels of experience. In psychotherapy as in art and science, these levels may consist also of conscious and unconscious, of cognitive and affective, or of different aspects of objective reality.

For example, in the metaphor "my hand was a bandage to his hurt,"[6] the "hurt" is readily understood as not literally signifying a physical wound, but as connoting human suffering. In equating a hand with a bandage, the metaphor brings to mind the hand's qualities of protectiveness, softness as well as strength, its clinging qualities, and other features that have parallels with the bandage's nature and function. The bandage at the same time adopts a shape that conforms to one's image of the shape of a hand. The concrete qualities of "hand" and "bandage" as well as "hurt" modify and interact with each other within the context. And concrete attributes are integrated with the abstract ones of human suffering and dependency. Dissimilar or disparate objects are equated in a dynamic interaction with one another, which heightens the appreciation of both. There is integration rather than additive combination, condensation, or compromise.[7] A neologism such as "handage" is not presented to combine aspects of hand and bandage. It does not in any way consist of a condensation or a compromise formation between "hand" and "bandage," "hurt" and "bandage," or "hurt" and "hand." The metaphor contains individually specified objects that are integrated into a larger unity with its own overall properties. "Hand" and "bandage" are identified, and they interact and modify each other constantly in the full expression.

"My hand was a bandage to his hurt" is a clear-cut example of the metaphor as an integrated entity. Creation of integrated entities in artworks, especially metaphors, are clear-cut manifestations of the use of the homospatial process. A similar type of creation occurred in the following instance: A 20-year-old woman came into treatment after having made a serious suicide attempt by jumping out of the second floor window of her college dormitory. In the course of the subsequent therapy, it became clear that she had a quite disturbed symbiotic relationship with her mother. She found it very difficult to see faults in her mother and tended always to criticize herself for having thoughts and feelings that her mother might not approve. One day, in order to emphasize to her therapist that her problems, such as a particular one of never wanting anyone to touch her, were entirely her own doing and did not in any way reflect on her mother, she said: "Do you know what my mother told me? She told me that even when I was an infant, around six months old, that I wouldn't allow her to touch me. Can you imagine that? A six-month-old baby that wouldn't even let her own mother touch her?"

At that, the therapist commented: "Your mother is a Brahmin, for without Brahmins there would be no Untouchables" (he was, of course, referring to the Indian caste system). Hesitating for a few moments, the patient became thoughtful, and then said: "Those people really do treat the Untouchables badly." After some further quiet thought, she began tentatively to explore the idea that in actuality the mother's account had been implausible. Hesitatingly, she wondered whether a six-month-old infant could possibly not want to be touched, or held, if that touching were done at all properly.

In subsequent sessions during the following weeks, and with clarification and support from the therapist, she returned to the matter and began to realize that a six-month-old infant could not possibly *prevent* a grown person from touching her. Even if she had shown discomfort when in her mother's arms, it may not have been due to the touching at all; rather, it may have arisen from a wide variety of things. Her mother misinterpreted the situation and, as she stated directly several sessions later, her mother was very likely uncomfortable about touching *her* in the first place. Just as the Untouchable class in India is defined as the lowest class and the Brahmins as the highest, with each category depending on the existence of the other, the infant may have been herself untouchable in relation to her mother's feelings about touching.

In this case the therapist had created a metaphor, "Your mother is a Brahmin," along with an aphorism regarding the relationship between Indian castes. In retracing the steps in the metaphor's creation, the therapist remembered that the patient herself had been talking of her interest in East Asian religion and culture some sessions before this interchange. When she spoke of her mother's recollection, he conceived the word "Untouchable" and the image of a shrunken Indian man looking somewhat like Gandhi came to his mind. Actively superimposing this word and the accompanying image with his mental percept of the patient's words and physical presence, he conceived the metaphor "Your mother is a Brahmin," and almost simultaneously thought of the aphorism as an elaboration as well. In a homospatial process, the therapist had created an apt metaphorical and interpretive intervention. Although he had earlier thought fleetingly of asking the patient whether she believed what her mother said, he rejected that prosaic literal construction for the metaphorical one.

Although the patient in this example was sophisticated and the metaphor somewhat elegant, metaphors in psychotherapy need not be couched in sophisticated or elegant terms. Indeed, in most cases, the language of the metaphor should not be overly polished or esoteric but should be drawn from the patient's world and experience. Thus, in one instance, a middle-aged female patient told a therapist that her marital problem was "99% my husband, and 1% me," and the therapist—thinking of the famous Ivory soap commercial slogan, "99 and $^{44}/_{100}$% pure; it floats"—said, "So you're a bar of Ivory soap, eh?" In response, this patient smiled slightly, and then shifted to talk about her own dissatisfaction with her marital sexual relations.

In another instance, a young female patient was talking about her inner feelings of emptiness and her constant need for her children and boyfriends. In this case, superimposing a mental image of a dry empty vessel onto the patient herself, the therapist commented that she seemed to arrange to have the kids and numerous men around "in an effort to plug up the holes."[8] To this, the patient replied that she really wanted to be alone, but felt very confused. Then, she began to pursue her concerns about being self-sufficient. In both of these cases the patients were high-school educated and the use of a metaphorical intervention employing language and content drawn from ordinary experience served to move the therapeutic process ahead.

The particular metaphoric intervention resulting from the homospatial process is not a linguistic phenomenon deriving primarily from associations or manipulations among words; it is a product of the active superimposition of complex mental images involving the patient's life, and words, and behavior. A 21-year-old male suffered from symptoms of depersonalization, withdrawal, and inability to concentrate. In the course of psychotherapy, he became more outgoing, began relating to his peers, and developed a close heterosexual relationship. This relationship, though stormy at times, was his first attempt at intimacy and sexual intercourse. At one point, however, when his partner herself became particularly disturbed and angry, his own symptoms of disconnectedness and withdrawal returned. Coming, then, into one of his therapy sessions, he yawned and wondered why he felt sleepy all the time. Although at first the therapist didn't understand the reason for this complaint, he attempted to pursue it against some resistance. Finally, the patient revealed that his girlfriend was constantly angry and woke him up three times each night. Although it seemed clear that this bothered him, he had said nothing and she had become even more agitated. Asking first what she actually said and receiving the reply, "I don't remember," the therapist simply suggested that the waking up, and the patient's feelings about that, might be the reason he was not sleeping. Then, the patient said: "I have no feelings; I'm in a daze all the time." To which the therapist commented: "Well, the benefit of being a sleepwalker is that you don't have to know or feel, but you can still move around and participate in what goes on."

The patient's response was strongly positive. He asked the therapist to repeat the entire formulation and said that he wanted to think a lot about it. Then he proceeded to talk about how he didn't allow himself to have feelings, or know about them, because he felt he didn't *deserve* to have them. For the remainder of the session, he productively pursued the important theme, for him, of the difficulty and danger of both having and expressing feelings. In this case, the therapist had created the metaphor of the patient as sleepwalker after superimposing a mental image both of the word "daze" and of a dazed but walking person upon the image of the sleepy patient sitting before him. Incorporated within the metaphor were also the numerous impressions the therapist had gathered in previous sessions of the patient actively withdrawing from painful situations. Additionally, the therapist was aware that the patient consistently used his withdrawal as an active weapon to control others, especially his mother. This metaphor, then, constituted a complex interpretation that stimulated awareness and an unfolding of factors relating to one of the patient's central symptoms, withdrawal.

All of the metaphorical interventions described so far have consisted of clear-cut and independent metaphors in which different levels of experience have been brought together, equated, and integrated. Whether they are couched in poetic or ordinary terms, therefore, they are equivalent to poetic metaphors, although used in a therapeutic context. Other types of metaphorical structures can also, in the therapeutic context, be creative manifestations of the homospatial process. Figurative language applied to, and arising out of, any specific emotional or behavioral context can function to produce effective or creative metaphors. Language as it is ordinarily used is perfused with such figurative expressions. We speak of a person making "a cutting remark" where "cutting" is a physical act that is in another realm of experience from words and "remarks." We speak of time "running fast" or of "having a long wait," where "running" and "long" are factors that pertain to space rather than being actual properties of the abstract entity of time. Or we speak of someone having a "foxy smile."

Although all of these expressions are spoken of as metaphorical according to a linguist's definition, they are not poetic metaphors because they have become so incorporated into ordinary language that they no longer evoke interaction among their elements. They do not cause us actively to integrate disparate levels of experience. When we hear these expressions we think neither about a smile on a fox's face, nor about measuring time by means of a distance between two points or by a figure running.[9] Commonly, these are called "dead" metaphors, meaning inactive and non-interactional, in distinction to "fresh" or poetic metaphors. Although they may once have been used poetically, or had the same impact that a fresh metaphor has, time and constant use have rendered them virtually literal. Therefore, use of such expressions has neither creative effect nor psychotherapeutic advantage. When, however, they are used with mental superimposition within a particular context, they may become effective metaphors and effective therapeutic tools. Poets constantly revivify dead metaphors within poetic contexts and, as shown in the next example, such revivifying can also be creative and meaningful in therapeutic contexts.

A 25-year-old female patient came into treatment because of a diffuse eczematous skin lesion covering the dorsum of her hands and forearms. Diagnostic evaluation, including a full dermatological workup, suggested that the symptom was primarily psychogenic in origin. The patient was evaluated as suffering from a severe conflict regarding her mother, which, together with intensely ambivalent feelings toward her, seemed to have something to do with the outbreak and persistence of the skin rash. During the fourth week of therapy, the patient, who characteristically avoided expressing any type of critical thoughts or feelings about members of her family, began the session by describing an experience of having been mildly disappointed by something her older sister did and said to her. Detecting that the patient's voice indicated stronger feelings than the mild disappointment she described, and mentally superimposing word and image representations of "skin," "defenses," "sister," and "patient," the therapist said, "She really gets under your skin, doesn't she?"

Following this comment, the patient elaborated on her feelings and began to acknowledge intense anger toward her sister, which she then continued to express throughout the session. Several weeks later, the patient returned to talking about her sister and, in passing, suggested that in some ways her sister's personality resembled that of the patient's mother. Noting the association, the therapist remarked, "She [the mother] gets under your skin, too, doesn't she?" Although the patient's eyes lit up in apparent recognition of the connection the therapist was making to her skin ailment, she did not refer to that directly; rather, she responded by beginning to acknowledge some ambivalent feelings toward her mother that previously she had denied. It was a turning point in the treatment because, following that session, the patient's skin ailment began to improve noticeably, and as the therapy progressed she became increasingly comfortable in discussing her ambivalent feelings and underlying conflict regarding her mother.

In this case, a cliché phrase or a dead metaphor, "get under the skin," was revitalized and freshened by application in a context where it had a new representation or meaning; it referred to an unconscious connection between the patient's skin ailment and her unspoken feelings about her sister and her mother. Note that it was not necessary for the patient to verbalize her understanding of the metaphor or for her to indicate any intellectual or conscious understanding of the connection between her feelings and her symptom. Her behavior, however, indicated that she possessed such an understanding regardless of whether it was on a conscious, preconscious, or unconscious level. The metaphor, as an integrated representation referring both to her underlying feelings of anger and to her skin (also to the fact that she was hiding her feelings under a coating or skin), allowed or encouraged her to speak of her previously prohibited thoughts about her sister and mother. We can assume that she registered the connection to her symptom without her explicitly saying so because she became motivated to talk about her feelings, and also because the symptom began to disappear after the therapist's repetition of the metaphorical intervention in reference to the mother.

Related to revivification of figurative language is the use of a proverb or aphorism to connect disparate elements and create a metaphor in context. Such occurred with the use of the proverb "nothing ventured, nothing gained" in connection with the interpretation of a dream in the 425th hour of an intensive psychotherapy with a 25-year-old man.[10] The patient arrived at the hour stating that he had been feeling upset and despondent after the previous day's session. He then recalled and reported a dream involving himself and a boyhood friend, P., as follows: The two of them are swimming at an inlet of a large lake. There are numerous inlets and rapids in this lake, and suddenly his friend warns him that there is danger and he should swim sideways across the current. Previously unnoticed by him, the dreamer-patient now realizes that the water has become quite turbulent and is sweeping him toward a wooden overflow dam and waterfall. The friend's advice to swim sideways is useless and he becomes frightened that he will be swept over the dam and killed. Suddenly, however, he is below the dam and safe. Later, he is walking on the shore together with his friend.

In discussing the dream, the patient brought up many associations that seemed to indicate that the friend in the dream represented the therapist, whose name also began with the letter P. When the therapist suggested this representation several times, the patient steadfastly objected. Finally, when the therapist pointed out that one of the elements in the patient's associations connected to some specific knowledge the latter had about him, the patient reluctantly accepted the possibility but stated that he was not at all sure. To this, the therapist commented: "It isn't important to be absolutely sure. After all, nothing ventured, nothing gained." This comment then led the patient to talk about his reluctance to take risks even though he had long harbored a wish to go on a canoe trip to Hudson Bay.

This trip, he knew, went through dangerous white water and canoers have been lost there with some regularity. Then, after gazing at a photograph of the Alaska wilderness on his therapist's desk, he admitted that he had been holding back. He had known that the therapist was a canoer and enjoyed outdoor activity, and he had longed to take the trip to Hudson Bay with the therapist. This acknowledgment was accompanied by feelings of shame and guilt.

In this case, the proverb "nothing ventured, nothing gained" was used to connect vividly the patient's fear of risking an insight about himself with the concrete elements of risk in the manifest dream. The concrete referents of the proverb, with overtones of tangible and material risk and subsequent achievement, were connected with the intangible world of psychological risk. Prior to using this intervention, the therapist had strongly suspected that the dream pertained to the therapy and to the therapist himself. Remembering that he had once been on a white water canoe expedition in which his own canoe had capsized, followed by a close and dangerous call, he superimposed the images of that experience upon the elements in the patient's dream. When the patient said that he was unsure, the therapist thought of the fact that he too had been unsure after his close call, but had decided to go on another white water expedition soon after. Out of this homospatial process involving superimposed images, words, and spaces, came the phrase "nothing ventured, nothing gained" and a created metaphor in context.

EFFECT OF METAPHORICAL INTERVENTIONS

Rather than continue at this point to cite more of the rich and varied possibilities or instances of the therapeutic use of created metaphors, I shall focus on those presented in order to spell out some reasons for the specific effect. A primary value of the therapeutic use of metaphor is the stimulation and subsequent understanding it provides for the therapist and the modeling it offers for the patient. The therapist is challenged to loosen up, be spontaneous, and to use his highest intuitive powers in order to create metaphors. While allowing himself to think freely and intuitively about the patient, he must also listen quite carefully in order to base the metaphors on what the patient brings to him. Particularly effective metaphors are often those that are based on something in the patient's experience, such as the skin metaphor for the patient with eczema, or on the patient's own language, such as in the "99% him and maybe 1% me" example. For the patient, the therapist's freedom and spontaneity, his willingness to take risks and to trust learning and working with intuitive processes provide a model for collaborative creative work. Appreciating the therapist's willingness to take risks, the patient can also loosen up, tap his own intuition, and take some daring risks at reformulation of his understanding of himself.

As a therapeutic tool, there are many specific reasons for metaphor's effectiveness. Used as an interpretation, metaphor has the significant power of having simultaneously a cognitive component and an affective one. Hence it embodies in its own structure the type of insight patients need to achieve. The metaphor has cognitive meaning: When a therapist says, "She gets under your skin," or refers to the patient as a sleepwalker, he is suggesting that skin irritation and a dazed state of consciousness, respectively, are related to internal feelings of anxiety and defensiveness; the vividness of such metaphors penetrates to affective levels as well. A concrete image connects the feeling to physical experience; the therapist is not prolix and punitive but brief, concise, and understanding.

Crucial to the effectiveness of metaphor is its affective power. In art, this aspect of the metaphor is taken for granted. It is one of the reasons that metaphor occupies a central place in every artistic field. The reasons for such power to stimulate affect are quite complex, but probably derive from the concrete imagery and vividness and from a homology between the metaphorical structure and unconscious processes. Although primary process thinking is not at all directly responsible for the creation of a metaphor, the completed metaphor manifests a compression of thought and imagery that is experienced as homologous with the primary process mechanism of condensation.[11]

Another major function of metaphorical intervention is its capacity to stimulate patient response. The stimulating property of an artistic metaphor is a vital and intrinsic aspect of its appeal. Metaphors such as the poetic "my hand was a bandage to his hurt" or the therapeutic "Your mother is a Brahmin, for without Brahmins, there would be no Untouchables" stimulate and evoke images and thoughts about caresses and injuries or exotic countries or—depending upon the audience's or the patient's sophistication—thoughts about eastern religions and intolerance. Sometimes there is only an affective response to metaphor initially but this is followed by some type of elaboration if the metaphor has been at all effective.

The capacity to stimulate response in art is due to the multiple meanings, the integration of dissonant or dissimilar elements, the intensity or vividness, and the homology with unconscious structures. Multiple meaning and dissonance are evocative on a conscious level and there probably is also some direct resonance with preconscious and unconscious levels. The use of an appropriate metaphor in therapy stimulates the patient to respond because of these factors operating together with a focus on pertinent content. Meaningful response, of course, occurs especially when the metaphorical interpretation is accurate. But even when it misses the mark to some extent it may help the patient to open up psychological areas that previously were unexplored. Sometimes this occurs when the metaphor incorporates something that the patient only touched on or only implicitly demonstrated to be a concern. For example, the metaphor involving Ivory soap led the compulsive patient to whom it was addressed to discuss later her concerns about being overly clean. Because the metaphor has concrete content, it opens up a patient's concrete issues of concern.

The sparse but highly suggestive scientific literature on the use of metaphor in therapy focuses primarily on this capacity to stimulate patient response.[12] Sledge emphasizes the ambiguity of metaphors and other linguistic factors as facilitating such response.[13] Caruth and Eckstein advocate the use of metaphor with both borderline and schizophrenic patients as a means of bringing together "remaining islands of ego functioning."[14] These authors, whose therapeutic use of metaphor consists primarily of picking up on metaphors or figurative language that the patient introduces, and elaborating or discussing the implications of such language, assert that metaphor serves important defensive functions. They believe that metaphors are effective because they allow the patient *not* to talk about his specific conflict but, instead, to reveal whatever related material he wants without being overcome by anxiety.

Reider, who describes a dramatic instance of his use of an aphorism with metaphorical qualities during treatment of a neurotic patient in psychoanalysis, states that metaphors penetrate to the patient's unconscious; he also emphasizes a defensive function.[15] To an hysterical woman with severe conflicts about seeing male genitalia, he said, "There's a saying in Japan that blind men are not afraid of snakes," and this allowed her to begin to talk about her fears. Reider asserts that the therapist's use of such metaphors allows the patient to respond more freely because he can concurrently defend against aspects of the interpretation that are too threatening. All of these writers, except Sledge, assume that metaphors are primarily primary process productions. This assumption is rooted in an erroneous belief that concrete, vivid mental productions, and elements containing visual imagery, are always direct resultants of primary process operations. There is a tendency to consider imagery or imagery-provoking types of thought as within the primary process domain.

In art, created metaphors have multiple meaning. The elements in a metaphor are in a state of tension with each other by virtue of the fact that they are dissimilar or disparate elements brought together. It is this tension of dissimilars within an integrated frame, in part, that stimulates aesthetic response. Because of the tension, we are stimulated to think about or otherwise experience the multiple meanings of the metaphor. There is no reason to believe that created metaphor operates any differently in therapy. While certain patients may use a therapist's metaphorical intervention defensively, just as any intervention can be used defensively, the major stimulus to response is within the structure of the metaphor itself. It is erroneous to think that an interpretation couched in such terms as "Your aggressive feelings toward your mother play a role in causing your skin ailment" would provide less of a defensive protection than "She gets under your skin, doesn't she?" or that "So you're a bar of Ivory soap, eh?" serves defensiveness more than "You want to believe that your husband is primarily at fault, but you must cause difficulties, too." Logical interpretations phrased in primarily literal language, in fact, may often provide the patient with an opportunity for defensive intellectualization. A compulsive patient, for instance, might use such explanations merely in the service of self-punitiveness. Both reaction formation and intellectualization would lead him to say, "Yes, I'm just terrible." Moreover, on the basis of linguistic and empirical studies, Glucksberg and his associates have shown that metaphorical language in context is more readily understood than literal language.[16]

A particular metaphor's effectiveness always depends a good deal on the type of metaphor used. Clearly, one would not use a complicated aphorism such as "Your mother is a Brahmin, for without Brahmins there would be no Untouchables" with a patient who has no familiarity with Indian culture. However, as many highly effective metaphors involve the reviving and restructuring of banal or cliché phrases and their contexts, there is great potential for using everyday expressions, slang, and other highly familiar language. Metaphorical interventions can therefore be used with patients from all socioeconomic classes and educational levels. Because they are vivid and often contain relatively simple and concrete terms, they are in fact often quite effective with tough adolescents and nonintellectual patients. Not only are metaphorical interventions comprehensible and stimulating to such patients but, because they function to a large degree on an affective level, they are readily assimilated.

FURTHER CLINICAL APPLICATIONS

Metaphorical interventions are effective in a variety of therapeutic circumstances and approaches. The following example demonstrates an application to the group therapy situation: A middle-aged female patient suffering

from manic-depressive illness had been quite disruptive in a series of therapeutic community meetings in a psychiatric hospital. She paced around
constantly and frequently would remove articles of clothing or otherwise
expose herself. She seemed to find it impossible to sit in one place; often,
she would make a loud remark to a staff member or another patient and
then get up and walk out of the meeting. Shortly she would return, sit in a
different place, and within a few minutes make another remark and repeat
her previous behavior. Observing that her verbal comments, though psychotic and highly disorganized, were hostile to other members of the
group, the staff member-leader of the group addressed her directly and said:
"Joyce, you are a hit-and-run driver."

The leader's comment produced laughter, both from the patient herself
and from other members of the group. She then stated that the comment
was correct and sat down. Members of the group began to talk with her
directly about the hostility in her comments, the discomfort caused by her
disrobing in the group, and some recognition developed for everyone (including Joyce herself) that this latter behavior had not been so much
sexually motivated as unconsciously hostile in intent. Although she again
became somewhat agitated toward the end of the same meeting, she then
merely got up and paced around but did not leave. During subsequent
meetings, when she again returned to some of the symptomatic behavior of
verbal attack followed by leaving or by attempts to leave the group, allusions were made to the metaphor "hit-and-run driver" by a member of the
group or sometimes by the patient herself. Frequently, there was further
discussion of her hostility and also of her hurting and of being hurt.
Gradually, her own hostile comments became more direct and clear and
were undisguised by psychotic disruptions and incoherencies.[17]

Related to the theory of metaphor as defense but different with respect
to method of application is the approach of Milton H. Erickson. For
Erickson, as for the psychoanalytic writers cited earlier, metaphor is a
nonthreatening and indirect means of reaching the patient's unconscious
mental realm, although his and the psychoanalytic definition of unconscious differ in some respects. Used as a major form of therapeutic intervention, his metaphors are applied both in interactive discourse with individual
patients and families, and in a practice that has been named the "embedded
metaphor" technique.[18] With this technique, he develops particular metaphors that he considers applicable to an individual or family constellation
and weaves them into stories and parables about life experiences. These
stories are sometimes about his own life experiences and those of his friends
and acquaintances, about childhood development in general, or about

other (unidentified) patients; they are chosen because of their pertinence to the problems of the patient to whom they are told.

For example, a psychology professor suffering from emotional difficulties in connection with the end of his 12-year marriage was told a story by Erickson about an artist who was painting a picture of a circus scene.[19] The artist of the story was also a teacher like the professor, Erickson said, and he was concerned about the use of the color blue in his painting. He had used blue on a coat jacket being worn by a clown, a ribbon on a horse's tail, and a merry-go-round, and wondered about whether they were all the same shade. After setting the stage in this fashion, Erickson then went on to describe the picture and tell the patient—without stipulating any connection to him—that this artist had marital difficulties. He said the following: "His first wife had kept him and treated him like the south end of a northbound horse, had made a clown out of him and kept him on a merry-go-round never knowing if he was going up or down. I don't believe yet that he knows what that picture means. It's out of his system." To this, it is reported, the patient nodded his head and smiled "with regular responses to each image in the picture."[20]

In this example, Erickson's metaphors connected with the color blue, i.e., "south end of a northbound horse," "clown," "merry-go-round," serve as indirect interpretations about the patient's submissive relationship with his wife. Because he did not encourage patient responsiveness and working-through, the primary effect of such interpretations tended to be teaching and influencing behavior. In this way, Erickson functioned in a manner similar to that of the creative artist or writer in relationship with society at large. Just as these use metaphor to teach, to move, and to influence their audiences and spectators, the Ericksonian approach produces similar effects with individual patients or families.

An important difference from the artistic production, however, lies in the particularity of Erickson's metaphorical constructions. He developed metaphors from the patients' own words and from his meticulously keen observations of patients' behavior and reactions. In this manner, his metaphors appear to result from a creative homospatial process arising from a particular therapeutic context in each case. Not a matter of using standard or cliché metaphors in therapy, such as those advocated by Barker,[21] Erickson's metaphors are new and unique. Although less extensively derived from verbal interaction than is usual in psychoanalytic psychotherapy, they seem to result from superimposition of mental imagery derived from Erickson's highly developed observational skills.

Creation of effective metaphor also plays a role in behavioral therapy approaches, albeit not manifestly an interpretative one. In the behavioral therapy desensitization procedure, for instance, a patient who is phobic about dirt may be asked to imagine scenes such as seeing himself opening the top of a garbage can and finding it swarming with cockroaches. Although the behavior therapist would very likely not explain the process in these terms, I believe one can characterize this in part as a metaphorical intervention. In choosing an appropriate desensitizing scene or image to use with a particular patient, the therapist spends a good deal of time trying to understand the conditions and circumstances of that patient's phobic reaction. Choice of an appropriate scene, then, would likely depend on the therapist's ability to superimpose a concrete image onto what he senses or believes is a source of the patient's conflict. Hence, an idea such as swarming cockroaches might properly pertain to a particular patient's fear of dirt because it represented underlying emotions of unbridled aggressiveness or sexuality. In addition to the behavioral response shaping aspects, the extent of success of the desensitization procedure may in this way depend a good deal on the therapist's appropriate choice of metaphor. This can be true for positive images or scenes as well as negative ones. As support for this conjecture, the following finding in a desensitization experiment is pertinent:

[Two] subjects revealed how their specific [desensitization] . . . images would, with repeated presentation, begin to change so that well-known individuals would appear, e. g., in an audience they were visualizing (family members, employers). They related that a surprising amount of affect would ensue and they were subsequently induced into making a series of insightful realizations about the origins of their PS [pre-sensitization] anxiety, why it was maintained, etc.[22]

ESSENTIALS AND CAVEATS FOR
METAPHORICAL INTERVENTIONS

As a last example of the often simple lucidity and essentials of this type of therapeutic intervention, I shall describe a minimal but creative metaphorical enactment directed toward the breaking of a therapeutic impasse. A 38-year-old man was unable to see that his whining, childish behavior, which characteristically alienated him from other people, was a replica of what he himself had described as his mother Louise's common mode of behavior toward him. Frequently, over several weeks, the therapist made attempts to clarify how the patient had alienated numerous different individuals by adopting his mother's whining, complaining tone. Comments such as: "Isn't that the way your mother would have done it?" or "You seem to have been behaving in that situation exactly as your mother did with you when your father went to work," or "That sounds just like your mother," were used to no avail. Each time the patient either disagreed or explained away the circumstances by referring to various other factors. Defensiveness and rejection of the interpretation characterized his response.

It was only at a point a few weeks later that this particular impasse was resolved. The patient then was recounting yet another experience in which he had antagonized someone and had also felt badly treated, when the therapist became aware that the patient was using a tone of voice that sounded precisely like the whining tone that his mother must characteristically have used. Thus, while the patient was continuing to describe the details of his experience, the therapist merely said, "Yes, Louise."[23]

This metaphorical attaching of the patient's mother's name directly to him had the effect of producing an immediate insight. The patient was momentarily surprised, but, with a silent laugh, then said, "You are absolutely right; that's just the way my mother talks." More elaboration of the pathological aspects of his identification with his mother followed.

Some important distinctions apply to conditions such as whether the therapist is initiating a metaphor himself, whether he is responding to a patient's metaphor with another metaphor, or whether he is encouraging the patient to elaborate on meanings and associations connected to his production. In art, it is a maxim that metaphors cannot be translated or elaborated in literal terms. When, for example, we attempt to explain the meaning of a metaphor such as "the branches were handles of stars," by pointing out that the stars are presented as reachable or holdable, we deprive the metaphor of some of its vitality. Even going somewhat further and pointing out the subtle nuances, such as an evocation of the idea of an eternal relationship between elements of nature, could excite some interest but does not compete aesthetically with the mere statement of the metaphor in the first place. Because artistic and literary critics constantly do elaborate on the meanings of metaphors in just this way, they are often attacked as being too analytical or too academic.

However, although analysis of a particular metaphor may indeed render it somewhat less interesting, it can also sensitize the viewer to a fuller, more immediate and wider appreciation of the next metaphor he encounters. These considerations also apply to psychotherapy. Encouraging a patient to elaborate on the meaning and association of his own characteristically used metaphors (and also figurative expressions) is an effective way of getting at unconscious meaning, as a metaphor is a compressed construction that brings together a number of a patient's conflicts.[24] Because it always has a strong affective component, analyzing a metaphorical construction can be a shortcut to important preconscious and unconscious emotional constellations. Exploring a phrase such as "My wife had her foot on my neck" could possibly lead to the patient's coming to understand some of the reasons that he gets himself into such a position—for example, because there are some pleasures in it. The concrete referents of the metaphor might derive from early childhood voyeuristic experiences of peering under women's skirts or from other sensual and sexual connections. Once such a metaphor is explored and the patient attains a grasp of the unconscious factors underlying it, his understanding may apply to other metaphors he or the therapist uses, and hence facilitate a rapid achievement of a fuller type of combined cognitive and affective insight.

Responding to the patient's metaphor with another metaphor, or with a literal discussion of what the therapist feels are its implications, can have the value connected with other types of metaphorical interventions, but there are some hazards. Elaborating on the patient's metaphor tends to be quite intellectually analytic and, just as in the artistic case, can deprive the metaphor of its affective component for the patient. When the therapist says, "By that, you mean to say, etc.," he tends to treat metaphor as a readily translatable type of verbal production and may thus inadvertently encourage the patient to communicate through metaphor on a regular and excessive basis. Even when the therapist avoids direct interpretation and responds to the patient's metaphor with another metaphor, he runs a large risk of missing the point of the initial metaphor. He then encourages a dramatic interaction which, while it may seem to be perfused with deep understanding on both participants' parts, may be totally wrong.

CHAPTER IV

Homospatial Process and Empathic Understanding

Empathy, and empathic understanding, constitute another type of creative effect of the homospatial process in psychotherapy. Initially described by workers in aesthetics, empathy is today a major clinical construct of treatment. This path from art and aesthetics to clinical theory and practice is by no means a new one. Sigmund Freud, the founder of the principle of modern psychotherapy, had a profound appreciation for the importance of art and literature and the insights of artists and writers throughout history. Indeed, he publicly acknowledged the deep understanding of the human psyche provided by writers and artists before him, as in the following: "But creative writers are valuable allies and their evidence is to be prized highly, for they are apt to know a whole host of things between heaven and earth of which our philosophy has not yet let us dream. In their knowledge of the mind they are far in advance of us everyday people, for they draw upon sources which we have not yet opened up for science."[1]

In line with this heritage, then, it can be no surprise that empathy and empathic understanding in treatment can be illuminated by considerations based on scientific research on creativity. The concept of empathy, introduced into clinical theory first by Freud, was earlier the cornerstone of a theory of artistic and aesthetic experience conceived by the German psychologist Theodor Lipps.[2] Lipps also influenced Freud extensively in his theory of the comic and, as has been shown by Kanzer, Lipps's concept of an unconscious antedated Freud and directly influenced him as well.[3]

Lipps's term "Einfühlung," literally meaning "feeling into" was translated into English as "empathy," based on Latin and Greek equivalents, by the psychologist Titchener.[4] The English aesthetician Vernon Lee (Violet Paget) elaborated the concept and experience of empathy and considered it to be the major factor in aesthetic pleasure.[5] For example, Lee pointed out that we react positively to a metaphor such as "the mountain rises [up in front of us]"[6] because we have experienced raising our own heads when looking at a tall mountain. Controversy about the precise nature of such empathy developed between Lipps and Lee, and also Groos[7] who was famous for his psychological studies of play. The art critic Worringer later attempted to shift aesthetics away from empathy toward what he called abstraction.[8] Psychologist Groos had focused on "inner imitation" in his discussion, and for several decades after him, experimental and sensory psychology also emphasized the imitative factors in empathy. In more recent years, empathy has been of interest to psychologists involved in clinical and experimental investigations and developmental studies of socialization, altruism, and social learning.[9]

Clinical interest in empathy has been strong since the introduction by Freud, and seminal papers on the mechanism of empathy in treatment have been written by Fliess, Greenson, Ferreira, Schafer, and Beres and Arlow.[10] Also, Rogers has put a good deal of emphasis on empathy in his non-directive therapy approach and it has been a focus of his psychotherapy research.[11]

A somewhat distinct development has been the work of Kohut[12] and his followers, in which a "central position"[13] of empathy in both human development and psychotherapy has been emphasized. Work of this group has focused on the role of empathy, and on the nature of empathy as a mode of understanding, more than on explanations of the mode of action or psychodynamic structure of empathy itself. Kohut, for instance, defines empathy as "vicarious introspection" and, while emphasizing an observational and data-gathering aspect to this function,[14] he does not explain how this type of introspection actually leads to understanding and knowledge. Historically, then, the empathy construct has passed from aesthetic discourse, involving considerations of the experience of pleasure and involvement in an artistic object, through Freud's work and into modern psychotherapy, where it is considered a factor in a treatment process involving both intrapsychic and interpersonal factors.

I have traced this history to throw into relief the variable nature of this construct, to put empathy in art and empathy in human relationships into a correct historico-theoretical perspective,[15] and to focus attention on the challenges connected with considering the nature of empathy in the treatment process. The term "empathy" has accrued a number of overtones and meanings through popular as well as technical usage, and these additions are not necessarily intrinsic either to the psychological properties of the phenomenon or to its therapeutic effect. For example, in common parlance the word empathy has come to be used as a virtual synonym for the word sympathy, but it is important to distinguish these terms with respect to therapy. Whereas sympathy means to feel the same as someone else, as when one says, "I am in sympathy with you," or "I share your feelings," empathy means to understand as well as to share in a manner that goes beyond having the same surface feelings. Being empathic with a depressed person in a therapeutic setting would not consist of becoming depressed oneself or saying "I also feel your future is black and therefore feel sorry for (or with) you," but it could involve understanding and responding to difficulties with aggression and self-esteem behind the depressive presentation and affect.[16]

Empathy is also often linked with love and warmth. People are described as warm and empathic or loving and empathic and, in therapy, warm interventions are often automatically described as empathic ones. Although I believe there are intrinsic connections between warmth, love, and empathy, they are not simple or direct.[17] A therapist's empathy may be experienced by a patient as warm, or even loving, but warmth or love does not directly generate empathy and empathic understanding.

Usually, also, empathy is considered similar or related to intuition. Kohut,[18] as well as Beres and Arlow,[19] draws distinctions between these phenomena. In this case, however, this commonly made connection does provide some special clues to the psychological properties of empathy and its therapeutic effect. Intuition is similar to empathy because both are, in some way, sources of knowledge. After Freud introduced the idea of empathy into psychoanalysis, he defined it as "the mechanism by means of which we are enabled to take up any attitude at all toward another's mental life"[20] and pointed to an essential elucidating or knowing function. While intuition consists of drawing conclusions from minimal cues and tends to be primarily a cognitive skill pertaining to all realms of knowledge, empathy pertains primarily to human experience and has strong affective components. Both, however, have distinct cognitive and knowledge-generating functions. These latter functions of empathy, as suggested in Freud's comment, are crucial to the conduct of a treatment based on understanding, both cognitive and affective, of another's mental life.

Although there are many different ways of understanding and being with a patient that relate to empathy, or are called empathy, I propose that the role and function of the empathic process in treatment derive closely from the initial construction of "feeling into" another object. From tracing the nature of this operation of "feeling into" comes an explanation of both the mode of transmission and the type of understanding and knowledge achieved about another's mental life. Not a self-evident operation, "feeling into" in treatment is related to empathy in aesthetic experience and is primarily a creative function.[21]

In the psychotherapeutic transaction, empathy involves the homospatial process. As with the creation of metaphors, the therapist cognitively and affectively formulates multiple entities as occupying the same space. However, beyond and including words and their meanings as in poetry, visual forms as in art, and sounds as in music, the therapist conceives his self representation together with the patient in the same space. In this process, the therapist actively "feels into" and superimposes his representation of himself with his mental model of the patient. He may conceive of himself as actually sitting where the patient is and also include in such a physical image the mentally represented word, visual, and sound experiences he has had in sessions with the patient. As the homospatial process can involve the visual, auditory, kinesthetic, tactile, olfactory, and gustatory sensory modes, the therapist experiences superimpositions of multiple sensory representations associated with the patient's location and psychological experience—how the patient sits, moves, experiences the taste of food, etc. Most important, there are superimpositions of the therapist's and patient's "lived space"[22]—the mental model of the patient's feelings, thoughts, and experiences and the therapist's mental representation of his own feelings, thoughts, and experiences. This mental model of the patient may—and, in the most effective and fully developed empathic experiences, usually does—derive from a rather long and protracted association with the patient. Also, the therapist must have a fundamental base of systematic knowledge together with a preconsciously available storehouse of experience with human conflict, crisis, and suffering. The longer the association with the patient and the more developed the mental model, the more complex and protracted the empathic experience.

Let us look first at an example of what is appropriately described as an empathic "event," a short-term phenomenon: A middle-aged hospitalized male patient with a long history of impotence reported to his therapist that he had begun a relationship with a female patient having strong sexual overtones. Because the patient had fairly recently been focusing on concerns about homosexual masturbation fantasies, it first appeared to the therapist that a fairly strong acting-out resistance had developed. Furthermore, the hospital had quite explicit prohibitions against sexual relations among patients, and the picture was further complicated by the appearance of what seemed to be the patient's overt rebellion against hospital rules.

While the patient talked about his relationship with the woman, the therapist listened and tried to find an effective way of confronting him with his resistant behavior. Experiencing the patient's account as increasingly defiant and closed off with respect to the possibility of insight, the therapist then began to change his mode of listening. He listened to this patient's words about his intense need to be with the woman and, actively but fleetingly, mentally represented himself sitting where the patient was and talking about this relationship. At that point he continued to hear the patient desperately trying to escape his homosexual concerns and also experienced another aspect of the patient's discourse. It sounded quite a lot like the words of an adolescent male who was having overdramatized feelings of love for a girl he had not known very long. Listening carefully to this aspect of the patient's production brought back his own feelings as an "in-love" adolescent and memories of concerns at that time. Specifically, he remembered the feeling of having something to live up to—he felt he had to live up to both the girl's and his own expectations. Remembering this, he commented directly to the patient about such a feeling, saying it seemed he felt he had something he had to live up to. In response to the intervention, the patient relaxed his defensive stance somewhat and began to talk of his fears of pursuing the relationship. The therapist then attempted to clarify the patient's fears; that led directly to the topic of his serious concerns about sexual performance.

In the therapeutic process, empathy is an active motivated function that leads to particular understanding of the patient's inner psychological state.[23] It is, as Schafer has described it, "a creative act" in personal relationships.[24] The product of a creative process is, as I have said, both new and valuable, and empathy produces useful interpersonal knowledge where it did not exist before. Therefore, it should come as no surprise that a creative operation present in other types of creative activity should be involved. Therapeutic empathy is not the same as the general developmental function Herbert Mead called "taking the role of the other."[25] Nor is therapeutic empathy the same as "getting with"[26] the patient, getting on his side, or simply conceiving how another person feels. These are probably early aspects of the empathic process, but simply being on a patient's side does not produce knowledge by itself about the patient's inner experience, nor does it necessarily lead to such knowledge.

Conceiving another person's feelings primarily involves a shift of perspective alone. Although shifting of perspective has importance, like Mead's construct it is not specific to therapeutic empathy but is an aspect of everyday human interaction and all functional relationships. Experimental support for this distinction comes from a study by Stotland in which instructions to subjects differentiated between imagining what another felt, imagining oneself in another person's situation, and simply watching another person carefully. Subjects who experienced distinct physiological and subjective responses to another person's pain were, to a significant degree, neither in the group instructed to imagine what the other person felt, nor in the one told to observe reactions carefully, but in the group specifically told to imagine themselves in the other person's place.[27]

Since Freud's initial formulation of the psychodynamic structure of empathy, i.e., "a path leads from identification by way of imitation to empathy," identification has been considered a core aspect of the phenomenon.[28] Fenichel emphasized the function of body imitation in producing the identification.[29] Schafer described the gradual building up of a structural identification with the patient that optimally remained segregated within the therapist's ego "as an object of actual or potential contemplation," while Fliess earlier, and Beres and Arlow later, took the position that the identification was a modified type they termed "transient."[30] Greenson, Shapiro, Buie, Basch, and others have criticized such formulations on the basis that classical identification involves a structural change in the ego that is not evident in empathic processes.[31] In support of such criticism, Meissner's careful and systematic discussion of the identification mechanism stresses the need to take its intrinsic defensive roots into consideration.[32]

Defense and empathy do not appear to be at all connected. Although some writers have pointed out that empathy can be used for defensive purposes[33] and some have shown deceptive confusions between countertransference factors and empathy,[34] it is difficult to provide an adequate psychodynamic account for a defensive genesis of the empathy phenomenon. Moreover, as a largely passive and unconscious mechanism,[35] it is difficult to connect identification with empathy's conscious, actively motivated aspects. Similar considerations apply to the proposition that projective identification is the basis of empathy.[36]

In the case example cited, the therapist did experience a subjective sense of feeling as the patient did, and some prior identification with the patient may possibly have been involved, but other aspects of the sequence of events need to be emphasized. For one thing, the therapist was clearly aware of his own separateness from the patient and the transient experience of being the same as the latter was succeeded by knowledge about the latter's preconscious contents. Such separateness within the empathic experience has been also cited by some of the above theorists emphasizing identification, but considered only as an indication of the functioning of a special *type* of identification, rather than as a contradictory piece of data.[37] More recognizable in the example is something similar to what Beres and Arlow call "signal affect,"[38] a premonitory sense of some event or change. The therapist experienced the patient as closed off and defiant but nothing happened automatically; he was then motivated to *change his mode of listening*. In this changed mode, he actively superimposed his self representation upon an image of the patient talking. He brought his own "lived space" into the same "lived space" as the patient and began the creative homospatial process leading to empathic understanding. He then continued to superimpose his self representation, specifically as an adolescent, upon the representation of the patient as an adolescent, in a continued "feeling into" process. This led to an understanding of the patient's preconscious concern that he formulated into a verbal interpretation.

In the creative process in art and in psychotherapy, the homospatial process is actively oriented to the achievement of a goal. In the creation of artworks, such a goal may be the formulation of metaphors and other integrations; in the psychotherapeutic process, the goals may be sharing the patient's thoughts and feelings and understanding them. Precise motivation for achieving particular goals differs in different activities; in the therapeutic process, distinct experiences often move the therapist toward the empathic event. This may be dysphoric lack of comprehension, signal affect, or other. Embarking on the homospatial process, in both art and therapy, first involves absorption in the material—whether it be particular words and meanings or dynamic psychological forces—next a focused type of concentration and attention, and then a breaking away from previous constellations and configurations. Thus, in the creation of the metaphors "the branches were handles of stars" and "tarantula rays of the lamp spread across the conference room," the first step in the homospatial process involved the focus on the sounds and meanings of the words, then each pair of words "branches" and "handles" or "tarantula" and "lamp" were taken out of their ordinary perceptual contexts and brought into physically impossible mental configurations within the same spatial location. In the empathic event in therapy, the homospatial process first moves patient and therapist out of their usual contexts as totally separated objects and brings them into an impossible configuration within the same space. Need I add that the therapeutic event also involves some psychological risks that are not as apparent—on the surface, at least—in the poetic homospatial process?

Following the break in the usual context, the therapist's mental superimposition of his self representation with the patient representation involves simultaneous togetherness and separation. Thus, the therapist in the example experienced himself talking along with the patient. This was neither "just as" the patient nor "as if" he were the patient. This was not the therapist simply substituting himself for the patient in a thought such as "How would I feel if I were in the patient's shoes?" In order to carry out a mental superimposition, a full-blown and active "feeling into" the patient, the therapist must have a clear and well-developed sense of his own self boundaries. Representing himself within the same space as the patient does not involve fusion or merging but a fleeting and highly unstable sense of dynamic interactive sharing. Because it is unstable, cognitively conflictual, and arousing, the mental conception becomes progressive and generates new images and articulations, such as the example of the therapist and patient both being adolescents in love. As these new mental events within the homospatial process continue, a particular factor of understanding is crystallized. This factor of understanding is an important constituent of the creative progression and effect. When used in interpretations, or otherwise conveyed to the patient in the mutual creative process, it functions to produce therapeutic movement and tangible insights. Creating insight is one of the major therapeutic actions of psychotherapy.[39]

THE NATURE OF EMPATHIC KNOWLEDGE
IN PSYCHOTHERAPY

We now must look more specifically at the factor of initial understanding itself to see how the homospatial process operates to bring it about. In pursuing this, I shall propose some answers to scientific questions regarding the nature of empathic knowledge in therapy and how that knowledge is transmitted. Three explanatory foci are pertinent: (1) self and object representation, (2) intrapsychic operations, (3) cognition.

In the therapist's empathic experience, the homospatial process involves bringing the image or representation of the self into the same mentally conceived space as the image, representation, or model[40] of the patient. Just as in the homospatial process leading to the creation of poetic and other artistic metaphors, the elements of the representations are in dynamic interaction with each other. Consisting of both unconscious and conscious memories, ideas, and affects, these interacting elements modify each other in a continuing dynamic elaboration and they still retain discrete identifying features. With self and object representations within the same mental space, conscious and unconscious elements of the self representation modify the object representation and vice versa. Particular ideas, memories, and feelings connected with the self representation interact with both experienced and postulated ideas, memories, and feelings incorporated within the representation of the object.

The bringing together has not been a matter of juxtaposition, condensation, or combination. Instead, there is mutual interaction and modification while self and object boundaries remain intact. Thus, with regard to the patient talking about his love affair, when the therapist conceived himself within the same space as this patient, he instantaneously experienced himself also as someone talking and thinking about love. Although the therapist's self representation was that of a mature person talking of love, the superimposition upon the patient's production led to interaction and subsequent modification of both self and object representations. Concomitantly, the therapist experienced the patient as an adolescent in love and felt himself to be a patient overdramatizing an infatuation. This led him to remember his own adolescent love affairs and to recognize his tendency to overdramatize himself at that time. He next thought of his concerns about living up to both his own and the adolescent girl's expectations; these concerns seemed to have a meaningful connection with the patient's productions.

Just as the poet's hazy mental superimposition of "branches" and "handles" or "tarantula" and "lamp" led to mutual modifications of shapes and word representations, and to new images and ideas of "stars" or "rays," respectively, so too the therapist's hazy and fleeting superimposition of himself and the patient led to a mental interaction involving mutual modifications together with a series of images and ideas regarding expectations. Then, applying these images and ideas to the therapeutic context, just as a poet applies mental imagery to the realm of words and the painter to the realm of shapes and colors, the therapist recognized that the patient was concerned about the expectations both of the real woman and of the therapist himself. With this recognition, he decided to make an interpretation about the former as an introduction to the issue of transference expectations with the latter. The decision to follow this particular interpretive sequence was a matter of technical procedure pertaining to the context of that particular therapy session and need not delay us with further explanation here.

Another example can serve to clarify achievement of knowledge through the homospatial process over a longer, more extended period of time. An anorexic young female patient, in therapy for several years, had consistently complained of difficulties with her female co-workers as a factor interfering with her ability to function effectively. Over the course of therapy, the therapist had gradually developed a model of the patient as highly competitive with other women, resorting often to projective and introjective defenses, but perfectionistic and successful in a way that might indeed instill competition and jealousy in others. They had worked together on her past difficulties with women. Recently she had repetitively complained over a series of sessions about being unable to sit in the company lunchroom with other women workers because of her inability to eat. She had also complained that these women gossiped too much. Unable to determine how the difficulty in eating related to the gossiping, or what was embodied in the patient's experience, the therapist focused primarily on her being excluded from the conversation.

In the next session, she started by talking about a woman friend—not a co-worker—who had bothered her. The therapist pointed out, in this particular instance, that this woman was attempting to provoke the patient's jealousy. To his distress and confusion, his comment induced a continuation of her complaints about not being able to sit with co-workers in the cafeteria. As the therapist then attempted to clarify whether the patient was being excluded or whether she excluded herself, he thought of an insight he had had one time about a problem of his own—he had believed that a girl friend had been too dependent on him, but instead he really had been too dependent on her. As he continued listening to the patient, who was now complaining that the other women talked about themselves all the time but she never did, he actively represented himself superimposed upon the patient's location in the cafeteria surrounded by women talking. He then experienced a feeling of both himself and the patient as dependent and overwhelmed in the situation. Concomitantly feeling both the patient's dependency and a sense of himself as excluded in the situation a moment later—in an interaction of mental representations—a feeling of jealousy became crystallized. He realized that the patient was jealous that the other women were free to gossip and talk about people as they liked.

The therapist commented to the young woman that the workers were not exclusive or jealous of her because she did not gossip, but that she was jealous of them. This then led, gradually and in an unfolding way, to the patient's exposing other areas of her jealousy. She spoke of jealousy of her boss and another worker and eventually of jealous feelings toward her younger sister. In the next phase of the homospatial process, superimposition did not persist, but the therapist actively aided the patient in making connections in the type of articulation process described in Chapter VII.

The steps in this empathic experience consisted of the long-term development of a model of the patient, the therapist's confusion and intensified motivation to understand the material, his recognition and specification of an important factor in himself, and a purposeful and active superimposition of the fully developed self representation upon his mental representation of the patient. Also illustrated in the detailed dissection of a fleeting mental experience are the factors of interaction of mental representations, followed by crystallization of understanding and a subsequent longer unfolding clarification and testing within the overall progression.

In another case, a middle-aged patient had led a highly schizoid isolated life and had been in therapy for over a year. In the course of a therapy session in which he was berating his elderly mother for cutting him out of her will, he talked of previous hatred for her and described himself as having tried to remove her completely from his life six years before. He stopped seeing her completely but "then," he said, with pain in his voice, "when I became desperate and really troubled I had no one to call but her. I had lived my life without any contacts at all with people and she was the only one I could call."

For a long moment, the therapist hearing this felt completely immersed in the patient's feeling and point of view. "Yes," the therapist said to himself, "this patient never had any real friends and sadly the only person he could turn to was his mother." He was, at this moment, feeling sympathy and oneness with the patient, not empathy. As he experienced the depth and intensity of the patient's feelings of helplessness and depression, however, he began to shift his perception. While continuing to experience the sad affect, he focused on the present circumstance in which he was sitting with the patient in the office. In a momentary but active shift, he represented himself both separated from and connected to the patient at once in a mental superimposition. The patient, he then realized, was also excluding *him* from those he could call on. Did the patient feel that way "right now?" he asked, and, receiving an affirmative reply, pursued the reasons. The pursuit led the patient to acknowledge, for the first time, that although he hated his mother he also continued to be tied to her.

The homospatial representation of therapist and patient superimposed in this case involved an interaction of component elements similar to previous ones. However, rather than generating a specific insight or a factor of similarity, this interaction primarily emphasized separateness of therapist and patient and thereby clarified that the therapist was himself a subject of the patient's feelings of alienation. The therapist felt at first merged with the patient until shifting to a homospatial conception involving discrete self and object representations superimposed and interacting. He shifted from a merged and sympathetic stance of experiencing the same conscious feelings as the patient to an empathic stance in which he experienced both the patient's preconscious and conscious feelings together. In the homospatial process, the patient was bereft as well as attacking to him and he himself was also feeling bereft but, now, *unlike the patient*, he was able to mobilize active resources to cope with such feelings. Through the dynamic interaction of these representations he was able to separate himself and enlarge the scope of the inquiry.

PRESENTED KNOWLEDGE

The type of knowledge achieved in these examples of self and object representation within the same space should be differentiated from directly verifiable or so-called propositional knowledge and can best be termed "presentational" or, more simply, "presented" knowledge.[41] Rather than literally spelling out a specifically formulated series of verbal propositions about truth or validity, such as is found in textbooks and expository accounts, truth is displayed in a presented or embodied form as it is in artistic products and metaphors. For instance, in the first example I gave of the patient talking about his love affair with a woman, instead of specific formulations pertaining to oedipal, pre-oedipal conflicts or self-object impairments, the homospatial conception initially embodied a complex representation of both patient and therapist as adolescents in love. This representation *presented*, rather than proposed, several truths and the patient's feelings of love were *experienced*, rather than only conceptualized, by the therapist. Through subsequent exploration and clarification in therapy, some of the truths may be rendered explicit but usually not all of them. In the same way, created metaphors present truth about broad and complicated issues of human concern. They present direct embodiments of truth – on both a cognitive and an affective level – and point also to specific areas of validity.

Going back to my early example of the metaphor "the branches were handles of stars," the entire construction should, if effective, strike one as containing truth or validity. Thus, one might experience a sense of continuity between the world of nature on earth and in the universe, or else see a natural configuration of physical objects seeming to attest to the grandeur of God, or see stars as the top of a torch in the woods leading the beholder out of darkness and disorientation. Presented in all these ideas is some element of truth: Earth and universe are common components of nature; the world of nature provides putative evidence for the working of God; stars do lead wanderers out of dark woods. Also, perceptually valid factors are present in this, as in any good metaphor. Branches can look like wooden handles of canes or torches, stars may touch and seem held by branches of tall trees, and so forth. As I continue to spell out these literal truths, it should be apparent, as I stated in the previous chapter, that I do some violence to the immediate and overall impact of the verbal phrase itself; at the same time, I do not exhaust the possible range and depth of truth it contains. Such presented or embodied truth of a metaphor is manifold, virtually inexhaustible, and more than the sum of its parts. This applies to metaphorical constructions ranging from "Life's but a walking shadow" from Macbeth's funeral dirge for his wife (Act V, Scene V), to "Oh let there be nothing on earth but laundry/ Nothing but rosy hands in the rising stream/ And clear dances done in the sight of heaven" from Richard Wilbur's poem, "Love Calls Us to the Things of this World,"[42] and to more extensive central aesthetic metaphors such as the character Blanche within the Williams play "Streetcar Named Desire," or to pictorial and metaphorical images such as the large man in the painting "Man With a Hoe" by Millet. Also, it applies to scientific metaphors such as the productive one, "black holes in space." Presented and experienced truths, such as the deceptive insubstantiality of life, the gratification of redemption from sin, the loneliness of promiscuity, the grandeur and importance of simple labor, and visual paradox in nature, all come forward in these metaphors and there is always a sense of more. Also, all of these presented or embodied truths point to testable propositions about reality. Certainly, this has been clear in the field of astrophysics, where the "black holes in space" metaphor has proved especially generative of propositions and testable hypotheses and formulations.

In therapeutic empathy, truths embodied in and derived from the homospatial superimposition are similarly both manifold and testable. Like created metaphors, empathic presentations contain the cognitive and affective components of lived experience. Also, just as we use the Blanche metaphor to say rationally to ourselves we will not risk Blanche's particular fate in carrying out some action, empathic presentations may be the basis for an informed and rational decision to interpret or not interpret a patient's defensive stance. Such presentations are themselves evaluated and tested through specific derived interpretations, clarifying interventions, and the patient's responses.[43]

INTRAPSYCHIC KNOWLEDGE

With respect to the second focus of knowledge I mentioned, the intrapsychic, I have in previous works explained how unconscious material is actually unearthed and brought to consciousness during the creative process because of the psychodynamic structure of the particular creative functions themselves.[44] I described a mirror reversal of dreaming function of both the homospatial and janusian processes. Both have a mirror image relationship with unconscious dream and primary process mechanisms in that, as in all mirrors and mirroring, there is *reversal* along with similarity. The consciously willed homospatial process is superficially similar to unconscious primary process condensation, but concomitantly involves motivational, cognitive, and affective reversal. The janusian process has a mirror reversal relationship with the equivalence of opposites primary process mechanism. Because of these reversal relationships, both processes serve a directing and formative template function within the ego. As a psychological template, the function is homologous with physical templates that lock in and direct biological and other physical processes—the double helix genetic template is one example.

One psychological template function of these creative ego processes is to direct and reverse primary process operations and bring unconscious material into consciousness. Unearthing of unconscious material, the production of quasi-insightful experiences (not the full insight occurring in psychotherapy), and both arousal and reduction of anxiety—which has need-gratifying functions in its own right—are goals for the person engaged in creative activity.[45] On a cognitive level, the reversal of condensation mechanisms by the homospatial process is manifest in the hazy and transitory images and representations, in contrast to the intense, vivid, and formed effects of the primary process. These hazy and transitory properties in themselves produce cognitive tension that evokes further mental progression rather than the binding and quasi-resolution of drive and drive-derivatives of primary process condensation.

Spatial configurations of conscious homospatial representations do, in a very broad and general way, resemble unconscious condensation configurations but, as the obverse of promoting concealment and repression, the homospatial process instigates uncovering and the appearance of unconscious derivatives in consciousness. This occurs following the superimposition phase. Because creative thinking has particular cognitive goals as well as cathexis for unearthing unconscious derivatives, the homospatial process subsequently brings condensation structures into consciousness and begins an unravelling sequence. This unravelling sequence operates somewhat similarly to an association sequence in a psychoanalytic session, except that the associations are not free but embedded within the creative activity. Fragments representing wishes, fantasies, and other unconscious contents are "decondensed" or expanded and are incorporated into the work in progress. However, without the help of a therapist "other" or guide, so to speak, they are usually not fully recognized as unconscious derivatives by the creative thinker himself. While condensation mechanisms facilitate drive discharge, but keep unconscious material from consciousness primarily through disguise and distortion, the homospatial process operates in the reverse direction and facilitates unearthing and unconscious revelation.

For example, in the instance of the creation through the homospatial process of the metaphor of a horse and rider mentioned in Chapter I, the poet later became progressively—albeit dimly—aware of unconscious connections between the horse and feelings about his mother. These feelings were also incorporated into particular other ideas and metaphors within the poem, as well as into the poem's central poetic statement. He had, however, no inkling whatsoever of these connections beforehand.[46] Similarly, prior to the creation of the metaphor "the branches were handles of stars," that author had thought only of the sound and shape connections between branches and handles. Afterward, he became dimly aware of images of branchlike maternal arms encompassing a child. During further creative work related to this metaphor, the firelike intensity of the star led to conscious thoughts of warm, erotic sensations and to unearthed unconscious fantasies of erotic sensations in the held child. The unravelling stopped short, however, of connecting himself to the held child.

In the homospatial conception of therapist and patient within the same mental space, a similar unearthing of unconscious material occurs. Beres and Arlow[47] emphasize the emergence of the therapist's unconscious fantasies in the empathic experience, and the clinical literature on empathy is replete with descriptions of the therapist's becoming aware of preconscious and unconscious contents both during and after dramatic empathic experiences.[48] Although conscious superimpositions of mental contents intrinsic to the homospatial process were not specified by the particular authors, a careful examination of the published reports strongly suggests such operations.

For example, Simon reports a dramatic empathic experience in regard to a patient who described being attracted to a stewardess on an airplane and then spilling a drink she gave him all over his lap. Documenting his own response to the patient's story, Simon reports his initial conception as follows: "Lusting after the stewardess—spilling the drink. Hmm, fouling his own nest. . . . "[49]After this actively formulated representation of a bird in a nest superimposed upon the image of the patient in the airplane, his thoughts then drift to other matters and the dramatic sequence of events occurs. Simon mentally envisions "a cormorant-like bird everting its stomach, as if through its belly button," and soon after the patient spontaneously talks about an image of "a black widow spider" who "turns her stomach out and her own digestive juices start to eat away at her body so that the little spiders can eat her up." Reporting that he felt hit "like a thunderbolt" by the concurrence between his thoughts and the patient's image, he then detailed the complex and manifold unconscious roots of his and the patient's constructions.

There is little doubt from this therapist's discussion that *both* constructions of bird and spider were primary process condensations; moreover, the therapist's condensation appeared not before but *after* he had conceived and actively superimposed the image of "fouling his own nest" upon a mental representation of the patient spilling his drink upon his lap. The active bringing of the image of "fouling" into the same space as the spilling of the drink in a homospatial conception was the beginning of the creative empathic process. The process then continued with the unearthing of the cormorant for the therapist, and a coincidental appearance of a similarly structured condensation by the patient. Following that, the therapist's condensation was unravelled and further clarification of unconscious material occurred to him.

Simon's example illustrates that the therapist's unearthing of his own unconscious contents leads to *valid understanding of the unconscious contents of the patient*. Although there is no necessary and sufficient reason for therapist's and patient's unconscious contents to coincide consistently or exactly, validity is nevertheless quite high. This is because the process is based both on the patient's production and on the therapist's model of the patient derived from the therapeutic experience. Based partly on the therapist's own memories and experiences as well, it differs from ordinary intuitions based on memory alone. Like other sources of a therapist's understanding, the products of the homospatial process are used as interpretations that are then subjected to mutual verification within the therapy itself. Seldom as dramatic as the Simon example, the unearthing process continues through later therapy sessions and is incorporated into an unfolding creative process within the treatment.

For a less dramatic example of a similar psychodynamic sequence there is the following: In the process of working out a termination of therapy, a young male patient became quite rebellious toward his therapist. He threatened to get a job that he thought the therapist strongly disapproved of, he missed sessions, or he came late. In one session during this period, he arrived early but then tauntingly said he actually had hoped he was late. He proceeded further with this provocative tone and little the therapist did, such as interpreting his anxiety, seemed to produce any effect. Then, the patient said, still provocatively, "I would like to go outside and just sit."

At first, the therapist experienced the remark as a hostile wish to escape the therapeutic situation. Still motivated to understand, however, he fleetingly thought of comfortably sitting outside on the lawn and then conceived a hazy image of the patient in the same spatial location. Remembering that it had always been extremely difficult for this patient to relax and enjoy himself, he commented appreciatively that it seemed that the patient was able to think of himself as relaxing. Immediately, the patient's hostile and provocative stance melted and he said: "Everybody says I'm so much better. But now I have to prove myself." With this, the patient had introduced preconscious material and thereby gave evidence of the validity of the therapist's interpretation. The remainder of the session consisted of a discussion of the patient's concerns about having to prove himself during and after termination. Later within this session and those following, the therapist also became specifically aware of some of his own passive and regressive wishes that seemed to have been unearthed by the homospatial process along with the empathic understanding.

That full superimposition of mental images is involved in the homospatial process rather than such factors as analogic thinking, or merely shifting to a positive or sharing mode of listening, is demonstrated by another example involving the same therapist. In this case, he made a mistaken interpretation in a distinct failure of empathy. In an advanced phase of therapy, a middle-aged male complained about a childlike closeness between his mother and his aunt, a closeness that had always excluded him. His mother had recently had an accident and, when the patient phoned to talk to her, his aunt answered and promptly told him that she had moved in to be at his mother's side. Listening to this, the therapist asked himself how the patient might be feeling. There were no superimpositions of images or representations. Instead, he remembered his own gratifying feelings of taking care of a sick mother and decided that positive feelings must underlie the patient's resentment and complaint. He stated that it sounded as if the patient wanted to be with his mother, even to take care of her, but that his aunt was interfering. Rejecting this interpretation, the patient said that the therapist was way off base — "I don't really want to take care of my mother. I have dreams about her sucking my blood." Merely listening for the patient's perspective, without a full superimposition of self and object representations, may put one on the patient's side but may not be empathically correct. The types of listening "from within the patient's state of mind" described by Lichtenberg[50] and as the subject rather than "object acted upon" described by Schwaber[51] are effective early means of entering into the empathic process but are not themselves sufficient means of providing understanding.

COGNITIVE KNOWLEDGE

The third type of knowledge derived from the homospatial process within the empathy experience, I designate as "cognitive" because it pertains most clearly to the thinking and perceptual field. It is, however, intricately tied up with affect, motives, and other intrapsychic and interpersonal dynamics. When, as is often the case, manifest perceptual imagery is involved in the mental superimposition, there is a *widening of the field of mental perception and of conscious thoughts*. Because the homospatial process involves elements occupying the same mentally conceived spatial location, composition displays and boundaries of component elements necessarily appear to change. Because of alterations in the dynamic balance and array of elements, aspects of the perceptual field that previously were unnoticed become more prominent or newly delineated. Background features may come to the foreground and previously empty areas appear full. Contours of shapes are altered and a new topography appears.

All of this is highly transitory and the mental perceptions are usually dimly in awareness; for those who seldom experience conscious mental imagery, there may be little perception of imagery at all. The sense of a widening of the field of conscious thought is nevertheless experienced, although it may not have been heretofore described in the literature or in clinical discussions in just this way. This widening of the field of conscious thought consists of becoming aware, or paying attention, to aspects of a patient's communication — verbal or nonverbal — that were previously ig-

nored. Such aspects may be features of the patient's current communication
or they may derive from communications and interactions of the past.
Cognitive widening of the field operates together with forces reversing the
countercathexis of repression to produce remembrance as well as insight. It
would be a mistake to postulate that either the cognitive function or the
overcoming of repression comes first or is causally responsible; these two
factors operate in conjunction with one another.

An example from Greenson of an empathic experience illustrates both
the homospatial superimposition and the widening of the cognitive field:

I had been treating a woman for several years and . . . in one hour she recounted
the events of a weekend and focused in particular on a Saturday night party.
Suddenly she began to cry. I was puzzled. I was not "with it"—the crying left me
cold—I couldn't understand it. I realized that I had been partially distracted by
something she had said. At the party she mentioned a certain analyst and I had
become side-tracked, wondering why he was present. Quickly reviewing the events
she recounted, I found no clues. *I then shifted from the outside to participant listening.*
I went to the party as if I were the patient. Now something clicked—an "aha"
experience. A fleeting event told to me as an outsider eluded me, now in my
empathy this event illuminated the crying. At the party a woman had graciously
served the patient with a copious portion of food. To me as the observer, this event
was meaningless. *But to me as the experiencer, this woman instantly stirred up the*
picture of the patient's good-hearted and big-breasted nursemaid. The "aha" I experienced
was my sudden recognition of this previously anonymous figure. Now I shifted
back to the position of observer and analyzer. Yes, the longing for the old nursemaid had come up in the last hour. In the meantime the patient herself had begun
to talk of the nursemaid. My empathic discovery seemed to be valid. When the
analyst's association precedes and coincides with the patient's, it confirms that the
analyst is on the right track.[52]

In this full and unusually detailed description, it is clear that the therapist's cognitive field was widened and new understanding, consisting partly
of the overcoming of repression, occurred. He took notice of a previously
ignored female food provider at a party. It is also worth noting that
Greenson's empathic experience was explicitly conscious and deliberately
motivated. It also involved the bringing together of self and object representations in such a manner that he continued to be aware of his separation
from the patient. This was not fusion, nor was it identification in the
traditional sense of a structural modification of the therapist's ego. It was a
process of superimposition of self and object representations in which
perceptual imagery, memories, and thoughts appear.[53]

Greenson's reported feeling of lack of comprehension is rather typical of the onset of the homospatial process in the empathic experience. Some emotional event usually signals or begins the sequence. Here again, Beres and Arlow's term, "signal affect,"[54] seems suitably descriptive; it points to a motivating factor of affective importance to the therapist. I would add to or modify their formulation and point out that the homospatial process in the empathic experience operates specifically to unearth unconscious factors intrinsic to the signaling emotion or affect.

EMPATHY IN THE CREATIVE
PROCESS OF PSYCHOTHERAPY

The sequence of events is directly analogous to a characteristic sequence in creative activities in the arts and sciences. Briefly summarized, it is, as follows: The creative process begins with what the aesthetician Beardsley colorfully termed an "incept."[55] In the interview studies that I performed, I found that for a poet this "incept" consisted of a word, phrase, image, or idea; for a visual artist it was colors and shapes; and for a scientist it was a metaphor, a puzzle, or a mathematical equation. All of these, including in a complicated way the puzzles and mathematical equations, had some personal and unconscious significance for the creative person.[56] Partly because of this unconscious factor, the person was motivated to engage in a creative process that aroused personal anxiety and eventually resulted in some degree of unearthing, however small, of the unconscious material. For a lengthy set of reasons that I will not repeat here, this sequence was clearly part of the naturally occurring creative process and not induced by my presence as a psychiatrist investigator.[57]

In addition to the anticipated gratification of increased knowledge— personal as well as other types—another important motivating factor is the absorption in, and love for, the particular materials involved in the creative work. The poet's absorption in and love for words include their sounds, meanings, histories, and uses. His manipulation of words is itself an intense gratification and the homospatial process in poetry therefore often begins with an idea or feeling that particular words or phrases ought to be the same or related in some way. Both of the word pairs, "branches" and "handles," and "tarantula" and "lamp," it will be remembered, were superimposed partly because they were assonantal and shared similar sounds. Similarly, the painter and musician are motivated to explore and bring together sensory images of colors, shapes, and sounds that are foci of intense interest, love, and absorption. In this absorption, narcissistic investment has to some extent been overcome and there is love for sensory experience, ideas, and physical materials in themselves.

For the therapist engaging in empathy as a creative process, there are also emotionally charged incepts, both long-term and short-term, that begin the process. Long-term incepts consist of complicated self and object interactions and symbolizations directed by the particular contract for treatment and the background characteristics of both therapist and patient. The incept for the short term may be a feeling of being blocked or of not understanding the patient, the intrusion of a personal fantasy as cited by many previous writers on empathy, or a recognition of some similarity between what the patient has said or done and something experienced by the therapist. In all these circumstances, the therapist's absorption in, and love for, the material—be it an intriguing and puzzling dream report, recurrence and recognition of a resistant pattern, subtle or dramatic symbolization, or the complexity of the interactional field, indication of change and growth together with the connections between all of this with the health and welfare of the patient—instigated a creative homospatial process. Once begun, the therapist takes a risk and actually courts experiences of personal anxiety[58] in order to achieve understanding. It is because of this experience of anxiety followed by understanding that empathic events sometimes seem dramatic to the therapist himself.

Nevertheless, rather than a mysteriously driven process carried on out of the therapist's control, there is an important measure of active and specific creative activity—however fleeting and undetected even by the therapist himself—when engaging in the homospatial process. The process has very likely been used regularly by competent and creative therapists heretofore, but because it is so fleeting, the volitional element and the experience of superimposition may often have been unattended. In the same way, creative subjects I worked with had by themselves never before traced the particular characteristics of their thinking in creative work.[59] It is not, therefore, a mechanical operation that can be mechanically applied but a creative skill that is both developed and learned, even though its detailed characteristics pass rapidly through awareness.

There may also be other more passive, or at least more automatic, types of empathy in the therapeutic context, but these are neither directly creative nor comparably productive of distinct understanding and knowledge. Regardless of the mode of knowledge achieved (and all three types are usually involved) through the homospatial process, there are always both affective and cognitive components. What I have called the widening of the cognitive field results from interactions between affective and motivational factors in the homospatial process and the effects of imagery manipulation through superimposition. The partial overcoming of repression concomitant with widening of the field is due in part to the template function of the homospatial conception—its mirror reversal with respect to primary process operations. Also, other particular creative operations with both cognitive and affective aspects, such as the janusian process, play a template role in unearthing unconscious materials. After the therapist achieves understanding and some measure of anxiety reduction through unearthing of unconscious material, he uses this understanding in his general approach or subjects it to verification through formulations and interpretations to the patient. These can be overtly or implicitly denied or accepted. When the approach or formulations are effective, the patient usually introduces new material or otherwise collaborates in a mutual creative process.

CHAPTER V

Janusian Process and
the Flash of Insight
and Discovery

Playwright Arthur Miller told me the following: "Simultaneity of opposite forces. I can't imagine anyone failing to see that at the earliest phases of creation this procedure has to happen. I have always felt that it—the cohabiting of the unlike or opposed—provides the energy to go on with the making of a work, not because it is a solution but because it is the matrix of the problem that the work will finally de-intensify. . . . The creator . . . in maturity has learned how to hold in suspension this illogical logic, a balancing act which a wisp of breeze can undo. . . ."[1]

According to my documentary and interview evidence, numerous other creators in art and science, like Miller, formulate simultaneous opposites and antitheses as a "matrix" of a problem or as a flash of insight and discovery. Eugene O'Neill conceived the idea for the play "The Iceman Cometh" after realizing that a friend of his youth had simultaneously wanted and not wanted his own wife to commit adultery.[2] A novelist's initial formulation for his Pulitzer Prize winning novel was of a revolutionary hero who was responsible for the deaths of hundreds of people but with his own hand killed only the one person he loved; a poet conceived a poem about the relationship between sex and violence after having the idea that rocks on a beach were weapons of violence and, at the same time, felt like smooth human skin; Picasso's initial conception of his painting "Guernica" was of a woman simultaneously looking inside a room and outside at a courtyard; in addition to Einstein, Bohr, and McMillan discussed earlier, Darwin formulated the simultaneous operation of maladaptation and adaptation in the struggle for existence in discovering the principle of natural selection, Watson conceived chemical chains as simultaneously identical and opposite in determining the double helix structure of DNA, and Pasteur conceived chickens as both diseased and not-diseased at the same time in discovering the principle of immunization.[3]

All of these are instances of the operation of the janusian process in creative accomplishment. For the therapist engaged in creative therapeutic collaboration, the janusian process also involves what Miller calls a matrix. In a flash of insight and discovery, the therapist conceives simultaneously operating opposites or antitheses regarding the patient's mental functioning and behavior. Frequently, these simultaneous opposites or antitheses are constitutive of the patient's particular psychic conflicts. Unlike ordinary stepwise understanding of conflict, however, janusian formulations are not derived directly from inductive, deductive, or analogic reasoning. Although based on both theoretical and clinical expertise, they involve actively formulated leaps of understanding at both early and later phases of therapy. Motivated by the therapist's intense desire to comprehend or by a feeling of being stymied, they serve as waystations—Miller's "matrix of the problem"—in the production of the final creative outcome.

The path to construction of these formulations is varied and complex, but the immediate precursor in the sequence is the therapist's recognition of salient patterns or themes in the patient's past and current feelings, thought, and behavior. A 33-year-old unmarried female patient with symptoms of anorexia nervosa and bulimia had a history of a good deal of success in school and work. Also, she had always, she said, been a "nice" girl who sacrificed herself in her early years by taking care of a seriously depressed mother. Despite her successes and past laudatory behavior, however, she suffered from very low self-esteem. Consciously, her preoccupations centered completely on food; she constantly talked in therapy of her eating difficulties and their interference in her interpersonal relationships. For one thing, she felt she could not attend parties because she was tempted by the presence of large quantities of food and drink.

After several months of therapy, she decided on one occasion to try to go to a party despite her fears and misgivings. Although managing to go and stay for a while, she soon felt she had to leave because of acute anxiety and revulsion when viewing all the food. When she discussed these circumstances with the therapist later, she first dwelt on the details about the food but, in response to his exploration and questioning, shifted to talk about the interpersonal contacts at the party. She had been talking with a female friend, and, during the course of the conversation, began thinking that she was really a lot nicer person than this friend. She added that she had had similar thoughts about another friend with whom she had talked earlier. Finding then that she felt highly critical of both of them, she decided that there was no value in being at the party after all. She left feeling lonely and miserable.

At this point, the therapist had the following thought: *She is both below and above everyone else at once and is therefore all alone.* Listening to her account of her experiences at the party, he first remembered numerous previous occasions on which she had compared herself with others. Frequently, she decided she was nicer or smarter and placed herself above them. He also thought of her success in school and work and her helpfulness to her mother, and felt somewhat puzzled about how to understand or help her with her loneliness. At that moment, he actively shifted to the opposite and thought of her very low self-esteem. Immediately conceiving her as fixated simultaneously above and below everyone else, he realized she was on no one's level and alone. He then decided to transmit this understanding to her in the form of an interpretation, pointing out that one of the reasons she felt lonely was that she felt only above and below other people and never together with them.

The validity of this leap of understanding seemed to be demonstrated by subsequent events. At first, the patient argued that she never put herself above anyone else, just below. While continuing to challenge that aspect of the interpretation in subsequent sessions, she at one point told the therapist for the first time that she liked him and also talked both of feeling better and of eating somewhat more regularly. Gradually, with further discussion and application of the interpretation, her challenge became milder and milder and she began to make active choices not to compare herself with others and started to make more friends. Much later in the therapy, she and the therapist made connections between her behavior with friends and feeling both above and below her mother in her earlier years. In taking care of her mother during the period of the latter's depression, she felt like both a mother and daughter to her.

The flash of insight contained in this sequence was neither a welling up of unconscious material for the therapist nor a theoretically derived construction. With respect to the former, it was a fully conscious shift and connection of opposites. With respect to the latter, it went beyond a theoretical recognition of grandiosity as a defense against feelings of low self-esteem. It involved a compressed grasp in context of one of the patient's specific conflicts. Although surely unconscious material as well as conscious knowledge factors played a role, as both do in all types of thinking, the attainment of insight in this case resulted directly from the operation of the creative janusian process. The therapist, like the scientists and artists described earlier, actively shifted to formulate the opposites of being above and below operating simultaneously in the patient's feelings and behavior. This construction of a conflictual theme was eventually connected with the patient's competitive above/below feelings about her mother. Also, in other aspects of the therapy I have not described in this brief vignette, connections were made with the patient's conflicts about success and failure.

The janusian process in therapy begins with assumptions and formulations about the patient that are based on experience and association with that particular person. In this way, it follows the same sequence as in any creative field. The artist has familiarity and experience with his materials, the scientist with the canons of knowledge, and creative persons generally know their fields exceptionally well. On the basis of this association and knowledge, the therapist is both consciously and unconsciously aware of particular patterns and themes of the patient's mental functioning and behavior. Also, because of transference, the themes develop within the therapeutic situation itself.

Such themes and patterns are identified and worked with on the basis of theory, experience, learned technique, and other defined aspects of the therapist's skill. Both early and late in therapy, when such themes and patterns are refractory to exploration, when deeper or more extensive explanations are called for, when striking discrepancies occur, or when countertransference blocks are present, the creative therapist considers shifts, reversals, and extremes. The artist similarly chooses themes and develops the opposites with which he works; both artists and creative scientists focus on opposites for deep explanations and shift to opposites when they are stymied. When opposites or antitheses are formulated as operating simultaneously, there is a feeling of surprise, sudden realization, and sometimes of breakthrough. These experiential components derive from the radical shift of comprehension, the seemingly self-contradictory nature of the formulation itself and also, as we shall see later in this chapter, from some aspects of the psychodynamic structure of the janusian process.

In art and science, janusian formulations may involve radical departures or paradigm shifts from previous styles, structures, or bodies of knowledge. Almost invariably, however, there are modifications and integrations of the simultaneous antitheses in the development of a final created product. In psychotherapy, the therapist's janusian formulations are similarly altered and integrated into the ongoing mutual creative process. Sometimes, as in the example, they are the basis for a particular interpretation, and sometimes they serve to guide the therapist in his subsequent overall approach and interventions. When they are used manifestly as interpretations they are further elaborated, connected with other aspects of a patient's functioning, and otherwise developed and changed. They function together with other creative and noncreative operations in the ensuing therapeutic process.

Because the opposites in a therapist's janusian formulation are derived from the specific context of the therapeutic interaction, they tend to be both specific and comprehensive. Rather than deriving from theoretical postulates about types of psychic conflict, the janusian process involves shifts in elements and themes derived from the specific patient. Instead of conceptualizing, primarily on the basis of theory, a general problem such as a conflict over homosexual impulses toward the patient's female friends—although these may also have been involved—the therapist's janusian formulation in the example pertained to a pertinent and specific conflict about feeling above and below others. Because the janusian process brings salient opposites together, from direct or extensive knowledge about the patient, it tends to compress central issues and therefore to be comprehensive. The opposites of above and below others included the patient's feelings about her mother and about the realm of success and failure as well.

Another illustration, taken from the therapeutic work of Theodore Reik,[4] elucidates the specificity and comprehensiveness of the janusian process further. Describing a series of events leading to an important insight, he introduces the therapeutic issue in the following way: "I will try to demonstrate the difference between knowledge experienced and knowledge learned by rote by an example from practice."[5] The case concerned a woman with symptoms of depression, inability to work, and a seriously troubled marriage on the verge of collapse. Husband and wife spoke only when necessary, had not had intercourse for a year, and the husband had "contracted a superficial intimacy with another woman."[6] During numerous rage attacks, the patient threatened to kill her husband.

Then Reik reports the following event: "One evening there was a fresh quarrel in which the couple said nearly everything to one another that they had on their minds. The next day in her treatment, she told how she had not been able to sleep for fury. When, towards morning, she was falling asleep, a mouse ran across her bed, so that she was kept awake. Then she resolved to leave her husband and return to her parents. During the day she so far altered her resolution that she decided to return to her parents that next morning, if the mouse ran across her bed again in the following night. When she came home from shopping about noon of that day, she found the mouse in a trap that she had set for it. She stayed."[7]

Discussing his understanding of this event reported by his patient, Reik points out that ordinarily a psychoanalyst would think that the mouse is an animal that often unconsciously symbolizes the male genital organ. This formulation would perhaps have penetrated to a hidden meaning of the patient's thought and the fact that she stayed after catching the mouse in the trap. The resulting comprehension, however, would be quite limited and would not reveal, as Reik says, "the varying impulses, of different sides of her character, nay, of the nature and secret purposes of the neurosis."[8] The actual path he took to understanding one of the hidden meanings of the event was, as follows: "At some point while he [Reik] listened to the woman's stories and accusations [about her husband] there occurred to him a surmise of the unconscious purpose of the violent excesses of rage, for which the husband's cold behavior and his aberration provided a sufficient conscious motive. . . . Unconsciously the patient wanted to regain her husband. . . . She knew nothing of this secret wish; *her conduct seemed to tend instinctively in the very opposite direction. . . .*"[9] He then went on to explain how this realization led him to understand the patient's superstitious contract regarding the mouse. If the mouse, and not her husband, came to her in bed on the next night as well, then she would leave and return to her parents.

In Reik's exposition, it is clear that he paid no attention to the mouse, but all at once came to the realization that her wish and behavior were opposites. He formulated the simultaneously antithetical idea that she wanted to drive her husband away and to regain him at the same time. This idea comprised a comprehensive and specific grasp of the "nature and secret purposes of the neurosis." As is characteristic of the creative sequence with such formulations, he then conceived of further elaborations and extensions as part of an integrated system of insights which seemed to be correct.[10]

In both of the examples so far, the janusian process led to sudden illuminative grasp of conflicting motivations. Within the context of the ongoing mutual creative process of these particular therapies, these illuminations were similar to the flashes of insight and discovery characteristic of creative activity in other fields. Because conflict has a prominent place in modern clinical theory and practice, however, it may be difficult to distinguish such specific formulations from general theory and, as Reik terms it, from knowledge learned by rote. It may be difficult to appreciate and identify the creative context of these illuminations. Therefore, to clarify the creative nature of these and other clinical janusian formulations further, and also to illustrate another instance of the creative janusian process in scientific theory and discovery, I shall turn to the general background developed by Sigmund Freud. From a platform of understanding the role of the janusian process in Freud's creative accomplishment, we may then proceed to further clarification of creative clinical practice.

FREUD AND JANUSIAN PROCESS

Opposition was a *sine qua non* of Freud's thinking. Formulations involving opposition, either in their content or in some critical aspect of their structure, are found throughout the substance of psychoanalytic theory. For example, there are: reaction formation; turning into the opposite; equivalence of opposites in primary process and dreams; representation by the opposite in jokes; sadism and masochism; reality and pleasure principles; sex and aggression; Eros and Thanatos; antithetical meanings of primal words; paranoid hatred based on homosexual love; ambivalent feelings; psychological conflict between opposing wishes, drives, defenses, structure, etc.; restitutional function of psychotic symptoms; and although it was not original with Freud, bisexuality. Also, phobic fears are based on wishes; symptom formation involves both a wish and an opposing defense; negation indicates the opposite in the unconscious; and the uncanny unfamiliar is based on unconscious familiarity. A comprehensive list would be far longer, erroneously fueling the common misconception that psychoanalysts turn everything around into the opposite.

Although Jung focused more explicitly on opposites and opposition than Freud, developing a theory of personality structure based on opposing faculties and opposing female and male orientations, as well as a theory of motivation based on resolving opposition, it is nevertheless safe to say that the latter's theoretical and clinical thinking was even more perfused with opposites than the former. There is no reason to become polemical about the matter, of course. Opposition was important in both these creative men's thinking and its influence has persisted in modern psychoanalysis and in most types of psychotherapy. To focus further on Freud, however, it seems clear that one reason for the pervasiveness of opposition was that the janusian process played an extensive role in his creative thinking.

In his dedication statement for *The Interpretation of Dreams*,[11] the work he considered to be his greatest accomplishment, Freud quoted Virgil as follows: "Flectere si nequeno superos, acheronta movebo" [If I cannot bend the Higher Powers, I will move the infernal regions]. Although telling Fliess that this quotation referred for him to symptom formation,[12] both the use as a dedication and the nature of his approach suggest that the overall idea also represented a guiding principle of his creative thinking. Typically, he turned from unbendable higher levels of psychic functioning toward polar opposite lower and "infernal" levels in order to understand both levels simultaneously. Searching the lowly regarded and disrespected areas of human experience, he discovered broad and meaningful truths. Dreams were a major focus of his interest when, as he himself pointed out, the prevailing professional attitude was "Träume sind Schäume" [Dreams are froth],[13] and sexuality was certainly a downgraded area in his time, considered unworthy of serious professional concern. Notably, with the psychology of error (see Chapter VIII), he combed the wastebaskets of human action in order to understand critical aspects of pathological as well as nonpathological human functioning; this was reflected in what was then a paradoxical title for his landmark study, *The Psychopathology of Everyday Life*.[14]

Beyond general issues of conceptual approach, an historical tracing of the development of some of his major breakthroughs show unmistakable earmarks of the janusian process. The discovery of transference and the nature of its critical importance in treatment was, as Bird described it, a creative leap and an "unbelievable discovery,"[15] and it involved the formulation of a simultaneous antithesis. The first gleaning of transference for Freud concerned a noxious development in treatment that had caused his colleague Breuer to flee in "distaste and repudiation"[16] from his patient Anna O. Also, Freud himself had experienced his own patients' excessive feelings of love for him to be quite bothersome. Applying the term "transference" for the first time to the source of these difficulties, he defined it as a "false connection" and described it as a resistance.[17] Not long after, while still considering it to be a resistance, he also called it the treatment's "most powerful ally."[18] Somewhat later in the *Introductory Lectures*, he described the full formulation as follows: "transference which, whether affectionate or hostile, seemed in every case to constitute the greatest threat to treatment, becomes its best tool, by whose help the most secret compartment of mental life can be opened."[19]

In this most dramatic, and for psychoanalytic treatment most generative, formulation, Freud had conceived that the central inhibitory and negative factor in treatment was simultaneously the core facilitator of that same treatment. Although from one perspective Freud was simply carrying out good practice by identifying a core of illness on which to focus treatment, the particular type of formulation was unprecedented in the annals of medicine. Never before had it been proposed that the treatment circumstance facilitated or allowed the development of a problem which, in turn, was the very problem to be treated. The formulation of transference as simultaneously antithetical, resistance and facilitator, has been a waystation to further elaboration and theoretical integration in an ongoing creative process.[20]

Freud's discovery of the equivalence of opposites in the unconscious also appears to have been a result of his creative janusian thinking.[21] In a sometimes cited, but not fully studied, description of his discovery of the equivalence of mutually exclusive or opposite factors in dreams, Freud listed the mutually exclusive reasons appearing in the so-called Irma dream that accounted for his failure with the patient. They were as follows: "(1) that she herself was responsible for her illness because, she would not accept my solution, (2) that her pains were of organic origin and were therefore no concern of mine, (3) that her pains were connected with her widowhood, for which I was evidently not responsible, and (4) that her pains were due to an injection from a contaminated syringe, which had been given her by someone else." Then, he stated his discovery in terms of identification of a simultaneous antithesis, as follows: "All these reasons stood side by side, *as though they were not mutually exclusive.*" Immediately after, he presented his understanding of the reason for the representation of simultaneous antithesis he discovered: "I was obliged to replace the 'and', of the dream by an 'either-or' in order to escape a charge of nonsense."[22]

As the explorer who saw the ways in which superficial nonsense of dreams made sense, Freud here stated how he came to postulate the principle of equivalence of mutually exclusive or opposite reasons. First formulating the presence of simultaneous antitheses in the dream, he then developed their underlying meaning as a function of the logic and representation of the dream itself. He replaced the "and" by "either-or" and explained to himself and to the world that the dream represented alternate and opposite reasons as equivalent. This was extended to equivalence of opposites in the unconscious and developed in other ways.

With other creative theoretical accomplishments, Freud's writings give further indications of a tendency to formulate simultaneous antitheses. In his earliest formulations regarding sexuality he wrote of the sadistic factor and said, "a sadist is always at the same time a masochist. . . . We find . . . that certain among the impulses to perversion occur regularly as pairs of opposites; and this, taken in conjunction with material which will be brought forth later, has a high theoretical significance [referring to a discussion of the basis of ambivalence]. It is, moreover, a suggestive fact that the existence of the pair of opposites formed by sadism and masochism cannot be attributed merely to the element of aggressiveness. We should rather be inclined to connect the simultaneous presence of these opposites with the opposing masculinity and femininity which are combined in bisexuality—a contrast which often has to be replaced in psychoanalysis by that between activity and passivity."[23]

Similarly, Freud's early conceptions of the role of conflict in neurosis have the feature contained in the last sentence quoted of initial formulation of simultaneous opposites as the basis for later transformation and elaboration, as in the following: "[The] true significance [of compulsive acts] lies in their being a representation of a conflict between two opposing impulses of approximately equal strength. . . . What regularly occurs in hysteria is that a compromise is arrived at which enables both the opposing tendencies to find expression simultaneously—which 'kills two birds with one stone.' . . ."[24]

Perhaps his most striking formulation of a simultaneous antithesis appears in his analysis of the origin of the feeling of the uncanny, an exploration of repression and of the basis of an aesthetic phenomenon.[25] Discovering, on the basis of individual cases, that the uncanny (*"unheimlich"*) was the class of frightening phenomena that derived from reappearance of the old and long familiar, he explained the structure of the idea as in the following excerpts: "The German word 'unheimlich,' is obviously the opposite of 'heimlich' ['homely'], 'heimisch' ['native']—the opposite of what is familiar; and we are tempted to conclude that what is 'uncanny' is frightening precisely because it is *not* known and familiar. Naturally not everything that is new and unfamiliar is frightening, however; the relation is not capable of inversion. . . . Among its different shades of meaning the word 'heimlich' exhibits one which is identical with its opposite, 'unheimlich'. . . . [In] *the notion of something hidden and dangerous . . . 'heimlich' comes to have the meaning usually ascribed to 'unheimlich'. . . .*"[26]

He goes on to assert that this meaning of heimlich, literally rendered in English as homelike, is the one that pertains specifically to the unheimlich or unhomelike effect. The uncanny is a word with simultaneously opposite meanings and the effect of uncanniness consists of the unhomelike operating together with the homelike. To quote his final formulation: "The uncanny [unheimlich] is something which is secretly familiar [heimlich-heimisch], which has undergone repression and then returned from it."[27]

Although, as I indicated earlier, the janusian process and dialectical reasoning are not the same,[28] many other suggestions of simultaneous antitheses and opposition stand side by side with Freud's famous dialectical approach. In the latter, he separates opposites and contradictions and attempts to resolve or combine them, discusses opposite positions in sequence, or relates opposites to each other. In the absence of detailed data about such thinking, however, it is difficult to determine whether the janusian process was involved.

JANUSIAN PROCESS IN THE COURSE OF TREATMENT

Freud's formulations of simultaneous opposition and the general oppositional structure of a good deal of psychoanalytic theory should be differentiated from janusian formulations in particular treatment contexts. This applies to Freud's own ongoing treatment of patients as well. Although many of his insights in context necessarily played a role in this creative thinker's general theoretical conclusions, they are also of interest as examples of factors operating in particular clinical processes. One example of these comes from one of his earliest documented cases described in the prepsychoanalytic paper entitled "A Case of Successful Treatment by Hypnotism."[29] Blum, in an article on psychoanalytic insight, singles out this paper of Freud's for the following reason: "We can observe the father of psychoanalysis arriving at the most extraordinary insights into the psychology of motherhood . . . long before he had turned particular attention to the study of mothering and the mother-child relationship."[30]

Freud was asked by Drs. Breuer and Lott to consult upon the case of a young woman of his own acquaintance, who was four days postpartum and unable to nurse her baby. A serious difficulty in those preformula days, this problem had existed in somewhat lesser form with her first child. She had had a poor flow of milk, lost her own appetite, been insomniac and rather agitated. On this second occasion, she was vomiting all her food, becoming agitated when the baby was brought to her bedside, and sleeping not at all. Freud found her "furious at her inability to feed the baby."[31] After carrying out a physical examination, he induced hypnosis and, as he described it, his next intervention was as follows: "I made use of suggestion to contradict all her fears and the feelings on which those fears were based: 'Have no fear! You will make an excellent nurse and the baby will thrive. Your stomach is perfectly quiet, your appetite is excellent, you are looking forward to your next meal, etc.'"[32]

In using posthypnotic suggestion to induce positive behavior, Freud had so far followed fairly standard therapeutic procedure. The patient did, therefore, respond well at first by eating two meals, sleeping, and feeding her baby "irreproachably."[33] However, the symptoms recurred after the next day's meal. Freud then induced a second hypnosis despite a rather cool reception to his therapeutic enthusiasm by both the patient and her family. In this induction, he did something surprising and dramatic; he told the patient that: "Five minutes after my departure she would break out against her family with some acrimony: what had happened to her dinner? did they mean to let her starve? how could she feed the baby if she had nothing to eat herself? and so on."[34]

The result was equally dramatic. The patient was soon able to eat, had plenty of milk, and there was no difficulty when the baby was put to the breast. This condition continued for the next eight months. The husband later volunteered to Freud that he thought it strange that she had clamored violently for food after his departure that night and, in a quite unaccustomed manner, had remonstrated with her mother.

Clearly, as Blum in his discussion insists, Freud's successful intervention was not based primarily on the phenomenon of hypnosis, but represented an interpretation to the patient ("an extraordinary, early psychoanalytic interpretation").[35] Also, although we have no description from Freud himself about the exact nature of his own insight in this case, it seems clear that, again to follow Blum, "Freud's interpretation conveyed his awareness of both her wish to feed the baby in accordance with her mature conscious personality inclinations and her unconscious infantile wishes to be fed."[36] Or, to state this formulation in another way, she wanted to mother her baby and to be mothered at the same time. With both wordings, the insight consisted of a janusian formulation of simultaneous opposition.

The interpretation surely points also to other psychodynamic factors. There is recognition of the patient's anger and a focus on oral aggression. Blum suggests that the case report shows Freud's burgeoning insight into the origins of depression, his appreciation of conflict and symptom formation, and of genetic factors. All such factors do appear to be present and background understanding of this type is intrinsic to the janusian process. Blum's emphasis on a seemingly mysterious factor he calls "intuition," however, can be supplanted by reviewing the complicated unfolding in this example of the creative function itself.

As stated earlier, the janusian process requires, first of all, an intensive knowledge of the particular field or object of creative endeavor. In assessing Freud's knowledge both of his general field, which he called "neuropathology," and of the particular patient, we can say with confidence that he was highly sophisticated in the former and keenly observant with the latter. As his article shows, he had been deriving conclusions about symptom formation for some time, and he documented the facts about this woman's family background, her medical history, and the circumstances of the consultation with his well-known careful and systematic detail. Out of this wealth of background, then, he began the next phase of the janusian process with an assessment and approach to the salient features of the patient's psychological problem.[37]

In explaining his first intervention, he had said: "I made use of suggestion to contradict all her fears and the feelings on which those fears were based." In addition to using the standard positive approach to hypnotic suggestion, Freud had identified a particular underlying factor of fear in the woman's symptoms. He recognized that fear about mothering functions and abilities was at the heart of her difficulties with nursing. While such a realization may, in this post-Freudian era, seem rather to be taken for granted, I venture to suggest that it would not have been so obvious in Freud's own time.

The critical point is that Freud's understanding of salient features helped develop the *context* in which an apparent janusian formulation in the form of specific insight and subsequent interpretation took place. The context of failure to nurse, vomiting, and fear of mothering contained the opposites of desire to mother and the desire not to mother. Deriving salient opposites is not necessarily a separate or explicit step in the janusian process, although it does occur with certain types of scientific creativity, and the setting up of context and opposites frequently occurs, as here, together. In his initial approach to the woman's difficulty, Freud helped set up the context by developing the first of the opposing alternatives: He believed that the woman wished to mother her infant. He supported this wish.

Then, buttressed by the positive effect of his first intervention, and not discounting its validity, he used an interpretation that involved the opposite alternative: The woman desired not to be a mother but to be mothered herself. At that point, he had apparently postulated both opposites simultaneously. This janusian formulation was conveyed in his suggestion to the patient and functioned as a recognition of her conflict as well as encouragement for the ventilation of angry feelings. Finally, although there is no indication in Freud's account that the woman consciously apprehended or formulated the exact insight contained in his interpretative intervention, the improvement in her symptoms suggests some type of integration of affect or insight.

FUNCTIONS OF THE JANUSIAN PROCESS
IN THE TREATMENT CONTEXT

As the creator of psychoanalysis, Freud is in the position where little distinction can be made between his creative functioning in therapy, theorizing, or discovery. The janusian process and other forms of creative thinking played a role in both his theory and therapy in an enriching and interactive way. For modern therapists, especially psychoanalytically oriented ones, the situation is different. Because recognition of a patient's intrapsychic conflict is such a central feature of psychodynamic psychotherapy, the creative janusian process is sometimes difficult to identify and appreciate. Moreover, there is a risk of routinizing and stultifying principles originally arrived at creatively by Freud. Each application of the janusian process must be attuned to a specific context. It provides a comprehensive grasp in context of a patient's specific conflicts.

Insights and discoveries about other types of clinical phenomena beside conflicts also result from the operation of the janusian process. These may range from the discovery of simultaneously opposite functions in particular symptomatic behavior to more extensive discoveries about therapeutic difficulties and impasses. In one instance, a therapist treating a patient with bulimia suddenly grasped the idea that her vomiting served *both pathological and restitutive functions simultaneously*. She was a woman with a highly restricted fantasy life, constantly feeling bored and empty as well as unable to consider inner motivations, thoughts, or affects. At the same time as her inducing of vomiting was a debilitating symptom of her illness, therefore, it was a symbolic attempt to focus on her inner experience. Although the focus was on inner gastrointestinal contents rather than psychological ones, it nevertheless had restitutional features.

In another case, a therapist had filled out an insurance form regarding a patient's treatment, in which he was required to describe the nature of the therapy, and he spelled out all the conditions and responsibilities of both partners, i.e., getting to sessions on time, freedom to speak or not to speak, payments, etc. Learning of the existence of this document, the patient asked the therapist to provide him with a copy. In an exploration of the reasons for this request, the patient indicated that this written material served as a type of closeness and binding with the therapist because everything seemed clear and ironclad. After some thought, the therapist decided to comply and give a copy to him.

The therapy progressed satisfactorily over an extended period of time and the patient referred positively on several occasions to the written material regarding his and the therapist's responsibilities.

Inexplicably, however, the patient became subsequently quite seriously upset and the treatment relationship deteriorated; without explanation, he insisted vehemently that the therapist tear up the original insurance report in his presence. Being not at all clear about the reasons for the change, the therapist at first demurred and attempted to explore what had happened. No matter what tack he took, however, the patient steadfastly refused to explain and insisted only that the written document be destroyed. At first coming late to his therapy sessions during this period, he soon started to miss them completely. Totally stymied, and at a loss to explain what had happened, the therapist then had the following thought: The same document that holds us close together is a concrete object and barrier that stands between us. With this formulation, he was able to solve the therapeutic impasse.

Because these discoveries and insights involve formulation of both sides of a contradiction at once, both positive and negative, or else what was previously accepted and believed together with its contrary, they are usually experienced as surprises, breakthroughs, or as leaps of understanding. Consequently, they are frequently considered to be intuitions. Because intuitions, in modern times, have been considered to be products of the unconscious, the products of the janusian process are sometimes automatically attributed to quasi-mysterious unconscious functions. The experiential features of surprise, etc., result in some degree from the dissonant and cognitively discrepant features of the consciously conceived simultaneous antithesis formulations themselves, however; they do not indicate that the ideas actually erupt from the unconscious. The janusian process accounts for what is sometimes called intuition but these functions are not identical. Intuition is a broader psychological operation that includes the janusian process as well as other conscious and unconscious dynamisms.

To return to the matter of the comprehensive grasp of specific conflict, an example that is highly relevant to modern psychotherapeutic practice comes from Arlow.[38] The sequence in the development of interpretations Arlow describes is one that he proposes to be applicable to all therapeutic work. It involves what he also labels as an "intuition"[39] about a patient's central conflict that leads to subsequent understanding of the patient's "dynamics, conflict and compromise formation." A female in her mid-twenties, who was transferred to him from another psychotherapist, complained of being depressed and of having difficulty relating to men. After a detailed exposition about her family and academic career, she turned, he says, to an "elaborately recited account of the onset of her menses," and described "serious endocrinological, metabolic, dermatological, arthritic" difficulties and confusing and problematic encounters with medical specialists. Describing his response to this account, he says, "On the one hand I felt deeply moved by the overwhelming suffering that so young a girl had to experience at such a crucial period in her life; on the other, however, I detected a certain challenging bitterness in her recital to me." He added that his reaction was summarized by the ironic thought, "What a welcome to womanhood!"

In this sequence ending in what he calls an ironic construction, Arlow indicates the development of a janusian formulation regarding the nature of her conflicts. The woman was distinctly a victim, as indicated by his feeling deeply moved by her account, and at the same time her challenging bitterness indicated the opposite. The ironic thought was sudden and comprehensive. It contained the literal idea of her being welcomed to womanhood with the onset of her menses together with the implicit opposite idea of not having been welcomed at all.

As the treatment continued, the patient recounted, and displayed in the transference with Arlow, experiences in which she played boyfriends or doctors against each other. Also, although constantly hurt in her relationship with a boyfriend, with whom she had had intercourse, she was unable to give him up. In attempting to understand this material further, the author states that he consciously had the ironic thought in mind, was aware of his own annoyance at the patient, and thought of her as playing cat and mouse games. He then subjected these ideas to "a cognitive process, namely, observing how certain ideas were repeated and how a similar theme ran through them, recognizing the contiguity and sequence in which the ideas appeared in the patient's mind and finally how they converged into two or three major ideas suggesting hostility toward physicians who had hurt her and upon whom she wished to take vengeance."[40]

Developing and elaborating the comprehensive grasp contained in his ironic formulation, he characterized her conflict and his approach to treatment in the following way: "The woman cannot give up the tie to the man who deflowered her because she has not yet exacted the full measure of the vengeance she wishes to wreak upon him. Knowledge of this sort enables us to plan the course of treatment, the hierarchy of interpretations to be given, in a rational manner."[41]

Arlow's proposal that the sequence he outlines is typical for the therapist's development of interpretations would suggest a critical early role for the janusian process in psychotherapy. Other writers, such as Greenacre, however, emphasize less dramatic inferences or tentative deductions as "early basic steps toward an understanding of the unconscious conflicts."[42] Nevertheless, Arlow's description of his creative work is a good example of the characteristic course of development of the janusian process when it operates at the beginning of treatment. First, there is an immediate grasp of simultaneously antithetical elements in the patient's presentation. As the treatment progresses, and more information is obtained, the antithetical or opposite elements in the conflict are separately elaborated and clarified. Factors in the initial janusian formulation are more clearly defined and also applied to a wider range of behavior and dynamic constellations. In this instance, Arlow extended his formulation about the traumatic nature of the patient's onset of menses to the circumstance of her sexual relationship with her boyfriend. He stated that the patient experienced a "defloration" and gave it an aggressive connotation. His use of what he called a cognitive process[43] in order to transform, rationalize, and clarify his early formulation is a characteristic feature of the transformations and modification of janusian formulations in all types of creative processes. In psychotherapy, such modifications and transformations may be initiated by the therapist but they are carried through primarily by the patient. For example, simultaneous antitheses may be separated out, weighed as alternatives and resolved, or worked through. They may also, as will be described in Chapter VII, be subjected to an articulation process.

In later portions of a creatively conducted psychotherapy, the janusian process has a similar course. A rather cold and unexpressive female patient was talking about plans for a weekend visit to her mother in a distant city. She made these visits fairly frequently, but more recently she had begun to speak disdainfully about them and concurrently reduced their number because of her growing sense of independence. With regard to the details of this trip, she said she was very surprised that her maternal aunt was especially planning to spend time at her mother's apartment that weekend in order to see the patient. Seldom had this aunt seen her during her weekend visits, although she lived in the same city, and the patient felt pleased and flattered about the plan. She added, however, that she wished that her mother did not lavish so much attention and indulgence on her when she visited, because the aunt was rather unstable emotionally and would probably become quite jealous and bothered while she was there.

Listening to this account, the therapist knew that there was ample evidence that the patient's mother was as indulgent and favoring as the patient claimed and the aunt would have ample reason to feel jealous and uncomfortable. The patient spoke with genuine feelings of concern—a change for her—about her aunt's discomfort. Focusing on her expression of positive feelings, the therapist suddenly conceived the following idea: She is terrified that the aunt will intrude on her time and her exclusive relationship with her mother. She fears her aunt's exclusion and intrusion at once. Deciding to present this idea to the patient, he developed an interpretation emphasizing both aspects of the simultaneous antithesis, her pleasure and genuine concern about the aunt's visit and her wish to have her mother to herself.

In response to the interpretation, the patient, who never readily acknowledged her possessiveness toward her mother, said that she had not thought of "that" before. In context, the "that" clearly meant the entire simultaneous antithesis, although she seemed particularly enlightened and relieved by the stipulation of the second portion of the formulation. There were further extensions and transformations of this material; later discussions about events on the weekend trip indicated that she had developed and integrated some important insights about her relationships with both mother and aunt that pertained to other relationships as well.

All formulation of opposition in therapy is not a janusian process, however. In another case, an experienced therapist shifted to formulate an opposite but it was not a janusian process and was not successful. Here, a middle-aged female patient complained to the therapist over a period of weeks that he had been forgetting important details about her life. He had not remembered that she had a male sibling who died when she was a child and also had forgotten a recent flirtation she had had with a married man. Reacting to these complaints, the therapist thought about the fact that, in her background, she had a good deal of difficulty performing well in school and was always concerned about letting her parents down. He thought about her complaining that he was letting *her* down and decided that she was really concerned about letting *him* down instead. He offered that formulation to her in the form of an interpretation and the patient flatly rejected it. That may have been true at other times, she said, but she really felt that he was not functioning effectively. In subsequent sessions, the therapist realized that he indeed was having difficulty with the patient and that his forgetting had been due to his own countertransference problems. In the circumstance, the therapist did not identify salient opposites and therefore did not come to an understanding of an important conflict. Moreover, he simply shifted to the contrary of the patient's complaint. The shift to the contrary or opposite served defensive purposes alone.

The janusian process in psychotherapy involves postulation of both sides of a patient's conflicts or of other antithetical factors simultaneously. Either the therapist all-at-once recognizes the patient's self-contradictory behavior, as in the Arlow example of a woman appearing to be both victim and victimizer, or else he realizes that his previous formulations have been correct but that their opposite is correct at the same time, as in the example of conceiving that the patient both wanted and did not want her aunt to be present at her mother's house. Such conceptions are experienced as a flash of insight and a comprehensive discovery; they encapsulate a number of features of a patient's psychodynamics and behavior and are both cognitively discordant and illuminating.

With respect to the particular opposites chosen, I have at some length previously pointed out that opposition is an abstract concept; it is neither factual nor present in the concrete physical environment.[44] Moreover, terms and definitions of opposites are relative to, and defined by, a particular context. As an example of this point, I referred to colors in painting where, because they are based on reflected light, complementaries such as blue and orange or green and red are often considered opposites. For the physicist who is concerned with transmitted light, however, violet, not green, is at the opposite side of the spectrum from red. Also, cold and hot may be suitably defined as opposite points of temperature to an ordinary person listening to a weather forecast, but a natural scientist would surely insist on the designations, freezing and boiling, as more appropriate. Then, depending on whether the scientist were working in a context where water or some other chemical such as nitrogen were the standard, he would either designate 0° and 100°C as freezing and boiling opposites or start with −273°F as the cold or freezing pole on the nitrogen scale. Opposites are also defined differently depending on whether they are derived from polar positions on a scale or from dichotomous qualities.

The components of any dichotomy may be designated as opposites. Thus, we speak of opposite sides of a room, or of men and women as opposite sexes. Extremes or poles of a scale are another type of opposite, however, and the extremes of the gender scale are male and female, or masculinity and femininity, rather than men and women. Furthermore, in a modern perspective of the overlapping features of gender, neither dichotomy nor scale might apply and none of these terms would be considered opposites at all.

Another case involving a meaningful and generative janusian formulation illustrates the designation of opposites within the particular context of a dream report. A relatively young and not-a-little-creative therapist had worked with a depressed, borderline woman for several months and identified a pattern of her running away from significant relationships with men.[45] Constantly, whenever a man started getting involved with her in a serious way, she brutally broke off the relationship or actually left the geographical area she lived in. She appeared motivated to betray any man who cared about her. To the therapist, it seemed that this behavior was related to her distant father and overindulgent mother. At a point when she again threw over a boyfriend and attached herself to yet another male, a member of the nursing profession, she reported the following dream: She was sitting in the front seat of a car with her mother driving and her previous boyfriend sitting in the back. She said something to her mother, who became immediately defensive and irritable, and she then turned around to look at the boyfriend. Seeing that he remained totally silent, the patient-dreamer jumped out of the car, sat down in the middle of the street, and started crying.

Without asking for specific associations, the therapist decided on the basis of his previous understanding that the dream revealed that the patient was feeling betrayed. The mother in the dream represented the patient's current boyfriend, a nurse and member of a nurturant profession. The boyfriend in the back seat, however, represented the patient's father, and the silence indicated the father's betrayal of her at a time of need. All at once, the therapist formulated the idea that the patient was both betrayer and betrayed at the same time. This was represented in the dream by her sitting crying in the middle of the road as one betrayed together with her own betrayal of having jumped out of the car. The patient ran away and betrayed her boyfriends but she felt herself to be betrayed by them and by her father.

When the therapist interpreted this understanding of her difficulties in relationships with males, the patient assented. In subsequent weeks, a distinct shift toward progress occurred. While another therapist might have focused on this patient's hostility to males, the opposites of betrayed and betrayal aptly applied to the patient's conflicting motivations and perceptions. At the same time as she betrayed her boyfriends she felt they were betraying her. Just as with the opposites which it develops, and on which it is based, the janusian process, whether in psychotherapy, art, or science, is dependent on context. Because literature involves temporal sequences, human behavior, and language, and because it often focuses on psychological content, the literary context bears the closest resemblance to the psychotherapeutic one. In literature, as in psychotherapy, the context and opposites emerge from narratives and from the subject matter of human interaction.

Once a conflict or other problem is creatively grasped and understood by the therapist, the remainder of the creative process is similar to other fields. In all types of art, janusian formulations are seldom explicitly manifest, but they are transformed, worked out further, and otherwise integrated into artworks. In science, they are usually subjected to logical exegesis and integration into theories and discoveries. Different types of psychotherapy, as I shall discuss in the following chapter, integrate the formulations in different ways. In dynamic psychotherapy a revealed conflict is usually worked through in a process that is similar to dialectical resolution. The patient and therapist separate the opposites, assess and experience them, combine or supersede them, and eventually resolve the conflict.

Schafer, using terminology that coordinates pointedly with the view of conflict I have presented here, defines conflict as paradoxical actions and describes the resolution as follows: "Such resolution would be viewed as the person's redefining the paradoxical actions and their situations in such a way that they are: (1) no longer paradoxical, (2) no longer the only possibilities envisaged, (3) no longer the principal issues, (4) no longer the actions to persist in, or (5) some combination of these."[46] The alternatives Schafer designates are familiar conditions of the Hegelian dialectic resolution. Hegel proposed that opposing principles or arguments are found either to be overlapping in some way, or to be nonconflictual on another level, or to be not the only considerations, or else to be susceptible to combination or other reconciliation.[47]

Neither Schafer, nor I in following him, means to indicate only a logical stepwise process of conflict resolution similar to the Hegelian one in psychotherapy. Much affect, experience, and many divergent pathways properly distinguish therapeutic working-through.[48] Nevertheless, it is important to note that dialectical resolution involves separation of opposites and comes *after* the janusian formulation in creative processes. Opposites, in dialectical reasoning, are considered sequentially, whereas in the janusian process opposites are postulated simultaneously.

COUNTERTRANSFERENCE AND THE JANUSIAN PROCESS

Just as the janusian process provides a leap of understanding of patient conflicts and other difficulties, it also serves to identify therapist countertransference effects. Such effects are, as we know, a major factor in producing therapeutic impasses and other obstacles to understanding patients. Indeed, in some of the examples I have cited throughout this chapter, speculations about the initial operation of countertransference difficulty might well arise. In these instances, and in blockages due to countertransference in general, the janusian process functions in two distinct ways. First, because of its psychodynamic structure, the janusian process, like the homospatial process, serves to provide some degree of insight for the creative thinker himself. When conceiving janusian formulations about the patient, the therapist may develop understanding of some of his own conflicts. This definitely occurred in the instance of the patient who placed herself both above and below others; later that therapist realized that he had similar tendencies himself. Second, the content of a janusian formulation may pertain directly to the therapist's countertransference difficulty. In this circumstance, the therapist uses the janusian process to gain a comprehensive grasp of his own conflict or other problem producing an obstacle or a therapeutic impasse.

With regard to the first function pertaining to the psychodynamic structure of the janusian process, I have previously pointed out that the defense mechanism operating together with the cognitive aspect is negation.[49] By means of defensive negation, in which the multiple oppositions of a janusian construct negate each other, unconscious material bypasses repression. This is an aspect of the mirror reversal process described in the previous chapter.[50] For the artistic creative thinker such bypassing of repression may lead to incorporation of unconscious material directly into an artwork. For the creative psychotherapist, the negated unconscious material comes into awareness and, because of his training in recognizing such material, it may lead to personal insight. Such insights into one's own unconscious motivation related to the janusian process sometimes results in the overcoming of countertransference difficulties. Even when the countertransference problem is not fully resolved, however, the bypassing of repression may overcome an obstacle produced by countertransference effects.

The second function of the janusian process for providing a grasp of countertransference effects is the same as in the flashes of insight and discovery described throughout this chapter. In working on the mutual creative process of psychotherapy, or in the face of a particular obstacle or impasse, the therapist turns frequently to an examination of countertransference factors. He identifies salient themes developing within the context of a particular therapy; these may also be similar to, or derive from, countertransference themes identified in his other therapies. Actively postulating a simultaneous antithesis, as in the following example, provides a comprehensive grasp of his countertransference conflicts and other difficulties as well.

A male patient in intensive therapy in a hospital setting had a great deal of difficulty deciding to leave the hospital. Although he had worked productively in psychotherapy, he suffered from an extremely passive and dependent character structure and was clinging to the hospital environment. His therapist, however, believed that the time had come when he needed to be in outpatient therapy in order to work out his difficulties in a real living environment.

It was clear that the patient would not respond to any suggestions or encouragement from the therapist regarding the prospect of leaving the hospital. He clung tenaciously to an idea that he had not yet fully participated in the hospital's milieu treatment program. The therapist found that attempts on his part to clarify the defensive rationalization in this belief were met by evasion and passive resistance. Much earlier in the therapy, in fact, the therapist had discerned that any efforts to promote leaving would be passively resisted and he always refrained from doing so. Indeed, he had then carefully analyzed his own needs and wishes to ascertain whether he had any countertransference investment in the patient's leaving the hospital as a mark of success of the treatment. Although he certainly wished the patient to be able to leave and do well, the therapist felt generally quite secure about his own competence and believed he needed no such public show of success.

From time to time, the patient put aside his rationalization about needing to participate in the hospital program and made some tentative comments about leaving, although all the while conveying a distinct sense of foreboding. In response, the therapist only pointed out the patient's foreboding tone, but took no stand at all on the plans. Sometimes, the patient brought up self-defeating plans for outside living; the therapist then raised questions about why the patient was considering plans that seemed doomed to failure. After each of these forays, the subject was dropped for a period until, gradually, the patient began to talk of leaving with some conviction and decisiveness. Nevertheless, he still carefully avoided working out any specifics of job, locale, and plans for future therapy.

Over a period of several weeks, the patient made a definite decision to leave by a particular date. Still not specifying his intentions, he only spoke in a general way about ideas of where to go and what to do, and said he would work things out when he left. At first, the therapist felt concerned about the patient's vague and general approach, but, after thoughtful consideration, he decided that the patient could not really decide to leave the hospital in any other way. If he became more demanding by challenging the adequacy of the plan it might upset the apple cart and delay the leaving excessively. After all, the patient now seemed really interested in leaving. The therapist's patience and non-involvement had paid off; so it would be best to leave well enough alone.

So far, so good, it would seem. The patient continued to plan for leaving, and the therapist listened and did not challenge at all. However, as the planned date for the discharge approached, the therapist suddenly realized that he had somehow shifted into another position. Despite his own carefully considered reasons for not intervening, he was now effectively on the side of abetting the leaving schedule. His nonchallenging silence displayed *both non-involvement and over-involvement at the same time*. Understanding this, he became aware, for the first time, of having developed feelings of deep investment in the patient's getting out of the hospital. Although the patient's leaving had not earlier been for him a mark of success of the treatment, he had unwittingly come to feel differently.

In the session after these realizations, therefore, the therapist explored why the patient had decided to leave at that particular time. Clarification followed and the patient recognized that he was conflicted about leaving or getting better. He needed to keep things vague in order to avoid giving himself or the therapist any credit for his being improved. However, instead of speaking only of his misgivings about leaving, he now spoke also of genuine wishes of his own to move on.

The therapist's formulation involved the recognition of opposite poles of personal investment in his patient's behavior and their simultaneous operation in his therapeutic stance of non-intervention. Following that, he developed insight into his own countertransference conflict about the success of the treatment. Although not concerned about the patient's leaving the hospital earlier, he had later become overconcerned and a previously appropriate nonchallenging approach had obscured the true state of affairs.

All insight into countertransference on a therapist's part is not a product of the janusian process, however. Just as with identification of patient conflicts, other types of dynamisms, some creative and some not, play a role in the constant monitoring and assessment of reactions and feelings engendered by the treatment situation. Some other creative ones will be described in Chapters VII and VIII.

Throughout treatment, the janusian process is called into play by the creative therapist to solve problems, make discoveries, identify specific patient conflicts, and formulate and overcome problematic circumstances. After conceiving a specific simultaneous antithesis, the therapist may or may not convey the specific content to the patient. It influences his subsequent interventions, however, and is in turn influenced and modified by the patient's reactions and responses. The janusian formulation functions to generate a new series of interactions between patient and therapist that results in an ultimately creative outcome.

CHAPTER VI

Janusian Process and Creative Intervention: Paradox, Irony

Although I have followed Schafer and applied the term "paradoxical actions" to psychological conflict, I have so far largely refrained from connecting paradox directly with the janusian process. Some commentators on my previous work have done so, and I am sure that many of my readers have considered similar ideas before reaching this point. I have abjured using the word "paradox" up to now for several reasons, the main one being that it is far too loose a term. Common usage has given it overtones of the mysterious and bizarre or even the absurd but, worse than that, there is a good deal of variation in its meaning. Its original, and most general usage is as, dictionary defined, "a tenet or proposition that is contrary to received opinion."[1] This meaning does not coincide with that of the janusian formulation of simultaneous antithesis, because a distinct feature of the latter is that it is *both contrary and confirmatory* of received opinion at the same time. The simultaneous antithesis contains more than one contrary aspect. Only in philosophical and other technical discourse do definitions of paradox emerge that resemble the definition of simultaneous antithesis. Such discourse, important as it is, and as it has been in the history of philosophy,[2] is often concerned with logic and with the possibility or nonpossibility of resolution of paradox, rather than—as we are concerned here—with ongoing psychological thought processes and their clinical function. Regardless of purpose and use, the variability of meaning renders the term problematic in relation to the psychology of the creative process.

Nevertheless, there clearly are connections between the idea of paradox and the janusian process. Notably, in relation to psychotherapy, the idea of paradox has caught the attention of a large group of practitioners in both family and individual therapy. In many instances, their clinical applications reflect the operation of janusian process. Particular interventions described as paradoxical seem either to result from the janusian process or to constitute aspects of its development.

In addition to paradox, another type of clinical phenomenon, irony and ironic intervention, is often reflective of a creative janusian process. Both paradox and irony (under the general rubric of humor) have been advocated by various theorists and practitioners for use as therapeutic interventions. In the previous chapter, I discussed the therapist's use of the janusian process primarily as a means to insight and understanding. I labeled this use as a waystation in an overall creative process in which the exact content of the understanding might or might not be transmitted directly to the patient. In this chapter I shall consider direct manifestations and applications of janusian process in treatment interventions.

PARADOX

An early use of the paradoxical type of therapeutic intervention was manifest in a famous case described by the psychoanalyst August Aichhorn. A 17-year-old delinquent boy had been in Aichhorn's institution for several months and no one had been able to develop a treatment relationship with him. Aichhorn thereupon induced the boy to *run away* on the supposition that he would find that the outside was no better than the inside of the institution. Although he became worried at first when the boy did not return after a week, ten days later he appeared and a positive alliance developed.[3]

The more recent interest of family therapists in the use of therapeutic paradox can be traced to the work of Bateson and other members of the so-called Palo Alto group on the double bind theory of schizophrenia.[4] These workers described a confusion in hierarchical levels—on the basis of Russell's theory of Logical Types—that was observed in families of schizophrenic patients. According to the double bind theory, a schizophrenic son or daughter was continually exposed to double binds from parents, such as verbal encouragement to express feelings together with nonverbal prohibition against such expression. Because of the apparent pervasiveness of this type of family interaction, the Palo Alto group recommended the use of what they called "therapeutic double binds" to reverse such patterns. This therapeutic tactic was later extended to other types of illness and referred to by Haley as paradoxical.[5]

Similar approaches of other therapists with both individuals and families, notably those of Milton Erickson, were also studied and adopted. The naming of a specific therapeutic technique with the word "paradox" seems to have originated with the existentialist therapist Frankl in his term "paradoxical intention."[6] As an intervention appropriate to family therapy, the paradoxical technique was further developed by Mara Selvini-Palazzoli and her Milan group.[7] Many other family therapists, including Haley, Watzlawick, Weakland, Fisch, Papp, Weeks, L'Abate, Madanes, and Rohrbaugh, have written about varying forms of paradoxical interventions.[8]

In the hands of the Milan group, the use of paradoxical intervention has consisted primarily of "prescribing the symptom" and more recently has been extended in various ways. Prescribing a symptom consists of instructing a family group to continue or intensify such behavior as catering to a ritual, phobia, etc., of the member of the family designated as the patient (the so-called "identified patient"). At the same time, the patient may be told to continue or intensify performance of the ritual, augment the range of phobia, etc. Such prescriptions may also be extended to a broader pattern of family behavior and are then designated as "prescribing the system." In such a case a rigid father may be instructed to become even more rigid, a mother may be told to be more docile, and a patient shown how to become even more manipulative. Properly applied, such instructions are accompanied by comments introducing new alternatives for other members of the family.

Other types of paradoxical interventions have also been described and analyzed. Particular terms that have been used to denote these other approaches are the following: restraining change; reframing and positive framing; benevolent ordeals; positioning. Restraining change consists of a therapist telling a patient that he cannot change or, less strongly, worrying with the patient about the dangers of improvement. Reframing involves redefining behavior from the point of view of another person, such as telling parents that a supposedly weak and mentally ill child is winning a power struggle over them. Positive reframing consists of redefining negative behavior in positive terms. For example, in a case described by Papp, a wife who complained about the overinvolvement between her husband and his mother was instructed to find ways to praise the "beauty" of the rare mother-son devotion; she was also advised to suggest that her husband spend even more time with his mother.[9] Prescribing benevolent ordeals, such as suggesting to an insomniac that he deliberately think of all the horrible things he could while lying in bed awake at night, or devising other tasks that are worse than a symptom, is a principle derived by Haley from his observation of the work of Milton Erickson.[10] Positioning involves the acceptance and exaggeration of a patient's problematic "position," i.e., an assertion that an individual is making about himself or his problem. As described by Rohrbaugh *et al.*, "when a patient's pessimism is reinforced or maintained by an optimistic or encouraging response from significant others, the therapist may 'outdo' the patient's pessimism by defining the situation as even more dismal than the patient had originally held it to be."[11]

All of these techniques of paradoxical intervention do involve opposites and opposition of some type, whether or not they would be logically considered to be paradoxes. All have been claimed to have successful therapeutic effects. In each case, their advocates have provided detailed specifications and injunctions for their proper use. Paying attention to such factors as tone of voice, patient susceptibility, and other more specific factors that I shall discuss presently has been considered critical in the successful application of such techniques. Recently, Haley advised that they be used with caution and advocated applying them in stages and paying attention to follow-through.[12] Many theoretical formulations about the reasons for success have been proposed, most of which emphasize the instilling or instigating of change in an individual patient or family system.

From the point of view of the therapeutic creative process, all of these approaches run the risk of becoming routinized techniques in which a certain formula is applied over and over in differing situations with little regard for freshness or appropriateness. As I pointed out in the previous chapter, such risk is also constantly present with routinely applying Freud's creatively discovered principles; each new application of the janusian process must be attuned to a specific context. Because these paradoxical techniques involve a series of particular actions rather than understanding alone, there may be even greater risk of stagnation. This may in part explain why it is that many family therapists today seem to find the work of the Milan group to be somewhat repetitious, and the group itself seems to be moving away from techniques described in their earlier works.

Although direct testimonial evidence is lacking, I believe that it is reasonable to assume that the janusian process played a role at the discovery phase of each type of paradoxical intervention approach and, beyond that, particular clinical applications in treatment frequently result from the therapist's use of the janusian process. In many cases described in the literature, and in ongoing clinical observations, there seems to be little doubt that the therapist formulating particular interventions is actively conceiving two or more opposites or antitheses operating simultaneously. A therapist developing paradoxical interventions in this way is similar to one who develops creative insights about a patient's specific conflicts. He is aware of principles of psychodynamics or system organization and operates creatively in the particular therapeutic context.

Such creative development and use of paradoxical intervention is illustrated in a case example presented by Wynne.[13] A 34-year-old woman suffering from severe anorexia nervosa with bulimia, her 34-year-old husband, and their 13-year-old daughter came for treatment and, as Wynne describes it, they were all "enmeshed in turmoil" over the mother's symptoms. In the initial consultation, Wynne was particularly impressed with the husband's involvement. The wife gorged food massively three times a day that she subsequently vomited; the husband both purchased the food and supervised the vomiting. Their lives were consumed by this cycle because of the time spent obtaining the food and cleaning both kitchen and bathroom where she would seclude herself. No ordinary relationships with friends had taken place for years.

In discussing the background of the problem, both marital partners spoke of a conflict between the wife and her mother, a problem the husband said he had "inherited." Both recognized the vomiting to be an aggressive, upsetting act and spoke of her "throwing money down the toilet" and of the enormous amount of food that was being "wasted." Her father, the husband emphasized, was a banker who was concerned about saving money. Although the wife spoke of feeling extremely guilty about the hurtfulness of this "waste," she cyclically experienced both remorse and anger followed by gorging and vomiting.

Wynne says: "At a point in the consultation when I felt able to identify the cyclical impasse of the family system, I decided to introduce a paradoxical family intervention." This intervention involved prescribing the symptom but, he emphasizes, he made a thoughtful choice of the particular symptom to be prescribed. He describes his intervention as follows: "I had her give me a list of the food she had prepared the previous day. Some thirty dollars worth of food had been vomited on that day. I stressed that she continue to prepare such food exactly the same except that she was now to put the food *directly* into the toilet, and skip the step of putting it into her mouth and stomach. . . . We worked out a plan in which the husband . . . was to make sure that she continue to prepare the same amount as previously. . . . He was also to supervise her putting this food in the toilet. . . ."[14]

Wynne goes on to describe further interaction and working out of this intervention with the family, the fact that at the next visit to him ten days later the vomiting had stopped, and his later use of other types of nonparadoxical interventions to ensure a lasting improvement. Up to this point, the elements of the janusian process sequence have been demonstrated in Wynne's approach. First, there was an early identification of the husband's involvement. The themes of aggressiveness and of wastefulness next emerged as the context became further defined and both partners focused on the financial loss caused by the wife's illness. The husband, Wynne observed, made a point of saying that the banker father was concerned with money. Instead of worrying about her self-destructiveness and precarious physical state, waste and money seemed a focus for them both. Because of Wynne's careful attention to interpersonal interaction and to understanding the background and psychodynamics, a particular context had been developed and salient themes identified that would be the basis for specific opposites and antitheses.

Although Wynne does not describe the detailed steps in his thinking, he makes it clear that he had decided to shift to an intervention involving the opposite of a particular theme. Instead of the symptom of vomiting, the aggressiveness *per se*, or even the husband's involvement, he focused on *waste* and *destructiveness* and the throwing of costly food down the toilet. In formulating this particular intervention, he had recognized the concrete importance of the toilet and had, therefore, very likely conceived of the patient's engaging in *both purging and not purging at the same time*. By throwing food directly into the toilet, the patient bypasses her own body but has the experience of discarding and purging nutriments nevertheless. The conception for this paradoxical intervention, therefore, appears to have been a janusian formulation and was, I would propose, a creative step.

It is important to emphasize that such a formulation is an aspect of an unfolding creative process. This means that additional factors need to come into play and that the particular paradoxical intervention used may or may not lead to a creative effect. This point shall warrant a good deal of our attention presently but first let us look further at the detailed outcome of the Wynne intervention to assess its nature.

After reporting the absence of the patient's vomiting, Wynne poses both an important question and its answer: "What was the mechanism of change? Let me look for clues in the next session. The wife said that this had been the most 'dynamic experience,' the most 'eye opening experience' she ever had in her life. . . . When she saw all that food going down the toilet, food that she had deliberately placed there and had not 'involuntarily' vomited, she realized for the first time what she had been doing. I did not need to make any interpretations whatsoever; *she* made them."[15]

There is evidence, therefore, that the paradoxical intervention produced some insight for the patient, an effect that was somewhat similar to the creation of insight I have discussed in previous chapters. Notably, Wynne emphasizes that the patient made interpretations and presented the insights on her own. In this way she developed his janusian formulation into a creative effect. Going on to describe a problem that developed in the interim between their sessions, he designates another type of creative outcome as well.

The couple reported that the husband, whose tendency to withdraw had consistently been a problem, had decided to spend both an afternoon and evening watching television and had inexplicably refused to talk with her. The patient responded, according to Wynne, as follows: "She felt rejected and, as in the past, she felt a great surge of motivation to gorge herself. She also, as in the past, felt physically chilled. Now, however, she suddenly realized that if she did gorge herself, the food and vomiting would make her feel 'warm.' Her husband insisted that she not gorge but, rather, throw the food down the toilet directly. It was then that she had a creative 'solution.' Instead of gorging herself, she went and cuddled up on her husband's lap and became warm in a new way. The husband, who had been hoping for such physical advances from her for years, now was nonplussed. He discovered, to his dismay, that he did not know how to respond to her. At this point we could move on to a new stage of therapy; the structure of the family system had changed."[16]

Wynne's designation of a creative effect seems quite justified. Although this was not as yet a final outcome, the wife's behavior was creative in that it was both new and positive in the family context. As is often the case with creative effects, it was also initially disruptive to someone. This is not a necessary result, but such a disruptive impact—creative or not—is often cited by family therapists as a desirable outcome of the use of paradoxical interventions. Emphasizing that the family is a system, and that any intervention in family therapy must take that into consideration, they argue that paradoxical interventions disrupt system homeostasis and initiate change.

I believe this claim to be correct, as far as it goes. In the family therapy situation, unlike individual therapy, active suggestions and directions are often necessary in order to ensure coordination and promote change in a pattern of relationships. Exclusive attention to resistance, which may be appropriate in individual therapy, may at times serve different family members in different ways. Exploring a child's resistances in front of a parent may serve to enhance or reinforce a parent's resistance, and vice versa. Insofar as a family manifests a "system" of fixed patterns of relationship and behavior, it seems necessary to disrupt these patterns actively to facilitate change. Notwithstanding, all disruptions are not equally appropriate and all change is not necessarily beneficial.

Many interesting extensions of this principle of inducing change have been developed that relate the effect of paradoxical interventions to the following: the larger framework of Taoism;[17] epistemological assumptions and the interpersonal context;[18] therapeutic "compression" involving the enhancement of proximity in the family system.[19] Also, broad theories of psychopathology and structural change have been explored with both implicit and explicit connections to paradoxical interventions. These have included extensions of the initial double bind theory of schizophrenia to other types of psychopathology,[20] the effect of "dissonance" in structure,[21] and an alternative focus on problematic and nonproblematic reflexive loops.[22] Clinical analyses of the effect of the prescribing-the-symptom type of paradoxical intervention have emphasized that such prescribing involves accepting the system at its current level of operation as well as getting on the patient's side before initiating change.[23] Others have focused on how paradoxical interventions provoke defiance in members of the family and thereby produce change.[24] However, all discussions, even those that focus on getting on the patient's side, emphasize the startling and disruptive effect of the paradoxical intervention and, like Wynne, posit that the disruption is a force for change. The presumption of disruption is, in turn, directly dependent on the core notion of paradox in all the prescriptions described.

Paradox is disrupting and disruption stimulates change. Although this proposition seems quite acceptable and applicable to the Wynne example just presented, as well as to many others, it deserves further assessment on a clinical basis. The logically paradoxical nature of interventions involving prescribing the symptom depends, as Rosenbaum has stated it, on the principle that the therapist offers two contradictory statements at once: (1) "This is therapy; thus whatever I say in this frame is a healing statement." (2) "I am not healing you (by insisting that the patient maintain or increase symptoms)."[25] To the extent that this formulation describes the therapeutic circumstance, it conforms to the philosophical definition of paradox given earlier. Also it suggests the presence of a janusian conception. It is critical to note, however, that the first of the two contradictory statements is never stated explicitly to the patient. Moreover, no indication is ever given that the therapist makes any effort at all to establish that the patient has actually adopted the healing view of the therapist and the therapy situation.

Patients do not necessarily believe, either consciously or unconsciously, that everything they hear in therapy is a healing statement, nor do they necessarily come to the therapy in the first place with the expectation that they will be healed. All we have learned about resistance and about patients' coming to therapy merely to be supported or agreed with—even when they know they are behaving in problematic or pathological ways—indicates that we cannot take the first statement for granted. Despite the therapist's good intentions, and despite all surface appearances and traditional beliefs about seeking treatment, a patient may be neither motivated nor convinced about being healed. At least, the patient may not be convinced enough for one to assert that a true logical paradox is engendered. In practical clinical terms, an individual or family may not experience a suggestion to continue or intensify a symptom—depending on which symptom it is, of course—as extremely discrepant and paradoxical, or even, in some cases, as different from expected.

With respect to the second and assumedly contradictory statement of a non-healing effect, much of what is done in practice serves to modify or otherwise reduce this aspect of the paradox. Therapists usually introduce an intervention together with an explanation about the need to go slow or with some other justification about a healing effect. Such proffered explanations cast the intervention as a positive therapeutic action and, more important, they tend to prevent feedback from the patient and family as to how the instruction is actually perceived. Adding an aversive element to the symptom prescription, as is advocated by Haley and sometimes done by Erickson, also very likely conveys to the patient that the therapist is primarily healing in his purpose.[26] For example, the purpose of Haley's directive to another insomniac patient that she stay up all night, but carry out strenuous and unpleasant housework during the night, was very likely not lost on the patient. She must have clearly inferred that Haley was introducing factors that would directly stop her from being insomniac.

Paradox, in the sense of self-contradictory propositions, is in the mind of the therapist, but not necessarily in the minds of patients. The therapist perceives himself as being self-contradictory whenever he prescribes a symptom or a negative behavior. In order for the patient or family to experience an impetus to therapeutic change and participate in producing a creative effect, however, additional factors must be considered. Critically important are the means of transmittal and the nature of the specific content of the paradoxical intervention, as well as the patient's or family's psychological set and ability to apprehend. Simply formulating what the therapist considers paradoxical does not ensure the patient's engagement in a creative process.

In the Wynne example, on the other hand, meaningful paradox was experienced and engagement in the creative process occurred. In reporting her feeling of having achieved new insight, the patient indicated that she had taken over and apprehended the purging/not-purging reference of the therapist's paradoxical intervention. She stated that she realized what her "involuntary" vomiting had been doing. Wynne points out emphatically that he made no interpretations but the patient made them all.

Also demonstrated in the Wynne example is a principle regarding the transmission and content of a paradoxical intervention. The principle is that such interventions are creatively formulated and transmitted to the patient and family when, as discussed in Chapter V, they concern specific salient conflicts. Symptoms represent embedded conflicts. A choice to represent a symptom in a simultaneously antithetical way is a choice to unearth or clarify a conflict. The particular injunction to throw the food down the toilet focused Wynne's patient on purging and not purging. This focus very likely also included her conflicted concerns with control and with anal functions. Patients with anorexia nervosa and bulimia are, as I have attempted to show elsewhere, beset with conflicts about anality and control[27] and Wynne's example throws these factors into sharp relief. The paradoxical intervention therefore functions as a dramatic enacted form of interpretation at the same time as it serves to disrupt ingrained patterns of the family system.

The janusian process leads to formulation of specific conflicts in context, and these formulations are incorporated into creative paradoxical interventions. In order to transmit the janusian formulation effectively, it is necessary to be sure about the patient's apprehension of the apparent self-contradiction. At the moment of transmitting the paradoxical intervention, it is important to ascertain that enough groundwork has been laid so that the patient and family will intrinsically accept the therapist as a healer. This groundwork cannot derive from the mere fact of seeking therapy, or solely from the benevolence of the therapist, or even from transference alone, as transference can be quite negative right at the start. On another level, the care and thoughtfulness with which the therapist chooses a particular symptom or identifies a conflict will have an impact on whether, and how much, the family apprehends the therapist as a healer.

So far, I have primarily discussed a particular prescribing-the-symptom type of paradoxical intervention. Other types of interventions also labeled as paradoxical may share similar strengths and pitfalls with respect to creativity and therapeutic effectiveness. They may: effectively disrupt routinized patterns and instigate change; identify specific conflict; facilitate the mutual creative process involving the therapist together with the patient and family. On the pitfall side, all may become too routinized and formulaic to be creative or therapeutically effective. All may not be apprehended or taken over by the patient as simultaneous antitheses.

The pitfall of lack of apprehension of simultaneous antitheses may loom even larger than with the symptom prescription in such paradoxical interventions as restraining change, reframing, positioning, and benevolent ordeals. These interventions often have the difficulty, to start with, of being paradoxical only in the limited sense of the common understanding of this term. They frequently involve only the contrary of what is expected instead of consisting of explicit or implicit self-contradictions. Rather than a set of simultaneous opposites or antitheses, they are simply reversals and opposing positions. For example, when a therapist suggests that a patient cannot change or may encounter dangers with improvement, this may be surprising only because it is not what was expected. It may instill defiance (or pessimism when it fails completely), but it would not very likely be experienced as dissonant with the therapist's task. After all, one of a therapist's time-honored functions is to give the patient a realistic appraisal of the chances for success and therefore such remarks often would be heard as serious appraisals. In similar fashion, the reframing of negative behavior as positive, or vice versa, may also be experienced as surprising and contrary to a previous belief. However, it is then only an opposite rather than a simultaneous antithesis or a set of simultaneous opposites.

In the examples I have discussed up to this point I have focused on family therapy because the term paradox is frequently used there. However, I have indicated at several points that some of the same considerations apply to work with individuals as with families. To focus on this more general use of paradox in treatment, I will turn to the work of the creative therapist, Milton Erickson.

MILTON ERICKSON AND PARADOX

Innovation and the unusual were characteristic of the work of Milton Erickson. Although many of his approaches, such as the use of metaphors and storytelling discussed earlier, his use of hypnosis and his focus on unconscious processes and unconscious learning, are derived from, or share features of, other disciplines and fields such as Zen Buddhism, Judaic teaching, Sufi poetry and storytelling, psychoanalysis, and subliminal perception, his investigative and clinical work is constantly shifting and exploratory with an emphasis on new tactics and ideas. Although such a focus on the new and different is sometimes thought to be synonymous with creativity, such is not the case. We have required that newness be accompanied by value in our definitions of creativity, and all judgments on the value and outcome of Erickson's new ideas and tactics have not yet come in. Erickson's work is, however, highly focused on the use of paradox and, in many cases, his paradoxical formulations seem to result from the operation of a janusian process. Overall, unlike Freud, he did not develop any systematic theory of his clinical approach or of the nature of human functioning, and his creativity has been manifest primarily in his formulations and interventions.

Although systematic theory is lacking and some, such as Hoffman,[28] maintain it is impossible to replicate his work, others have attempted to describe distinct principles and clinical procedures, both with Erickson's help and on their own. Haley has used the term "strategic therapy" for the type of treatment done by Erickson and has called him "the master" of this approach.[29] Many of the particular strategies and precepts that Haley defines as part of this therapy appear to have involved a janusian process at some point in their development. For instance, "encouraging resistance," "providing a worse alternative," "encouraging a relapse," "encouraging a response by frustrating it," and "amplifying a deviation" all bear the stamp of self-contradiction and simultaneous antithesis.[30] Although we do not know the actual way these principles were developed, Erickson's own statement on his thinking and orientation is highly suggestive of the process I have described. In his preface to Watzlawick, Weakland, and Fisch's book entitled *Change*, Erickson says: "I have viewed much of what I have done as expediting the currents of change already seething within the person and the family—but currents that need the 'unexpected,' the 'illogical,' and the 'sudden' to lead them into tangible fruition."[31]

The precepts described by Haley are now all familiar components of paradoxical techniques used in family therapy; this is one reason Erickson has been called "the grandfather of family therapy."[32] With regard to his landmark work with hypnotic induction, which he used both with families and with individual patients, he developed a principle of indirect suggestion and elaborated it throughout his life. This principle implicitly involves a distinct janusian formulation. The idea of suggestion in relation to hypnotic states is clearly much stronger than its conception in everyday common usage. In the latter it is a proposal, but in hypnosis it is a form of directiveness or direction. The idea of indirect suggestion in hypnosis, therefore, is more appropriately considered as *indirect direction* – a simultaneous antithesis.

As a concrete example of this idea in practice, here is the verbatim beginning of one of Erickson's trance inductions:

Look at the far upper corner of that picture. Now you [speaking an aside to an observer] watch her face. [To the patient again] The far upper corner of that picture. Now I'm going to talk to you. When you first went to kindergarten, grade school, this matter of learning letters and numerals seemed to be a big insurmountable task. To recognize the letter A, to tell a Q from an O was very, very difficult. And then, too, script and print were so different. But you learned to form a mental image of some kind. You didn't know it at the time, but it was a permanent mental image. And later on in grammar school you formed other mental images of words, or pictures of sentences. You developed more and more mental images without knowing you were developing mental images. And you can recall all those images. Now you can go anywhere you wish, and transport yourself to any situation. You can do anything you want. You don't even have to listen to my voice because your unconscious will hear it. Your unconscious can try anything it wishes. But your conscious mind isn't going to do anything of importance. . . .[33]

This monologue induction was spoken, as Erickson's inductions always were, very slowly and regularly. The feature of indirect direction is, I believe, readily apparent in his shifting away from commands to enter a trance or fall asleep while at the same time directing the subject to believe in, and focus on, mental imagery. Furthermore, by using the idea of the unconscious mind, he both directs her to listen to his voice and permits her not to do so at once.

Other particular types of hypnotic induction developed by Erickson also reflect his tendency to formulate simultaneous antitheses. For instance, he slowly proclaims a series of opposite and contradictory statements which, he says, require the patient to seek understanding or meaning at another level. Frequently, he uses a type of contrary directive that, he believes, instigates the opposite at the same time, such as giving an example of a forgotten experience of childhood to facilitate both forgetting and recall, and emphatically admonishing withholding patients to withhold vital information "until the latter part of next week" as a procedure inducing them both to resist and to yield at once.[34]

Much has been written by both Erickson and his associates attempting to explain the effectiveness of his approach to hypnotic induction. In distinction to dramatic, commanding approaches, there may possibly be less instigation of a patient's dependency on the therapist. Erickson, Rossi and Rossi, Lankton and Lankton, all claim that it facilitates the patient's own capacities for change.[35] Erickson says, "the less the operator does and *the more he confidently and expectantly allows the subject to do*, the easier and more effective will the hypnotic state and hypnotic phenomena be elicited in accord with the subject's own capabilities and uncolored by efforts to please the operator."[36] Also, the claim is made that these procedures encourage the patient's creativity and that some aspects of it give "free reign to the creative process."[37] Leveton draws analogies between Erickson's later work involving induction of light trance, Bachelard's focus on reverie, and Winnicott's designation of transitional phenomena and emphasizes the therapeutic importance of eliciting what he calls the "between" realm of experience.[38]

Whether or not the indirect direction of Erickson's hypnotic induction stimulates further creative elaboration on the patient's part is hard to ascertain. If the technique is applied to everyone without regard to the principles of application of the janusian process I have outlined, it is unlikely to have a creative effect. For instance, the oppositions compliance and defiance are implicitly addressed in this approach. If these specific opposites are not important for a particular patient, a creative janusian process will not likely ensue.

Several of Erickson's own interventions in his ongoing relationships with his patients, however, are decidedly directed toward salient features of their difficulties. In the examples to follow we see a phenomenon similar to the clinical use of the janusian process by Freud described in the last chapter. With the vomiting mother, Freud's use of hypnosis seemed less important than his identification of a central conflict. Erickson's identification of conflict also seems to be a primary factor in his therapeutic effect.

In the case of a young adult male with a history of enuresis since puberty,[39] a case that has also been discussed by Hoffman,[40] Erickson reports that he first determined that the patient had been cystoscoped and had taken "barrels of medicine" for his difficulty. Also, he gathered the particular information that the patient lived at home and it was his mother who found his bed wet every morning. Then, assuring the patient that his problem was psychological in origin, Erickson told him to carry out a particular series of actions. First, he was to go to a neighboring city and engage a hotel room. While there, and preparing to sleep in the bed, he was to consider how frightened and distressed he would be when the maid, like his mother, discovered a wet bed the next morning. Then, thinking constantly of how humiliating and anxious he would feel, he would begin to think of what an amazing but bitter joke on himself it would be if, after all his worrying, the maid were surprised by a *dry* bed. He would focus on this latter idea and begin to feel shame, anxiety, and embarrassment when thinking about the maid discovering a dry bed rather than a wet one. If this program were successful, he was to remain in the room another day and again to worry about the maid's discovering the bed to be dry.

Erickson reports that this intervention was indeed successful in interrupting the enuretic symptom. Although the suggestion was carried out under hypnosis, and some other directives regarding the patient's grandparents were also included,[41] the presentation illustrates an identification of a central conflict. Erickson structures the situation to convey a circumstance in which the patient simultaneously wishes to wet the bed and not to wet the bed. Also, he experiences anxiety about both wishes. In either case, he is in the position of defying the maid who is represented as a displaced substitute for the mother. Therefore, it is a conflict about the desire to defy the mother that causes the patient anxiety. The patient is presented with a janusian formulation which serves as a nonverbalized or action-embedded interpretation of conflict.[42]

In another case of a man suffering from phantom pain in his legs, Erickson began the treatment by telling the patient stories about his own life. Two circumstances were described in which he experienced uncomfortable physical sensations as nonexistent or even comforting. Watching the man's reactions carefully while he talked, Erickson asked him directly where he felt the pain. The man replied that he felt it in his foot and (reminded by his wife) added "where there is no foot." Thereupon, Erickson told the man about a psychiatrist friend of his with a wooden leg. One day, while this friend and he were talking, the friend reached down to scratch his ankle. Then Erickson, referring to the itch as though it were real, asked the friend how the limb felt after the scratching. He replied, "good." Addressing the patient directly, Erickson said: "You can have good feelings in the foot, not just painful ones. . . . If you have phantom pain in a limb, you may also have phantom good feelings."[43]

Again, although couched in terms of storytelling, Erickson's central intervention constructed the simultaneous opposites of pain and pleasure together in the symptom. This was therefore a dramatized type of interpretation focusing on conflict either about masochistic gratification or else the secondary gain aspects of the symptom, or both. That secondary gain was likely a factor in the case is suggested by the fact that the patient next began to protest gratuitously that he did *not* want his wife to spend so much time taking care of him.[44]

Erickson used a similar type of interpretation in the case of a young bridegroom who sought help because he was unable to achieve erection during a two-week honeymoon.[45] Instructing the man to experience both his sense of shame and humiliation over the events and a wish to do "anything, *just anything*, to escape from that completely wretched feeling," he then suggested that the patient imagine himself and his wife in the nude. At the same time, however, he would feel that he had no control over his entire body. This would lead to the discovery that he sensed physical contact with his bride that was intimate and exciting him to action but there was "nothing he could do to control his physical responses." From Erickson's report that this intervention led to successful intercourse the same night, it appears that the simultaneously antithetical prescription to want to do something and nothing was successful. Very likely, this dramatized type of interpretation focused the young man on his conflicts about control, i.e., whether to be in control or to be controlled in the sexual relationship.

Conflicts about control are, of course, found routinely in obsessive-compulsive disorders, and conflicts about masochistic gratifications or secondary gain are found in a range of different conditions. Neither Erickson nor his associates discuss diagnostic factors or principles of psychopathology in describing his approach. However, verbatim transcripts of his work, his own commentary, plus the testimony of those who have worked directly with him,[46] indicate his continual and penetrating observation of his patients' verbal and nonverbal reactions. While delivering a monologue, either story or other type of trance induction, he modified, shifted, or honed in on a particular area touched upon, after noting nuances of reaction or response. It may be remembered, in the verbatim hypnotic induction I quoted above, that Erickson told the observer to watch the patient's face. In this way, his approach is exquisitely responsive to a particular person's psychological makeup.

His skill in observation is, I believe, the factor that gives specific creative impact to his work. The examples of janusian formulations I gave are only a small sampling of the numerous interventions of this type found throughout his and others' writings about his cases. Those used seem to demonstrate the choice of salient opposites despite the relative absence of information about how Erickson went about selecting them. In numerous other cases, his persistent use of reversals and paradox — in the commonly understood sense of contrary to the expected — seems also to have resulted in creative effects. In these, a mutual janusian formulation may have been developed in which the patient's understanding provided an aspect of the simultaneous antithesis. In such cases, and in those I have discussed, it seems fair to presume that Erickson's observations, though not described, functioned to determine important thematic factors and salient opposites.

The janusian process requires, for its creative effect, such specificity of themes, antitheses, and opposites. Use of techniques involving routine reversals, contraries of expected actions or behaviors, or even a routine introduction of the unusual would not be applications of janusian process and would not have creative effects. It is often said that Erickson's work cannot be replicated. One reason for this may be that those who attempt to use his approaches do not also possess, or work to learn, his sensitivity to and observation of conflict.

IRONY

Another type of intervention manifesting a simultaneously antithetical structure is irony. Unlike paradox, irony has not received much attention in psychotherapy literature and has not been incorporated into a defined technique.[47] It does share common features with some of the paradoxical interventions described here, in that its structure and effect are highly dependent on context. Irony consists of a verbal construction in which the opposite of what is literally stated is implied.[48] Consequently, an ironic statement cannot be understood to be one unless the implication is conveyed by the context. In psychotherapy, if a patient does not apprehend that the therapist is implying the opposite or intending a comment to be ironic, it will be taken literally. For instance, after having delivered a flood of hostile invective at the therapist and getting no response, a patient says, "You're really all right, doctor." The therapist then ironically says, "Whew, what a relief!" If this therapist response is not given with the right tone of voice, or if the patient has reason to believe that the therapist has been truly intimidated, the irony will be lost.

Irony is often considered to be a type of wit or humor, but many types of irony are not at all evocative of laughter. These are usually found in art and literature and range from serious to skeptical to tragic. Such irony usually is presented in the artistic context in a complicated unfolding way and is used to connote and express both superficial and profound truths. Considered the fundamental basis of poetry and drama by many critics, much has been written about its aesthetic and philosophical importance.[49] In art and literature, irony serves to exemplify, instruct, charm, humor, provoke, enrage, and otherwise deeply move both readers and viewers. In the therapeutic context, irony used by the therapist as interpretation is most commonly associated with humor. This is partly because ironies contained in relatively short constructions involve an apposition of opposites and, as Freud has shown, opposites brought together are often experienced as humorous.[50] More important to the therapeutic use, however, humor serves as a cue to the patient that something other than a literal meaning is intended.[51]

The use of any type of humor in therapy has been a topic of some controversy.[52] A therapist's display of wit or humor is considered by some to be, at a minimum, either seductive or competitive or self-aggrandizing and, at a maximum, a way of shortcutting and suppressing the exploration of a patient's dynamic concerns. This latter effect allegedly results because humor functions to release and alleviate anxiety about a particular issue or topic, and so the issue or topic is dismissed before the roots of the anxiety are explored. In such circumstances, the criticism goes, the therapist using humor is acting out his own countertransference conflicts and suppressing patient issues that are anxiety-provoking to him.

With each of the former effects, some countertransference factor is acted out as well. With seductiveness, the therapist exploits the capacity of humor to generate warmth, friendliness, and even sexual feelings in circumstances where he either cannot tolerate hostility or a feeling of distance from the patient or also needs the patient's love. With competitiveness, both the aggressive factor in humor and the humorist's demonstration of skill are seen to play a role. Aggressiveness, as Freud succinctly demonstrated, is an almost invariant component of jokes and other forms of humor.[53] Any type of therapist joking or casting of comments in a humorous way may be at the patient's expense and may also often be an indirect vehicle for the therapist to discharge hostile feelings. Demonstration of skill in a competitive way enters the picture because humor often involves cleverness, perceptiveness, wit, and other valued social capacities. Putting the patient down may be the therapist's purpose, without his realizing or knowing it. Also related to this factor of demonstration of skill is the self-aggrandizing and "show-off" function of displaying virtuosity and seemingly superior capacities to the patient. This serves only to reassure the therapist about himself and has little value for the patient. Particular types of highly fragile or paranoid patients may invariably misunderstand and be damaged by humor.

All of these criticisms are potentially valid but they need not deter the proper use of humor in therapy. They serve both to emphasize the potentially useful functions of therapeutic humor and as cautions or limits regarding improper use. First, although it can be used seductively by the therapist, humor does have the function of facilitating intimacy and warm relationships. It can be used to help the patient to feel intimate with the therapist without an accompanying feeling of guilt and fear. It can demonstrate a therapist's genuine positive feelings toward the patient and his willingness to relax and be friendly, and it can allow the patient to experience similar feelings in return. With some patients, relaxed or positive feelings are far more risky and guilt-ridden than are negative hostile ones.

Second, although humor can be used to obscure and bury issues that are anxiety-provoking both to patients and therapists, it also serves as a valuable release of anxiety in circumstances where therapy has become bogged down or where anxiety has reached an insupportable level. Each and every conflict that a patient brings to therapy is not necessarily explorable and, especially in working with seriously disturbed patients, use of humor to modulate anxiety may be the only way therapy can proceed. Done with care, this can be true for paranoid patients as well.

Third, although humor can be used just to display the cleverness and wit of the therapist, it nevertheless does derive from positive skills. It requires a certain degree of flexibility and freedom on the therapist's part and usually the same type of skill with words that is required in every psychotherapy. Also, it often requires a certain degree of perceptiveness and insight and, as I shall discuss presently, in the case of irony, a creative capacity. To expose these skills to the patient is not a detriment and can serve to facilitate the therapeutic alliance. Moreover, as some identification with the therapist always occurs, exposing these skills and attributes may serve as a positive model for patient development.

Finally, although humor often has an aggressive component, it is not therefore necessarily hostile to the patient. Aggressiveness in humor may not be at all greater than that in literal admonitions, confrontations, or even direct interpretations. As a positive feature, the therapist's ability to express aggressiveness in a socially acceptable way may also have a modeling function. The tendency of humor to be conveyed through exaggeration and dramatization, with the use of alterations in tone of voice and manner, additionally serves as a special check on aggressiveness. It is relatively easy for the therapist himself to recognize when his aggressiveness has changed to hostility in any particular humorous remark. This allows him to monitor his countertransference hostility and to correct it and, as with other types of errors I shall discuss in Chapter VIII, to use it therapeutically.

When humor and humorously stated irony become charged with hostility, there is a shift into *sarcasm*. Although technically sarcasm is considered to be a form of humor, it does not share any of the positive characteristics I have just outlined. Seldom, if ever, does sarcasm or a sarcastic intervention have a use or valuable function in therapy. Although sarcastic interchanges between two individuals may seem humorous to a third party, they are always hostile attacks at the expense of one or the other individual. It is just at the point that a remark intended to be friendly and ironically humorous becomes tinged with sarcasm that a therapist must become aware of the influence of countertransference hostility.

The dividing line between friendly humor and sarcasm is sometimes rather thin and for this reason humor must be used with care in the therapeutic situation. Only elements of context, such as the exact shading of the tone of voice, expression on the therapist's face, and other shared vehicles of meaning between patient and therapist, can determine the difference. With an ironic remark such as "What a relief!" any defensive quality to the tone on the therapist's part or any indication that he may not be as amused as he pretends to be will be properly experienced as a hostile rebuff by the patient. Also, if either the literal aspect of the remark or the implied opposite meaning receives undue emphasis, then the intervention will shade into sarcasm.

The simultaneously antithetical character of an ironic remark is critical both for its nonhostile effect and for its operation as a therapeutic intervention. When both the literal aspect and its implied opposite are conveyed and experienced as meaningful and applicable, the ironic remark then functions as an interpretation of conflict. When the therapist says, "What a relief!" after a hostile barrage followed by a compliment, he conveys his understanding that the patient wished to injure him but was also feeling guilty about that wish. The literal aspect regarding relief acknowledges the wish to injure and the implied opposite conveys that the therapist is perfectly all right. Beyond a simply literal interpretation, moreover, the humorous ironic intervention provides an affective acceptance of the patient's hostile wish. Rather than literally telling the patient that he is all right and uninjured, he enacts and demonstrates his comfortable state of being with his good humor.

An ironic intervention is a janusian formulation identifying both sides of specific patient conflict. Because one of the opposites in an irony is implied, there is often a more telling sense of simultaneity than with more explicit types of janusian formulations. This is because making each opposite explicit technically requires stating the substance sequentially. Even if that were not the case, however, the ironic intervention can convey a greater degree of acceptance by the therapist than other types of interpretations. A moderately depressed person, for example, may pour out a series of complaints about himself, such as: "I try to be nice to people but it never seems to work. Everybody acts as though I'm antagonistic, or lazy, or a bother. I used to be able to make friends; I used to have a lot of energy. I don't know why I try; I feel like giving up." To these, the therapist may ironically reply: "So, I guess you're just a worthless, nasty bum." Such a comment conveys the therapist's implied formulation of the opposite, i.e., "you're not worthless," and it also conveys an understanding that the patient actually does feel worthless. Moreover, instead of simply reassuring the patient, it acknowledges both sides of the conflict. On the one side, there is the element of truth in the self-deprecatory content of the complaint that commonly appears in depressed states. The patient is, and wishes to be, passive and nasty. On the other side, there is the wish to be active, make friends, and feel a sense of self-esteem and worth. Both sides are interpreted and, because of the friendly, humorous tone, acceptance of both sides is conveyed.

On another level, Stein, in an article on irony in psychoanalysis,[54] has pointed out that the entire analytic situation is an ironic one. Patients are expected to develop a transference but transference must be analyzed and hopefully renounced; the more intense and florid the erotic attachment in the transference, the more likely is it to be accompanied by, or be a defense against, hostility; the more the analyst feels himself responding, the more he has to understand his feelings; the patient sees the analyst as an omniscient and loving parent and is also aware that he is being charged a substantial fee; the procedure is conducted on the basis of psychic determinism as well as the implicit assumption of purposeful and moral choice. Although many attempts have been made in psychoanalytic literature to reduce and explain these ironies, Stein recommends that the analyst adopt an ironic but not cynical stance. This must involve some degree of detachment in conjunction with a deep commitment. Schafer also advocates what he calls an "ironic vision" for the psychoanalyst, and he quotes Freud as having said that psychoanalysis shows man to be more moral as well as less moral than he thought.[55]

With regard to the creative effect of irony, whether general stance or vision as Stein and Schafer describe or as a particular ironic intervention, it is necessary that the patient both apprehend the irony and apply it in the ongoing therapeutic process. Usually, this is manifested by a development of insight which may or may not be expressed by the patient as a propositional or intellectual formulation. For example, a patient was considering terminating therapy but the therapist knew that he was deeply ambivalent about doing so. Beginning a therapy hour with the description of a highly problematic situation at his office, his rendition of the details made it clear that he had become entangled in, for him, a repeated constellation of difficulties. He was being downgraded by his co-workers and his boss, a circumstance in which he characteristically responded with passive withdrawal. As he recounted the story, he began to talk about his growing awareness of the constellation and of his own tendency to withdraw. Reporting that he had this awareness in mind while working in the office the previous day, he described himself taking an active stance. He told his co-workers how much he resented their scapegoating and, in addition, took on a job for the boss that he completed successfully. Although he told all this to the therapist with some hesitation and discomfort, a distinct tone of pleasure also crept into his voice as he reported his effectiveness and success.

The therapist at that moment became aware of the patient's simultaneous wishes for both success and failure conveyed by the content of the tale and the manner of presentation. Thus, in a friendly tone of voice, he said: "Well, now, we can't have that kind of behavior! For all we know, you're going to continue doing this kind of thing; you're going to keep on understanding the source of your difficulties and correcting them. You're going to begin to be able to handle yourself in all kinds of difficult situations. The next thing we know you'll feel that you're better and will want to terminate therapy. Then, you may even feel cured. We can't have that! What are we going to do then?"

The tone, as I said, was friendly. The patient, who had heard ironic comments from the therapist before, smiled and immediately replied, "Yes, we can't have that. What am I going to say to my friends and my wife if I'm better?" Following this, he started tentatively exploring some specific goals in that session that might lead to termination of therapy. He continued to work on these goals in subsequent weeks.

In this ironic janusian formulation, the therapist conveyed that he was aware of the patient's conflict about success and failure and interpreted both sides at once. He spoke literally of the sequence of the desired events that might follow the therapeutic movement and also acknowledged the patient's desired opposite in his negating and humorous phrasing. He indicated uncritically that the patient might wish to fail in order not to leave therapy and still be perceived as being ill—an aspect of the interpretation verified by the patient's own ironically stated and insight-containing response. Also, he showed support and friendly pleasure for the patient's genuine wishes to improve and be on his own.

As with paradoxical interventions, it is important that an ironic intervention be related to the patient's specific conflicts and that the opposites involved develop from the particular context. Routine types of interventions will not be janusian formulations developed from the therapeutic interaction and will not lead to creative effects. Using humor for its own sake also will not necessarily touch on a patient's concerns and may have all the negative features discussed as cautions above. Using humor in the form of jokes told to the patient, or in the form of witty aphorisms, is similar to other types of storytelling or to the Erickson "embedded metaphor" technique. It will be effective if it derives from careful observation and understanding of a patient's specific concerns. To know that this is so requires confirmatory responses from the patient. All humor is not ironic and even ironic humor requires patient confirmation that it has been apprehended.

A 22-year-old schizophrenic female was acutely sensitized to being abandoned because her parents had traveled all over the world and often left her behind in a punitive way. Extremely wealthy and given to taking frequent vacations, they would invite the patient to accompany them when she behaved as they had wanted and not offer, or withdraw, an invitation when she did not measure up. After several months in psychotherapy, she had benefitted a fair amount and had fewer and fewer psychotic episodes. Although often manifesting massive denial, she displayed some capacity for humor. At a point when the therapist announced that he would be away for a month's vacation, the following interchange occurred at the beginning of a therapy session.

P: I'm really glad you're going away and I won't have to come to therapy. My mother wants me to ask you where you are going.

TH: Your *mother* wants to know?

P: OK, where are you going on vacation?

TH: (smiling) As *far* away from you as I can get!

P: Vermont? (N.B. the treatment took place in Massachusetts)

TH: Not far enough.

P: Florida?

TH: Much too close.

P: Europe?

TH: Right around the corner.

P: South America?

TH: Not far enough, thousands more miles away.

P: Maybe I can go with you.

TH: (still smiling) Ugh!!

In the remainder of the session the patient continued to focus on the therapist's vacation and, becoming more and more serious, she acknowledged feelings of jealousy and resentment about his going away. She also touched on some of her feelings about her parents' controlling behavior in connection with their vacations and other facets of their relationship with her. In this case it was clear that the apprehension of irony depended both on the therapist's ability to convey his genuinely genial feelings and on the patient's capacity for humor. Despite the extremity of her illness, however, there is no question, from a consideration of the verbatim interchange, that she fully understood and reacted to the therapist's creative interpretation. In stating that he wanted to get far away from her, he acknowledged her literal wish that she not be tied to therapy and, at the same time, he implicitly interpreted her fear that she was driving him away. Moreover, his affect indicated that she wasn't driving him away at all. This was further demonstrated by the continuing irony of the interchange. Each time the patient half jokingly and half seriously tested the therapist's interpretation of her conflict and fear, he increased the polarity of the oppositions and conveyed the feeling that he did not wish to get rid of her at all. At the same time, the patient designated locations to which her parents had gone, both with and without her. Thus, the interchange in this case represented a compressed reenactment, together with some working-through, of experiences she had had with her parents.

That some degree of working-through occurred is indicated by her revealing openly her wish to go with the therapist on his vacation. At that point, the therapist again reacted with irony and, compressed as it was, a telling interpretation. The use of the sham grunt of "Ugh" conveyed to the patient both an understanding of her fear that he would be repelled by her and her request, and an assurance he did not feel that way at all.

In addition to particular short interchanges, ironic interventions can be developed over longer periods of time and can also be quite serious in tone. For instance, a therapist developed the idea with a schizoid patient that at the end of therapy he would become more independent and then his loneliness would change to a feeling of really being alone. In another case, a therapist brought home to an idealizing patient who was seeking to attain physical prowess that, after consulting with many therapists, he had ironically chosen one who was far shorter than he as well as appearing to be physically inept. And then, of course, there are the myriad instances in therapy when one points out that a patient is carrying out the very behavior he abhors in others, that he has become identified with an aggressor, that he has difficulty functioning heterosexually because he cannot accept latent homosexual wishes, and that he cannot become truly independent because he has not accepted his feelings of dependency. Sometimes such formulations are constructed and used creatively by the therapist and patient together in a particular context, and sometimes they derive from other types of useful but not manifestly creative processes.

It is important to emphasize, however, that all life experience is perfused with irony and paradox. Life ends in death; wars are waged for moral reasons; evil is banal. Beyond any particular creative derivation or effect, it is probably safe to say that many of the formulations I have discussed ultimately derive their validity from the intrinsically paradoxical and ironic nature of life itself.

CHAPTER VII

The Articulation
Process in Psychotherapy

The therapist focuses on form and structure and uses both homospatial and janusian processes to develop understanding and construct particular interventions. Responding to the therapist's guidance and activity, the patient develops insight, resolves conflicts, and works to create new and valuable personality attributes and structure. As I have emphasized throughout, in order to engage in this mutual creative process, active choice and selection are necessary. The patient must, at many points along the way, actively choose to adopt a new pattern of behavior, just as the creative artist actively chooses to produce new patterns of form and content and the creative scientist actively chooses new theoretical formulations. Such active selection and choice are cardinal features of a particular factor that operates prominently in all creative processes. This is the factor of *articulation*.

ARTICULATION AND THE CREATIVE PROCESS

In the process of creation in any field, there is a progression from emptiness or disarray to the development of tangible order. Every piece of literature begins with an empty page, every painting starts with a blank canvas, music arises from the absence or obliterating profusion of sound, and scientific discovery from confusion, loose ends, and disorder. Responsible to a large degree for progression to tangible order is the factor of articulation. Articulation, which technically means simply to join, is a word with a double sense. The articulation or joining of an element with another one produces both a coming together and a separation at the same time. This is demonstrated quite clearly in the common use of the word "articulate." A person described as "articulate" or as an "articulate speaker" is a person who is able to present ideas and words clearly and smoothly. Such a person articulates or joins his words and ideas by bringing them together and keeping them clearly distinct and separate at once. It is in this double sense that articulation characterizes creative processes. These processes involve a constant bringing together and separating, separating and bringing together, throughout their course. This occurs in many different dimensions—conceptual, perceptual, volitional, affective, and physical. Both janusian and homospatial processes are types of articulation. The janusian process involves articulation of propositional ideas; the homospatial process involves the articulation of mental imagery. However, articulation functions throughout creative activity; it includes both processes and follows after them, leading directly to a creative result.

In producing a work of literature or art, as well as in developing a scientific theory, the creative person separates out critical aspects of the material he works with, and he fuses or brings these separated elements together. For example, in Eugene O'Neill's creation of the play "The Iceman Cometh," the metaphoric title of the play developed from a process of articulation.[1] Conceived by O'Neill from the idea of Christ as an epiphanic bridegroom coming to the virgins (Matthew 25:5–6) and from an old bawdy joke about an adulterous iceman, the iceman cometh metaphor simultaneously brought together and separated out elements of the sacred and the profane, salvation and icy death, sexuality and chastity, marriage and adultery, and other complex factors. On the basis of evidence from manuscripts of the play, several of these factors were in O'Neill's consciousness when he created the metaphor, and some are both felt and comprehended by a thoughtful audience hearing "The Iceman Cometh" as a serious phrase. The fully articulated sense of numerous factors brought together and separated out, however, is only experienced by an audience after seeing or reading the entire play.

As with homospatial and janusian processes, articulation differs from ordinary problem-solving by analogic, inductive, and deductive reasoning. All of these types of reasoning may play a role at some point, but they do not account for the phenomena of making, presenting, and creating that directly result from articulation. In scientific fields, the creative thinker uses ordinary problem-solving modes but approaches large questions in his field by separating out and bringing together key factors underlying controversy and confusion. In the example of Einstein's use of a janusian process in the development of the general theory of relativity, cited in Chapter I, he had separated and brought together, as an articulation, the physical facts and principles of motion and rest. This step resulted from neither inductive consideration of a series of empirical findings, nor a direct deduction from theory, nor consideration of an analogy. Such processes primarily set the stage for the particular articulating conceptualization and also operated later in the working out of the fully developed theory of general relativity. In a similar way, Niels Bohr's janusian formulation in the development of the principle of complementarity involved the separating out and bringing together of the conflicting elements of wave and particle theories of electron and light behavior.

Articulation in the creative process serves many functions. Its creative function is to produce tangible entities that are new and separate from previously existing entities and, at the same time, are connected to their forebears. Creations always bear resemblance to preexisting natural entities and events, such as Cezanne's resemblance to the Impressionists mentioned in Chapter I. However, they are also separate and *sharply* different in some way. With respect to the natural world, they are separated out and joined to nature rather than being a submerged part of it. Hence, they are to some extent free both of nature and past events.

In art, articulation functions to produce tangible created products and also has direct psychological functions for the artist himself. Together with articulating an artwork, the creative artist struggles to articulate aspects of his own inner world. His struggle to articulate on both aesthetic and psychological levels concomitantly produces effects that are important for the emotional appeal of art.

A short and concise example of aesthetic effects of articulation in an artwork is the beginning passage of Herman Melville's *Moby Dick*. This literary creation manifests separating and bringing together in many ways. The speaker indicates his own uniqueness and separateness from other men—a strangely erudite sometime-sailor who calls himself by the name of the biblical outcast Ishmael—and at the same time indicates his connectedness to all humanity. The language itself is highly articulate—rhythmically clear and distinct and yet flowing smoothly together, e.g., "Whenever I find myself growing grim . . . ; whenever it is a damp, drizzly November." The entire passage is unified and can be appreciated separately and alone, and at the same time it strongly connects and leads into a story to come. Here is the passage:

Call me Ishmael. Some years ago—never mind how long precisely—having little or no money in my purse, and nothing particular to interest me on shore, I thought I would sail about a little and see the watery part of the world. It is a way I have of driving off the spleen, and regulating the circulation. Whenever I find myself growing grim about the mouth; whenever it is a damp, drizzly November in my soul; whenever I find myself involuntarily pausing before a coffin warehouse, and bringing up the rear of every funeral I meet; and especially whenever my hopes get such an upper hand of me, that it requires a strong moral principle to prevent me from deliberately stepping into the street, and methodically knocking people's hats off—then, I account it high time to get to sea as soon as I can. This is my substitute for pistol and ball. With a philosophical flourish, Cato throws himself upon his sword; I quietly take to the ship. There is nothing surprising in this. If they but knew it, almost all men in their degree, sometime or other, cherish very nearly the same feelings towards the ocean with me.[2]

Note the explication of the speaker's unique and separate way of dealing with depressive feelings and his immediate insistence on a similarity and connection with "almost all men." Although we can only guess at the manner in which this passage was created, and its relationship to the author himself, data I have collected on the creation of a poetic metaphor from a poet research subject is directly pertinent to such matters. It is the metaphor "A mastermind/Kept track above the mantel" in the following two stanzas from a poem entitled "18 West 11th St.":[3]

> The carpet—its days numbered—
> Hatched another generation
> Of strong-jawed, light besotted saboteurs.
> A mastermind
> Kept track above the mantel. The cold caught,
> One birthday in its shallows, racked [The weak frame . . .]

The poem is about a house in Greenwich Village where the poet lived as a child and which the Weather Underground organization, in a famous incident, accidentally destroyed in 1971 while making bombs in the basement. The metaphor "A mastermind/Kept track above the mantel" is pivotal in the poem because the "mastermind" is a mirror that allows a passing through in imagination of both the poet's childhood images and the world of the Weather Underground. The poem took more than two years to create. In articulating this particular metaphor, the poet wrote at least 33 versions of the lines. The first version contained no reference to a mantel, but suggested the reflection of another world in a mirror by a reference to a "magic room," as follows:

> Or is it Christmas
> And from the first queen mother evergreen

> Stark with unmelting ornament
> I am running toward a further
> Magic room. Jamb and lintel of scarred leaf
> Tilt benevolently forward. From its depths [A little boy is
> running . . .]

The articulation of the final version of the metaphor from this beginning involved dogged and persistent bringing together and separating for the purpose of making and creating. The phrase "jamb and lintel" was brought together several times with the idea of an ideal room in the mirror, then with an idea of a mirror "leaning forward like a matriarch," and next with an idea of "an abstract realm," until the term *"mantel"*[4] was actually separated out and formulated. It developed from superimposition of the words "lintel" and "mantel," in a homospatial process, resulting in the phrase: "The lintel gleams/The magic world above the mantel." After that, the poet proceeded to bring "mantel" and the areas or realms above the mantel together within 15 different variations, e.g., "Above the mantel/A realm of infinite shabbiest poverty began," and "Another realm began over the mantel/Its catching cold/Glazed the flowers as with sleet." In one of these 15 versions, he returned to the earlier phrase "jamb and lintel" and brought that together with the mantel idea, as follows: "Another realm/Began over the mantel. Jamb and lintel of gilt." Then, the precursor to the "mastermind" metaphor was separated out in the following form: "A mental world/Began above the mantel." After bringing together "mental world" and "mantel" in six different ways, the poet formulated *"A mental world/Kept track above the mantel."*[5]

The poet made no further changes in those lines for several months, but he continued to work on other portions of the poem. When he hit on the final idea of using "mastermind" instead of mental world, his verbatim description of the process to me was as follows:

Well, I just thought it ["mastermind"] was better than the "mental world" and it connected obviously with "saboteurs." I mean one . . . one imagines behind any plot there is a mind. And to make it the mirror! . . . I just turned my attention to that line and . . . and then, that came to me. I suppose from the word "mental" it's not so far to get to "mind." *But it seemed to me it was already there, in a way, an embryo in the original phrase.* But in a way obscured by the temptation of rhyme—mental and mantel.[6]

In this final sequence of articulating steps producing the metaphor, the poet had focused on the off-rhymed, i.e., an inexact rhyme, pair "mental" and "mantel." He separated out the idea of *mind,* which, as he put it, was "obscured by the temptation of rhyme"—referring to a poet's tendency to make and hold onto rhymes. At the same time as he separated out the mind idea, he brought it together with another idea in the poem, the idea of "saboteurs," and articulated the word "mastermind" into the metaphor and the poem. This step also had connections with earlier versions in that "mastermind" is related to all of the following: the "abstract" aspect of "abstract realm"; the "magic" of the earlier "magic world"; the idea of the use of a mirror; and in the "master" aspect, to the earlier "matriarch."

The poet's sense that "mastermind" was already present as an embryo in his original phrase was an apt and meaningful description. He had indeed articulated it from the original phrase and the original idea in several different ways. Through progressive separating and bringing together, he produced a metaphor that joined an aspect of the magic room idea of his childhood to the idea of saboteurs of the Weather Underground organization. Also, although he did not refer to this in our sessions, he separated out the initial consonants of the off-rhymed words, "mental" and "mantel," and, in a final step, joined them into another poetically effective sound similarity. In using "mastermind" with "mantel" he produced both an alliteration of "m" sounds and an assonance of "a" sounds together. On another level, I have reason to believe—from information I have from my previous intensive work with this research subject—that he associated mirrors with his mother (N.B. the early idea of the mirror leaning forward like a matriarch) and that the mastermind idea could readily relate to her intelligence and domination. Therefore, in settling on the word "mastermind," he articulated an underlying unconscious meaning of the original idea focusing on the mirror. This was not a breakthrough of unconscious material but a gradual unearthing and shaping of what the poet indicated to be "already there."

The final created metaphor, "mastermind keeps track above the mantel," suggests many of these personal and poetic articulations and, in itself, it is an articulated structure. It is unique and stands alone at the same time as it connects to other aspects of the poem. It evokes ideas of the realms of an inanimate mirror (or family portrait) and an animate mind that are separated but also connected to each other. These independent ideas relate to and modify each other and dynamically interact within the whole metaphorical phrase. This metaphor, therefore, is a dynamic and aesthetically effective literary structure that both separates and connects many levels of meaning and of word use, all at once.

Another more extensive illustration from the literary process concerns the creation of a novel by John Hersey.[7] This novel, *Too Far to Walk,* concerns a college student embroiled in a struggle for identity and self-esteem in the America of the 1960s. Caught in a web of rapid value changes and a concomitant sense of unbridled impulses and temptations, he loses interest in his classes and school work and searches for gratification in debasement, sex, and drugs. Much of the novel involves the student's relationship with his parents. Through a series of scenes involving telephone calls to the parents, a visit home, and an LSD fantasy in which the parents appear, the novel unfolds a complex son-parent interaction. It is the unfolding and development of this interaction that accounts in part for the aesthetic effectiveness of the novel. The son's efforts to cope with his past and to move onward catch us up in the story. These are efforts at what I have described as articulation. In his movement toward freedom and independence, the son articulates his experience and his personality; he attempts to separate himself from those elements in his past and his parents that he finds unacceptable and to clarify and continue those that he accepts. He joins himself to the past, present, and future by both separating and bringing together.

In my work with Mr. Hersey during the course of his writing the novel, in which we systematically discussed the sections as they were written, it appeared that he too was engaged in a process of articulation on both a psychological and an aesthetic level. Thinking about his own sons during the period of time the novel was being written, he alternatively shifted his vantage point between the generations. At various points throughout the process, he sometimes felt himself to be in sympathy with the viewpoint of the son, and at other points he felt in sympathy with the parental view, particularly the view of the father. This meant that a process of temporary and shifting identifications was taking place. In the creation of the father-son relationship, the author alternatively identified with his own sons in relation to himself as the father, with himself as father in relation to his sons, and with himself as son in relation to his own father. In our discussion of scenes or events in the novel, Hersey indicated connections to his experience as a father, his sons' experience with him, and his feelings about his father or a father-figure.

Also, during the course of writing the book, he made a decision to move to Yale and to a position involving active daily contact with young adult college students, and thoughts related to this move connected to various elements and scenes. This does not mean that the characters in the novel were copied from the author's sons, his father, particular young adults from Yale, or even from himself. On the contrary, they were independent, created characters produced in a process of articulation in which the author attempted to separate and bring together elements from his own past, present, and future relationships. Fueled by his involvement with his sons, his relationship with his father, and his anticipation of his future move, Hersey juxtaposed a father and a son in order to separate out and bring together elements in that relationship. At the same time as he consciously articulated a story, he was articulating some of the unconscious factors in his own relationship with his sons, and in his relationship with his own father. It is this struggle to articulate unconscious factors in the course of the process that accounts for some of the aesthetic power of this novel, indeed such a process seems to relate to this power in any novel. The struggle to articulate is a struggle to become free of the past; it is a struggle to become independent in the sense of being both separated from the past and brought together in a meaningful continuity with the past. An audience senses this struggle and participates in it vicariously. Contrary to the view of many psychoanalytic critics, it is not the successful appearance (symbolic or direct) of unconscious factors in the work of art that is gratifying to an audience. It is the dynamic process of struggle toward independence and freedom. I say this for many reasons stated elsewhere[8] but will only repeat again here that an author is never very successful in gaining much insight into his own unconscious content when he is creating. This is not to say that he should be; it is merely an affirmation that *artistic* creating is not, in itself, a form of psychotherapy.

From early on in the conception of the novel, Hersey had juxtaposed the father with the son in a significant way. The son is seen as following the father's footsteps. He has enrolled in his father's college and he is taking the same history course with the same professor his father had 26 years before. And the professor still remembers the father and his work! Indeed, it is a particular incident with this professor in the novel that accelerates the young man's anti-academic slide.

In the first face-to-face meeting between son and father in the novel, the son John has brought a young woman home for the weekend, and there is an immediate air of male competition established as follows: "The principal feature of her costume, drawing John's father's eyes ever down, down, down, was a pair of black patent-leather knee length boots." As the scene at home continues, however, the father is described rather sympathetically and there is a feeling of closeness between the older and younger man.

When writing the first draft of this scene, Hersey had constantly separated the two and also brought them together. This can be seen most clearly in his initial changes and revisions in this chapter, as follows: When the son says his girlfriend is mature for her age, Hersey first wrote a separating phrase for the father's response: "Everything seems to happen earlier these days," but crossed that out and wrote a bringing-together one instead: "I suppose she is (as if something of the sort hadn't occurred to Daddy-O)." Later in the text, at an important point, he described the father as feeling he had to be stern in order to give his son something concrete to rebel against. This sharp separating of father and son he then revised and modulated by writing that the father was "pretending to be" stern, and adding the phrase "How out of character!" In the very next sentence in this scene, he at first described the father as talking together "man to man" with his son, and then changed "man" to "boy" to make it a separating idea of talking together as "man to boy."

In the subsequent major change in the following paragraph, Hersey initially described the father as weak and permissive but after that inserted the bringing together phrase "until now, John really thought himself wiser than his father." Finally, he ended this chapter by vacillating between a separation and a bringing together of the father and son in these three versions of the son's leave-taking encounter:[9] (1) "Excuse me, Pop (he said, going into his bedroom to dress, leaving the *non-king* staring at himself in the mirror)"; (2) "Excuse me, Pop (he said, going into his bedroom to dress, leaving *his friend* staring at himself in the mirror)"; (3) "Excuse me, Pop (he said, going into his bedroom to dress, leaving the *old man* staring at himself in the mirror)." He started with a description of the father as a *non-king*, a phrase related to an earlier discussion in the chapter of the competitive separation between the two. He changed this to a bringing-together phrase, *his friend*, and ended with the separating reference to the discrepancy in their ages: *old man*.

In the chapter following, the son has an argument with his parents and angrily leaves without saying goodbye. When the author and I discussed these two chapters shortly after he wrote them, he told me that he had felt primarily identified with the son during their composition. At the point when he described the young man leaving in anger, however, Hersey felt that he "resumed the role of the father." He therefore experienced the shifting identifications involved in juxtaposing father and son and articulating their relationship.

Finally, the son decides to take LSD, following which he "sees" himself as in Vietnam along with his father. The father in the hallucinatory experience is the commanding officer of the company and a sniper is slowly killing off their "good" compatriots. The following section, beautifully written and articulated on a verbal level, had been revised several times in the course of the first writing:

They were moving again. John's eyes roved through the noble woods. There! Ten feet off the ground. In the crotch of a twin-trunked giant—was it a species of beech? *Fagus grandifolia?* In the vee, a roundness. A burl? No! Surely a helmetless head; surely the sniper himself. Word came forward to hold up a minute, the bearers were having it rough. The men stood in fear. John, saying nothing, stared at the tree crotch. Now he felt the familiar onrush of feelings, the flood of everything at once, in every direction. With unprecedented force. He spoke to his father:

— The whole operation is ridiculous.

— We can't help that, son. It's out of our hands.

— Is it really? I mean, that idea gives me a real pain in the ass. Aren't you in charge?

— Keep your shirt on, fellow.

As they talked, John felt that he was maneuvering his father. There were some slender saplings between where they stood and the tree-crotch where the round shape was. Stepping aside little by little keeping the talk going so that his father, too, inched sidewise to catch the murmured words, John constantly faced the tree-crotch; his father's body, shielding his own, was placed with its back exposed to the double tree. Now they were in the open. John, his heart on the run, suddenly became convinced that the odd shape was, after all, a queer growth, a burl, perhaps a paper wasp nest. But then a whine came ridden hard by a snap.

As his father fell, with the faintest sign of reproach on his otherwise empty face, John felt such an exquisite pain in his chest that he thought the bullet must have passed through both generations.[10]

The author's decision to include a scene in which the father was, as he later put it, "killed off" was made shortly before he wrote this section. He had planned it neither when starting the novel nor at earlier points along the way. The clarification of the son's impulse to murder the father as a factor in the father-son relationship, therefore, resulted from the articulation of unconscious factors during the course of the writing and the concomitant working out of the novel's plot and of the nature of its father-son relationship. I know it did not come from other sources, such as therapy or any direct exploration by Hersey of his own feelings toward his father or his sons, because I saw him shortly before and shortly after the decision and we explored the circumstances under which it occurred.[11]

By clarifying and articulating the murderous impulse, the author was also able to describe the psychological articulation between the father and son in a moving and telling way. Describing the sniper's bullet passing "through both generations," he indicated that the son was more definitively linked to the father than he realized. And he suggested the nature of the link. Through dropping out of school, corrupting himself and taking drugs, the son was trying to destroy his father, his internal father, and was thereby destroying himself. Still separated from the father, as indicated by "the faintest sign of reproach on the father's face," the son was also brought together with him, and they were articulated.

ARTICULATION AND THE CREATION OF PERSONALITY ATTRIBUTES AND STRUCTURE

Unlike the individual literary artist engaged in creating a literary work on his own, the therapist and patient in psychotherapy are together engaged in creating the patient's personality attributes and structure. Together, they embark on a process of articulation, separating and bringing together elements from the patient's past, present, and future. As an end result of this process, the patient achieves active psychic separation from factors in the past and concomitant clarification and acceptance of continuity with his own past experience. In this sense, the patient develops meaningful independence and psychological freedom. Because of the psychic separation of the past and the present, the patient is freed from the need to repeat the past. On the other hand, because there is also an active affirmation of his connections with his own past, there is also preservation and affirmation of the patient's unique experience and individuality. Articulation is both the enemy of the repetition compulsion and the ally of uniqueness. Therefore, it is one of the prime modes through which patient and therapist accomplish the creation of attributes of personality and self.

I will briefly emphasize the difference between this perspective on creativity in the therapeutic process from traditional ones that focus on inspiratory experiences or from those that derive from Kris's formulation of creativity as a "regression in the service of the ego."[12] Inspiratory experiences, prototypically, are sudden bursts of understanding or new ideas that seem to come from nowhere, usually accompanied by feelings of excitement and gratification. Because these bursts are dramatic and exciting, they have often been erroneously considered to be the exemplification of creativity. Although such inspiratory experiences do sometimes occur in creative processes, they are by no means a major factor producing creations. They are decidedly not a major feature of the creative process involved in psychotherapy. While inspiratory experiences involve an experience of understanding and illumination, and may therefore seem to be the same as, or similar to, attainment of psychological insight, such is not the case. Inspiratory experiences are properly related to defensive or abreactive phenomena. The feeling of dramatic illumination and certainty, usually accompanied by a good deal of affect, results often from a partial defensive repudiation incorporated in the inspiratory ideas.[13] Abreactive discharge of pent-up emotions with temporary overcoming of repression may also often operate to produce a sense of certainty and an affective experience of relief. Psychological insight, however, consists of both affective and cognitive apprehension of unconscious and preconscious contents rather than either discharge or repudiation. Usually far less dramatic than inspiration, insight is psychologically a more productive phenomenon. Although an inspiratory experience can at times lead to psychological insight, those therapists who seek for constant inspiratory breakthroughs, or for an inspiratory experience as a therapeutic endpoint, are practicing in a spiritual rather than in a scientific mode.

I do not mean to disregard inspiration altogether in creative processes, because it plays a role at certain points. I do mean to indicate that inspiration is neither the *sine qua non* of creativity nor a proper goal of therapy, nor is it the usual mode of appearance of new ideas. As seen in the example of the poet's creation of the "mastermind" metaphor described earlier, new ideas occur in a nondramatic manner—as he said, "I just turned my attention to that line and . . . and then that came to me"—as a result of a long process of articulation. Because creative ideas appear most often in just this way, they are properly included within a discussion of the articulation process rather than considered as radically separate events.

As for creativity in therapy as a "regression in the service of the ego," Beres[14] has presented a model of therapeutic collaboration in which the patient regresses and characteristically presents primary process material to a therapist, who characteristically reacts on a secondary process level, until such times as the patient can control the regression with his own observing ego. In other places, I have presented extensive data and observations that challenge the validity of "regression in the service of the ego" as a formulation of the dynamic structure of creative processes in general.[15] This challenge also pertains to the creative process in therapy. The dynamic structure there also does not consist of a "regression in the service of the ego"; rather, it is a mutual articulation by therapist and patient on many different psychic levels. Although guided by the therapist, both participants engage in bringing together and separating throughout the process; both may use secondary process, or sometimes primary process, concomitantly, and both articulate material from conscious, preconscious, and unconscious levels, and from cognitive and affective modes at different points along the way.

The two case examples following shall, in some detail, illustrate the process of articulation in psychotherapy. They represent two different types or levels, as follows: (1) verbal or linguistic articulation; (2) articulation of a mother-daughter relationship.

VERBAL OR LINGUISTIC ARTICULATION IN THERAPY

The most immediate and straightforward illustration of the process of articulation in psychotherapy is on the level of verbalization and the use of language. This should come as no surprise, of course, because therapy is carried out verbally and, therefore, there must be intrinsic connections between laws of verbal or linguistic interaction and psychological change. This precept has been emphasized in varying degrees by Jacques Lacan,[16] Edelson,[17] Rosen,[18] and Rycroft.[19] I do not, however, mean to say that therapy is a process of helping a patient to speak better in the traditional sense of the term, to articulate. That would be patently absurd and misleading, as the skill of articulation in speech has little to do with psychological health except in a most remote way. I am rather speaking of the verbal and language interchange between therapist and patient as a concomitant bringing together and separating in psychological and verbal spheres. Much of the actual verbal interaction going on in a therapy hour can be understood in just this way.

Presenting the matter schematically, the patient talking in therapy puts forth a series of verbal phrases that manifest varying degrees of organization and connectedness. As we well know, elements that appear consciously quite organized and connected may represent severe disorganization and disconnectedness on a preconscious or unconscious level. Contrariwise, disconnected conscious elements often have both preconscious and unconscious connectedness and organization. As the therapist listens and interacts, he endeavors to identify numerous factors in the patient's productions, such as: anxiety, conflict, affect, nature of object relations, defenses, and so on. In his attempt to facilitate insight, he is most often interested in identifying preconscious and unconscious matters. He uses both janusian and homospatial processes to develop his own conceptual and empathic understanding.

Also, because he is aware of the need of persons to have secure ego boundaries and to function effectively as individuals, he is interested in identifying the qualities of independence, separation, and uniqueness as well as identifying connections with other persons and with society. He helps the patient to verbalize and elaborate in order to accomplish many different psychodynamic goals. Although he may not have been explicitly aware of it, a major mode of the therapist's interaction with the patient, in order to accomplish these goals, is to engage in an overall process of articulation similar to that in the examples of literary creativity I have described.

The following excerpt is from a psychotherapy session occurring at a middle point in the course of a two-and-a-half-year treatment. In a manner similar to the poet's articulation of the "mastermind" metaphor, this therapist and patient separate and bring together elements of the patient's psychic life. While the poet articulated the metaphor by himself and was concerned with aesthetic effect, the therapist and patient carry out the articulation together and are directly concerned with psychological effect. The session begins with the patient focused on his problems with money, which he attributes to his upbringing and family background. The therapist's first comment, "Is it too late to correct this?" functions to separate out the factor of learning and the patient's apparent stagnation in this area. At the same time, it brings together the patient's past with a possible future. From then on, separation and bringing together occur on both sides. The patient's fear, for instance, is separated out and brought together with other elements in several ways.

P: I've been thinking about my problems with handling money [pause]. I've always had money; money has always been given to me but I don't know how or why. Having money that way has stopped me from learning to do anything.

TH: Is it too late to correct this?

P: I'm scared shitless of taking responsibility for myself.

TH: How does that make you feel afraid?

P: I'm afraid I might fail.

TH: Are you really afraid of failing?

P: Maybe I'm . . . afraid of doing . . . well; that's . . . possible [in saying this, the patient has paused and hesitated repeatedly].

TH: You seem also to be afraid of doing well in this session with me — afraid of doing well in therapy.

P: I seem to feel that I must punish myself for something.

TH: Is it just *one* thing?

P: I'm not sure. I think it's one thing. It has to do with sex, I think [pause]. I always liked climbing trees; did a lot of that in my life.

TH: What is the connection?

P: [several pauses] There was a tree in front of my house. I climbed

it when I was three years old . . . never was able to climb to the
top, but later I did a lot of tree climbing. [At this point, the
patient looked very anxious and began staring.]

TH: What happened just then?

P: I feel vacant.

TH: Perhaps that feeling in here has something to do with a feeling
that you are climbing high up and succeeding in something.

The therapist's interpretation, just stated, served to relieve the patient's
anxiety. He then went on to clarify that he had a sexual sensation when
climbing the tree. This issue became further clarified in the sessions
throughout the remaining months of therapy as the patient increasingly
connected his fear of success to sexual issues with his mother.

Just as the poet earlier brought together and separated ideas of "realms,"
"jamb and lintel," and "mental world" in his several versions leading to the
articulation of the "mastermind" metaphor, in this session the patient and
therapist separate out and bring together several contexts and words pertaining to the patient's feeling of being afraid. The patient says first that he
is afraid of responsibility, then of failure, and then of success. When he
falters on the idea of success—at this point, he pauses repeatedly and
literally becomes verbally inarticulate—the therapist connects his fear of
success with a current fear of success right in the session. This focus on
form and sequence is the same as I described in Chapter II, and is a factor in
the articulation process.

Following the connecting remark, the patient separates out a new issue,
the issue of punishment, and the therapist responds with a question geared
directly toward separating out the factors in the punishment, "Is it just one
thing?" When the patient separates out the sexual issue and the climbing of
trees, the therapist then directly asks for a connection. Finally, in this
particular excerpt, a specific formulation is articulated by means of the
therapist's interpretation. This interpretation brings together the elements
of the patient's past tree climbing with his present fear of success as well as
with his symptom of vacancy.

That the therapist's interpretation was psychologically meaningful is
indicated by the patient's response of introducing new and important material which had thereby separated out yet another factor, sexuality, in his
anxiety. Effective interpretations are cardinal examples of articulating interventions on a therapist's part. Indeed, a prototypical interpretation—one
that connects a factor in the transference to an ongoing issue in his present
life and to his past life as well—represents an extensive articulation. Al-

though bringing together and separating often are temporally distinct—i.e., alternating or sequential, as in this particular session—the overall effect is one of joining or articulation. Thus, other interventions, such as clarifications, may all at times contribute to an overall effect and serve as part of the articulation process.

In the excerpt presented, many psychological issues enter into and affect the course and effectiveness of the articulation process. There is the apparent trust in the therapist, the patient's drive toward improved interpersonal relations blocked by his fear of growing up and taking responsibility, his guilt about sexuality, and an apparent yearning for a lost childhood. The therapist's awareness of and sensitivity to such issues play a critical role in the therapeutic movement, but his ability to participate in the articulation process is also important. Meaning and psychodynamic significance of the issues articulated, as well as factors such as timing, defensive state, and level of personality integration, are vital factors in the therapeutic effect. So, too, meaning and expressive features of the "mastermind" metaphor presented earlier were vital aspects of the aesthetic effect. For the poet, as well as for the therapist and patient, however, articulation is the means for facilitating restructuring, integration, and creation.

ARTICULATION OF A
MOTHER-DAUGHTER RELATIONSHIP

Another example will serve to illustrate broader effects on the total context or content of the patient's life. The previous example primarily illustrated formal aspects of articulation; the next example, like the earlier description of the novelist's creative process, traces articulation on the levels of both form and content together.

A 28-year-old woman executive with a borderline personality became severely depressed and excessively suspicious of friends and co-workers shortly after receiving an important job promotion. Previously, she had suffered from depressive episodes, and at the age of 19 she had required a brief psychiatric hospitalization. Following that hospitalization, she became enrolled in a business training program that later enabled her to get a job with a very large corporation. Starting at the bottom of the clerical ladder, she was extremely perfectionistic and very highly organized in her work, and so experienced a surprisingly rapid rise through the ranks of the organization to a rather high level of administrative responsibility. She could not, however, face the idea of another promotion that involved a major change to another department and even more responsibility. She quit her job.

The background of these events showed that the patient had been able to accomplish her rapid rise partly because of a very supportive therapy with the same therapist over the entire nine-year period, but especially because of the constant rock-bound support of her mother. Throughout this period of the patient's life, her mother, just as in the years before, had made virtually all her decisions and cared for her hand and foot. Despite having a full-time job of her own, the mother did all the cooking and cleaning in their shared apartment. She accompanied the patient on all shopping trips and decided on her clothes, chose her friends, wrote all letters and cared for all money affairs, and reviewed with her on a daily basis every detailed event of her life. With respect to her therapy, the mother insisted that she tell her everything that was said and then provided her own formulations. When working on her job, the patient would call her mother several times a day to ask for support and solace. And on several occasions, she called her every 15 minutes throughout the day!

In the course of psychotherapy within a hospital setting, many aspects of the patient's relationship with her mother were addressed. At the beginning, the patient forcefully and flatly asserted: "I have only one friend in the world—my mother." Gradually, however, she began to modify that assertion and recognize some strongly negative feelings. Indeed, the ambivalence toward her mother emerged as so extreme that soon she began to attribute the worst of motives to her, believing that she was intensely jealous and wanted her to be always sick or dead. At the same time, she displayed the characteristic splitting of borderline patients and came to believe that the therapist was completely responsible for her noxious view of her parent.

A turning point in the therapy occurred after the development of a peculiar financial difficulty. On the basis of an unforeseen technicality, it appeared that her hospitalization insurance coverage would run out much sooner than expected. Therefore, she had to make plans to leave the hospital before she felt ready. Because she now felt that it would be impossible for her to return home and live with her mother, and because she could think of no other alternatives, she believed this to be a disaster.

The therapist, however, while well aware of the seriously problematic symbiosis of mother and daughter, decided to challenge this position. Each time she brought up the impossibility of her living together with her mother, he, to her surprise and chagrin, questioned why that seemed to be so. Over and over, in session after session, this issue was a central theme. With rage and anger, the patient talked about her relationship with her mother. She spoke of her mother's undue influence and apparent need for her, and also of her own feelings of attachment and disgust for her mother.

Out of this therapeutic juxtaposition of herself with her mother, produced primarily by the therapist's challenge to the patient's splitting defenses and false pretense of separation from her mother, an effective articulation began. Together, the patient and therapist were able to designate a continued lack of separation between daughter and mother (and between patient and therapist as well). By continually juxtaposing and bringing herself together with her mother in the therapy sessions, she began to look for, specify, and try out some of her own separate and real attributes. This was the beginning of an ongoing process of articulation of her relationship with her mother. In the process of separating and bringing together, she, for the first time, came to recognize and acknowledge that, like her mother, she experienced feelings of jealousy and possessiveness. This led to a reduction in suspicious and paranoid thinking about other people in her life.

While attempting to articulate her relationship with her mother, the patient was also articulating her own personality. She began to take on increasing responsibility for herself and to feel better. In her mind, however, she reserved many areas of nonseparation and fusion with her mother. One was the working out of her financial responsibility for her treatment. Telling herself that "this is the last thing I will let my mother do for me," she took no action whatsoever to work out the insurance problem. Instead, her mother made constant calls to the insurance company, to a lawyer, and to the hospital administration.

Although it appeared on the surface that there was little the patient could do—she received a good deal of sympathy for her difficulties with finances from other patients and some members of the staff—the therapist again challenged her position. He raised the question of why the mother, rather than she, was working out the problem. Thus, the mother and daughter were again actively brought together and separated in the therapy. This led to a severe outburst on the patient's part; she at first became outraged at the suggestion that she should do anything more. Then, accusing the therapist of not helping her with the financial problem, she furiously insisted that she was being cast away and thereby forced again to live with her mother and be under her domination.

The fury gradually subsided and, in subsequent sessions, the patient and therapist both pursued the articulation of her relationship to her mother. Together they clarified areas of overlap between some of her symptomatic behavior and her mother's behavior toward her as a child. They clarified how she was carrying out in her life her mother's explicit as well as implicit wishes. And, again, they tried to separate out her own goals and wishes. Frequently, during this time, the patient became quite moody and depressed. As the process of bringing together and separating continued, she became increasingly aware of the possibility of choice and intention in her life. Although not conceptualizing it in this way, she became increasingly aware of articulating her own personality. She experienced the challenge of creating aspects of her self.

In the face of this challenge, sometimes this patient yearned for death and for self-destruction. In her moodiness and depression, she hovered between creation and destruction. It was a very difficult time. In continuing to work and to articulate, she chose the course of creation.

ARTICULATION IN THE PRACTICE OF PSYCHOTHERAPY

Although patient and therapist together do not create an entire personality anew in the way that an artist creates an entire artwork or a scientist a complete theory, aspects of the patient's personality are distinctly new. These aspects, as discussed in Chapter I, are stamped with the patient's uniqueness, new to the patient himself, but often also related to ordinary ways of functioning. The articulation process, taken as a whole, consists of helping the patient to develop his uniqueness while recognizing and accepting intrinsic connections with others. Because it clarifies and produces connections and separations within the patient's personality, it results in a structural personality integration.

While the creative artist's or scientist's struggle to create is often quite dramatic and socially far-reaching, patient and therapist together struggle toward less dramatic but, for the individual, often far-reaching effects. Creative artists or scientists develop new ideas and discoveries as a result of an overall articulation including homospatial and janusian processes; they separate and bring together and make what is potential into actuality. The patient and therapist develop insight and personality structures by also articulating the patient's potential into actuality. Articulation of insight is the specific process leading directly to the creation of insight referred to by Loewald.[20]

Articulation in any creative process applies both to form and to content. In these examples of the literary creative process and therapy, the emphasis alternated between form and structural factors and more extensive aesthetic or psychodynamic content. In both of the examples emphasizing form and structure, i.e., creation of the "mastermind" metaphor and the excerpt from

a therapy session, however, many content psychodynamic factors also operated in the choice of particular elements articulated. The nature of the
poet's relationship with his mother, for instance, entered into the creation
of the metaphor. In the therapy session excerpt, there were aggressive
transference elements as well as probable additional factors of primal scene
experience and masturbation fears. In both the examples emphasizing more
extensive content, the writing of the novel and the mother-daughter relationship, formal verbal and interaction factors as well as structural issues of
ego boundaries[21] played a prominent role.

Awareness of the articulation process can serve as a special guideline to
creative practice. While facilitating goals of attainment of insight and understanding, analysis of character and of symptoms, and working-through,
awareness of articulation can help the therapist to listen and interact directly on the basis of goals of creating personality attributes and structure. The
creative process involves making as well as understanding. The constant
focus on bringing together as well as separating in each therapeutic session
and in the longer sequences of the ongoing therapeutic interaction serves to
facilitate insight and understanding together with creation and personality
integration.

Focus on the articulation process entails a type of concentration on the
therapist's part that is receptive, wide ranging, and not persistently evalua-
tive or judgmental. Keeping in mind the dual goals of separating and
bringing together, the therapist is interested in encouraging the patient to
speak and elaborate on what he says and feels. Within this wealth of
material, the therapist seeks to separate out pertinent issues and trends,
largely by questions and other clarifying interventions. Simultaneously, the
therapist bears in mind possible analogies and connections between what
the patient is immediately addressing and other areas of the patient's life,
past, present, or future. For example, the therapist may listen for analogies
between material about a boss or a teacher and issues in the transference.
Or, he may hear connections between hostile feelings toward a spouse and
competitive feelings with a sibling or hostility to a parent. Although he
does not necessarily comment about these connections at any given point,
he is actively listening in this manner. Such listening involves a specific type
of concentration primarily on the formal aspects of the interaction in the
therapeutic session. Concentration on articulation as a formal aspect of
therapeutic interaction serves to reduce various tendencies to judge, dissect,
categorize, or compartmentalize in a persistent way the content of the
patient's productions.

The principles of neutrality and nonjudgmental acceptance of the con-

FIGURE 2: Henri Matisse, *Bather* (summer 1909). Oil on canvas, $36^1/2'' \times 29^1/8''$. Collection, The Museum of Modern Art, New York. Gift of Abby Aldrich Rockefeller.

tent of a patient's productions are not mechanically or artificially applied in a therapeutic hour, but arise intrinsically and naturally in conjunction with an active focus on articulation. Persistent judging, categorizing, and compartmentalizing of content have little to do with the goals of restructuring, making, and creating. Rather than the fluid flow of articulation with its alternating or simultaneous separating and bringing together, the operations of judging, categorizing, and compartmentalizing involve either firm and static separation or connection alone. Moreover, the state of mind associated with intense concentration on articulation involves a sense of broadened awareness. In this state of mind, the therapist is constantly receptive to, and is himself developing, new ideas. He is able to hear new material introduced by the patient and to develop new formulations from what has already been presented. While the process of therapeutic articulation is an ego function, this does not mean that it operates solely on a secondary process level. The therapist is focused on both primary and secondary process cognition in the patient, and he uses both modes himself. He searches for separations and connections on the levels of unconscious, preconscious, and conscious in both the patient and himself. Many psychic levels are articulated conjointly. This is similar to the state of mind of the creative artist.

The patient also needs to adopt a state of mind that is similar to certain aspects of the state of mind of the creative artist. This was recognized and stated by Freud in an early exposition of the methodology of the therapeutic process. In *The Interpretation of Dreams*, he cited the poet Schiller's famous exposition of the mode of facilitating creative thinking as the model for dream analysis as follows: "Where there is a creative mind, Reason—so it seems to me—relaxes its watch upon the gates, and the ideas rush in pell-mell, and only then does it look them through and examine them in a mass.—You critics . . . complain of your unfruitfulness because you reject too soon and *discriminate too severely*."[22] Although dream analysis is somewhat more specialized and routinized than other aspects of the therapeutic process, the actions of separating associations and connecting them to other elements and experiences in the patient's life are prototypes for much of therapeutic activity and prototypes of the articulation process.

The creative process of therapy is a matter of integrating rather than simply combining or reconciling. By this I mean that combining and reconciling may involve only adding together, submerging, or compromising—bringing together *without* separating—of various component elements. Integration, on the other hand, involves component elements operating together in an organic whole. These component elements of personality maintain separateness and identity while connected and interconnected with each other. They are therefore related and connected, rather than added, submerged into one another, or combined. Homologous with the structure of the nervous system of the physical organism, which is integrated through the joints or articulations known as synapses and synaptic functions, personality and behavior are also integrated through articulations.

CHAPTER VIII

Articulation of Error in the Creative Process of Psychotherapy

I am now, both in topic and approach, especially involved in risk. Having reached some high ground between the complex and converging paths of creativity and psychotherapy, I shall not yet pause to survey and take stock. Instead I shall hazard a rocky and seemingly divergent incline of errors, risks, and mistakes. I shall attempt to relate the psychology of error to the practice and theory of psychotherapy as a creative process.

What does error have to do with creativity or, more complicated than that, with the creative practice of psychotherapy? Some years ago, in one of my research explorations of the creative process in visual art, I met with a woman sculptor who did large scale abstract work in perfectly smooth white plastic material. These sculptures had perfectly clean lines and perfectly even coloration and were obviously proportioned according to exact specifications. I marvelled at their seeming perfection, and she described to me the detailed engineering process involved in creating such elaborate and elegant works. Then she took me over to look at one of the large surfaces more closely. Pointing to a gnarled and slightly raised blemish on the surface on one of her works, she said, "Do you see that blip on the surface there? Well, that's *me*."

This sculptor's dramatic and metaphoric reference to the single error on an otherwise absolutely perfect constructed sculpture may readily be related to poetic and philosophical conceptions of the human condition. To err is to be human. The sculptor's equating of her self and her own individuality with the error on her creation is consistent with philosophical emphases on celebration of humanness and of individual style and performance. There are surely other meanings, too, both aesthetic and psychodynamic, but we can surmise that she may also have felt uncomfortable and disavowing about the mechanistic and technological perfection of her creations. The unbroken sleek lines and machine-produced smooth surface in those works of art certainly produced some discomfort in me.

There is, I believe, more than personal psychological issues to be taken from this sculptor's remark, however. It is not only that erring is human and that artists assert their humanness or individuality in the errors they make, but error itself and a special orientation to error are intrinsic to the creative process. Both commission of errors and handling of errors are important and special matters in creative processes. First, errors are not merely allowed but, given a requisite very high level of technical skill, they are actually courted to some extent in the process of creating products in art, as well as in other fields. Second, in a significant way, errors are linked and integrated into such created products. The sculptor was not merely acknowledging an error in her creation; she was embracing that error and including it as a significant part of the product itself. Indeed, she considered it to be the sign of her handiwork and style, and thereby indicated what is referred to as the artist's "signature." Broader in meaning than the literal name written on a canvas or a sculpture pedestal, her signature was the error that figuratively represented herself in her creation. This way of handling, thinking about, and using error is a particular application of the articulation process. The articulation of error involves both separation and connection of aspects of both abstract and tangible material.

Before saying any more about the way in which articulation of error operates in creative processes, I will turn to a brief consideration of error as a topic in itself. To do so, I once again come straightaway to Freud's creative achievement.

FREUD ON ERROR

Although there had been some scholarly work on speech and hearing errors prior to the work of Freud, such as that of linguists and philologists Paul,[1] von der Gabelentz,[2] Jesperson,[3] Delbrück,[4] and especially Meringer,[5] his analysis of the psychological meaning of such errors was groundbreaking. Moreover, his work on the psychopathology of everyday life was systematic and well documented, and in the years following, it has been repeatedly reconfirmed.[6] It stands today as a well established scientific discovery, even among persons who are otherwise severe critics of psychoanalysis. Although some modern linguists challenge whether every speech error necessarily results from the actions of the unconscious, of repression, and of the primary process, these factors are widely accepted as operative and important in many errors and are included in both theoretical and empirical linguistic analyses.[7]

Freud's interest in error, of course, went beyond the errors of speech and written language for which his name has become used in everyday parlance. In the corpus of his work, he showed the operation of unconscious factors in forgetting, bungled actions, chance actions, and errors of memory. A general principle derivable from his explorations, therefore, is that *any error effect consisting of a discrepancy between intent and execution results from the operation of unconscious factors.*[8]

Freud focused a good deal on the role of primary process mechanisms in parapraxes and other types of error, but I am concerned here with his broader findings that erroneous *actions* are produced by unconscious factors, and that the substance of a particular erroneous action derives from, and to some extent represents, the unconscious factor itself. This finding points the way to a clarification of another one of the routes, in addition to the janusian and homospatial processes,[9] by which unconscious representations appear in creative works. For, while many theorists have rushed forward with a dogged insistence that unconscious representations appear regularly in creative works, e.g., oedipal and pre-oedipal conflicts in literature, fusions and sexual symbolism in art and sculpture, few — including Kris[10] — have provided more than teleological or *post hoc ergo propter hoc* psychodynamic explanations of the phenomenon. Errors provide an additional route for unconscious material to appear in creative works because of the special management of errors in the creative process. This applies to creative work in art and in other intellectual fields, and, as I shall show below, it applies in some measure to creative work in therapy as well.

Later in his life, in a paper entitled "The Subtleties of a Faulty Action," Freud discussed his own mistaken insertion of a word with a double meaning in a salutation accompanying a birthday present. In addition to a rich and interesting analysis of the particular error, which I will not repeat, Freud introduced a new conception and pushed the general understanding of error further. In this case, he said, "A mistake gained its purpose not by being *made*, but only after it had been *corrected.* . . . A variant, not without interest, of the mechanism of a parapraxis."[11] According to this, the purpose of an error could be realized after the error had been made, specifically in an act of correcting the error. With regard to articulation of error, I too am referring to a process in which realization or representation of unconscious meaning and other material occurs after the error is made. Although articulation of error and correction of error are not the same operation, there is a psychodynamic relationship.

In a broad sense, Freud's scientific creative processes in his early and later work on error are themselves instances of the creative articulation of error. In the earlier work, he articulated the entire topic of error within a body of psychological knowledge, and in the later piece he focused on his own specific error and subsequently clarified its distinct psychological meaning in connection with an overall psychodynamic structure.

ARTICULATION OF ERROR IN THE CREATIVE PROCESS

Creative people have an orientation to error that is out of the ordinary. Most people, when they are engaged in difficult work, tend to be quite careful or controlled; they are wary of making errors. Mistakes are irritating and bothersome, and sometimes are of a type and magnitude to provoke discouragement and cessation of the task. Although creative work itself is almost always quite difficult, and is very highly fraught with error, creative people characteristically deal with errors and mistakes in a different way. While engaged in the creative process, they think in a highly free and wide ranging fashion and take risks and chances that invariably lead to error. When errors occur, they may or may not be subjectively felt as bothersome, but characteristically they are directly noticed, assessed, and, if possible, articulated with the creative work in progress. Valuable or interesting elements within the error are clarified and elaborated, and are joined with the developing product as a whole. The error elements may be connected and incorporated within the product or they may lead its development into new directions. Articulation of error is not a matter of rejecting material because it is wrong or of turning away from an incorrect approach. Unlike what is generally called trial and error thinking, wherein errors are removed or corrected, articulation of error involves preservation in the whole work of new, interesting, or valuable elements within a miss or a mistake. It involves both separation and connection at once.

An illustration of how the process operates in artistic creative work, is provided by the painting "The Bather" by the modern artist Matisse (Figure 2). In the major proportion of his artworks, Matisse was interested in organizing color and pattern on a two-dimensional surface. He was a master of constructing patterns, and one of his achievements was the invention of the collage style of painting. In this oil on canvas painting done in 1909, it is rather easy to see the use of a bright, strong color design and the emphasis on the nude body of the male bather as a pattern of lines on an essentially two-dimensional surface. While the body is presented with some traditional line perspective, and there is some degree of depth and solidity, this effect is somewhat secondary to the effect of strong lines, contours, and especially a sense of movement on the flat surface.

How is such an aesthetic effect achieved? First, of course, the lines outlining the body contour are thick and black, and they stand out. But, did Matisse draw out these lines all at once with a perfect unbroken motion, much as we have seen Picasso do in his filmed demonstrations of spontaneous drawings using pen lights in the empty air? Not at all. Close inspection of the painting shows numerous repetitious and erroneously placed lines: in the hand region, behind the back, and on the legs. And now, it is important to note that when I say erroneously placed I am not describing the aesthetic effect of this painting, because these lines do not appear to be unnecessary or wrong in the total context of this artwork. Indeed, these seemingly stray lines emphasize and enhance the rounded contour of the body; they impart dynamism and a feeling of movement to the whole. That is precisely the point of such articulation of error! While a careful examination of the painting indicates that Matisse's hand strayed several times while drawing the nude figure, he was able to articulate these strayings with the overall final pattern he produced. Not only are the strayed lines part of the aesthetic form of the painting, but one could also take deeper implications and meanings from the crude and erroneous lines, meanings similar to those involved in the sculptor's remarks I quoted earlier.

Other illustrations of the principle of articulation of error in visual art come from artists of different styles, times, and schools. In the school of abstract expressionism, the working approach of the founder, Jackson Pollock, exemplifies the use of this principle. Although we know that Pollock planned his patterned canvases carefully and that he dripped buckets of paint on them with a highly skilled and practiced hand, much occurred that was not intended. These erroneous developments of lines, textures, and color effects were immediately and on-the-spot articulated by him into the overall design. With brilliant proficiency, Pollock, and other abstract expressionists who have come after him, introduced lines and colors that connected these errors to other aspects of the design. The errors became articulations within the whole design because they appeared as separations which were, at the same time, connected.

It is difficult to distinguish between error and either chance or randomness in such events because, as I shall make clear shortly, these factors are interrelated. For the moment, however, I shall refer only to error because of the clear-cut deviation of intent, or at least of expectations, in the straying of the artist's skilled and expert hand. The word "error" derives from the Latin word for "a wandering," and it is the wandering from a particular contour, line, or texture that introduces an initial separation. This separation is connected with the whole in an articulation contributing to overall integration, together with a final product or creation.

Moving away from modern art to a time-honored instance of articulation of error in visual art, there is the process of creative water coloring. With the water coloring technique, as even a beginning water colorist knows, the trick is to be able to work with thin liquid paint that runs down the surface of the paper as it is applied. Increasing skill with this medium allows the water colorist to anticipate the direction and extent of the run, and also to have an idea of the effects of running paint merging with surrounding lines and colors. However, there is no way to be sure of these effects beforehand—and this is where articulation of error comes in. The creative water colorist learns especially to capitalize on the dripping, runny effect and to use it as a means of producing an overall aesthetic result. In the course of producing this result, merged and connected lines and colors may, for instance, be separated out and emphasized by repeating them in an approximate way on other parts of the paper. Separated and dripping lines and colors may be immediately brushed into, and connected with, other lines and colors. The process is one of continual recognition and assessment of error and wandering, with both separation and connection into an integrated whole.

In the literary sphere, a telling depiction of articulation of error appears in a passage from Shakespeare's play "The Merchant of Venice."[12] Portia says to Antonio: "One half of me is yours, the other half yours—Mine own, I would say; *but if mine, then yours*, And so all yours" (Act III, Scene II, emphasis added). In her elaboration of the error, Portia brilliantly clarifies the separation of the first and second person pronoun referents and connects herself together with Antonio at the same time.

With respect to the process of creation in literature, Arthur Miller spoke to me at length about freeing himself up and making mistakes in order to use those mistakes to develop his ideas and his writing. Sometimes he felt he needed to try to write like a novice in order to generate emotion and error. John Hersey, also over a series of sessions, spoke of the importance of "blurts" and "inner mistakes" as the essence of what a writer did that made his work unique and idiosyncratic. He believed that mistakes allowed a writer to bring emotion into his work and, like Miller, he thought that novice writers sometimes brought more emotion than experienced writers into their work as a direct result of aesthetic mistakes.

An illustration of the articulation of error during the literary creative process comes from this latter author's writing of *Too Far to Walk*.[13] In a passage describing the hero's interaction with a sophisticated young college-town whore he had ironically and rebelliously brought home to meet his parents, the author first wrote the somewhat discordant following description:

She was a sharp girl, one who, it could surely be said, lived by her wits, and her conversation was far more intelligent than (at random) Wagner's or Gibbon's [names of John's, the hero's, friends]. She was college material—a dropout in the sense that it would never have occurred to her to try to get in. She began talking about Dahomey: something she had picked up from some pipe smoker [faculty member]. As she was talking of this, John suddenly thought of having sat in the Freshman Dean's office, one day the year before, and having caught a glimpse of a number beside his name on his record card on the Dean's desk: 3M242526. He had seen the number only a few moments, but it was seared on his brain. What was it? Was it a code for all his abilities and accomplishments? Or did it stand for *him*—his machine card self? He was at home; his excited mother was trembling upstairs for her cub—yet as Mona [the whore] spoke of the African ritualist bending over the girl with his special knives, John was overcome with a horror of the impersonality, the inhumanity of the big machine of life for which he was being educated. At any moment buttons might be pressed in that machine that would make of his number something for a GI dog tag. . . .[14]

In discussing this passage with me, the author commented on something that also would have struck a reader of this very first manuscript draft as being discrepant and out of place. Why the esoteric reference to the country Dahomey and Africa in the mouth of the young whore? It seems a definite mistake in the passage and the author himself wondered why he put it in. Instead of deciding to delete it, however, he proceeded to articulate this error by making some changes. He clarified and separated out an issue in the Africa reference, and connected it to the rest of the material in the passage. He changed "She began talking about Dahomey" to the more detailed and clear "She began talking about, *of all things, the cicatrization of the faces, arms and thighs of young girls in puberty rites in* Dahomey." And he also changed the sentence about the number on his record card from "He had seen the number only a few moments, but it was seared on his brain" to the connected phrasing of the following: "He had seen the number only a few moments, but it was *as if cicatrized across his forehead.*"[15]

Thus, with these changes, he gave the passage a unified and telling metaphorical impact relating the young man's college experience to a violent African puberty rite. Also, of course, the psychoanalyst reader will see the introduction of material referring to cicatrization as suggesting unconscious castration fears that relate meaningfully to a rebellious young man's experience and concerns with a whore. Interestingly, after making these changes—and here we have a dynamic similar to Freud's correction of a faulty action—the author himself became aware of a specific unconscious connection to an event in his life the previous day. This was that he and his wife had been at a meeting of the Institute of Arts and Letters in which awards were bestowed to several outstanding American writers. Because of the large number of people at the affair, some persons got confused about some of the attendees' names, and the author's wife commented that she thought everybody should have one's name *printed on one's forehead.* Thus, the textual change to refer to a cicatrix or scar on the hero's forehead brought out, and incorporated, an unconscious issue in the passage. This unconscious issue—pertaining to feelings about the Institute of Arts and Letters award ritual—came to the fore as a result of an articulation of the awkward and initially erroneous use of the idea of Africa.

To clarify the psychodynamic structure of this event, it is important to note that it was not a matter of the upsurge of unconscious material that was subsequently subjected to ego modification and control. It was not, therefore, a manifestation of what would be expected according to the traditional and problematic "regression in the service of the ego" theory of creativity.[16] Instead, the unconscious material was gradually brought closer to consciousness; it was rendered into consciousness and represented by means of an ego process of articulation of error. While errors are generally produced by unconscious wishes—and the Africa error was surely no exception—the active representation of this unconscious content in the work of art, and in the author's consciousness, was due to an articulation process.

Another illustration of the articulation of error in the literary creative process comes from my previously mentioned study of Eugene O'Neill's creation of the play "The Iceman Cometh."[17] As the articulation of error process was not described in the original report because it had not yet been formulated, I shall recapitulate that material briefly now. The iceman of the title of O'Neill's epic drama is not a character in the play or an actual person, but the subject of a joke about adultery told by the leading character, a salesman and evangelistic former alcoholic named Hickey. Also, as I stated above, the nonexistent iceman has other tacit and explicit symbolic meanings—the iceman of death and Christ the bridegroom. On the basis of O'Neill's explicit comments in his notes for the play and his specific use of the biblical "bridegroom cometh" phraseology in an earlier written play,[18] there is no doubt that he had in mind a symbolic iceman rather than a real one from the first.

However, in his very first reference to an iceman during the writing of the play, O'Neill constructed the following: A character, Harry, who is waiting for the salesman Hickey to appear, says, "Remember the way he always lies about his wife and the Iceman?" and another character replies: "Maybe that's what's keeping him, Harry. There's an old belief among savages that it's bad luck to call something too much, unless you're sure you want it because, if you keep calling it, it'll come to you. Hickey's done enough calling the Iceman and Fate has a bum sense of humor. Maybe it wouldn't know he was joking." Harry then becomes angry and says, "There was nothing to Hickey's bull about the Iceman. Only a joke, and he wouldn't give a damn if it was true, anyway." Without going further into the many references to the iceman of this type throughout the first manuscript draft, I want to point out that O'Neill introduced the idea of a *real, corporeal iceman*—an actual adulterer—right away in his very first writing out of the play. That this suggestion of a real iceman was an error on O'Neill's part—a discrepancy between intent and execution—is clearly indicated by his own revisions on the manuscript. He extensively cut the dialogue I just quoted, saving only the very first line, which he changed to: "Remember that gag he always pulls about his wife and the Iceman?" And more than that, he systematically altered phraseology indicating a real iceman in *every single one of the sixteen written contexts* in which a reference to an iceman appears in first and later drafts.

This systematic alteration of every single context demonstrates the fact of error, and to an investigator of the manuscript material it is a remarkable event. One perceives a virtually uncanny sensitivity in O'Neill, a sensitivity that removed all denotations of a real flesh and blood iceman—thereby delineating and establishing the symbolic feature—but managed at the same time to preserve a certain ambiguity about both real and symbolic aspects. In this way, the erroneous initial references to a real iceman adulterer became both separate and connected within the overall context of the play. Particular instances of this articulation process are also seen in the following small, but very specific, alterations: There is a subtle dialect change from the expression "cheatin' wit de Iceman or somebody?" to "cheatin' wid de

Iceman or nobody." In the latter, the erroneous idea of somebody, i.e., a real person, as an equivalent alternative to the iceman is removed, but an ambiguity remains. There is a change in the reply to the question: "How's de Iceman, Hickey? How's he doing at your house?" from the elaborated description, "Fine! He's moved in for keeps," to the slightly ambiguous but simple, "Fine."

A more extensive example of the process is as follows:[19] At the end of the second act, a character says to Hickey in the first draft version, "I notice you didn't answer me about the Iceman or deny it. Did this great revelation come to you when you found him in her bed? . . . Was it you caught the Iceman in the arms of your dear [wife] Evelyn at last, and had to make the best of it and shake hands with him?" In the initial aspect of articulation of this passage, O'Neill on the second draft completely deleted the very vivid reality reference beginning with the words "*Was it you caught the Iceman*" and ending with " . . . *shake hands with him?*" In the next version, he continued the articulation of his error by deleting the phrase "*found him in her bed*," and he produced the final construction he used in the play: "I notice you didn't deny it when I asked you about the Iceman. Did this great revelation of the evil habit of dreaming about tomorrow come to you after you found your wife was sick of you?"

In addition to literature and the visual arts, articulation of error operates widely in creative activities. In music, an empirical exploration by the psychologist Bahle of the compositional methods of 32 European composers, including Schönberg, Honegger, Malipiero, Orff, and R. Strauss, reportedly demonstrated as an intrinsic part of the musical creative process, "the discovery of musical values which at first he [the composer] has not intended or sought intentionally."[20] Also, in a unique study by Reitman, involving detailed recording of an American composer's vocal description of everything he was thinking and doing while he worked, the composer was found to engage frequently in "modifying a plan after the fact, as it were, so as to make it conform to something the problem solver has discovered or created by accident and now wishes to preserve."[21]

Shifting to scientific creativity, the remarkable cases of Sir Arthur Fleming's discovery of penicillin, Roentgen's discovery of the X-ray effect, and Pasteur's development of the concept of immunology were particular instances of the articulation of error. All have been cited in scientific and popular writings as instances of so-called serendipity, a wonderful but mysterious term meaning the productive use of phenomena appearing by chance. In all of these cases, however, an error occurred that the scientist was able to comprehend and develop. The substance of the error was connected, in each case, with the accumulated corpus of knowledge of the field. Instead of only correcting a mistake or turning away from it toward to a presumably correct direction, these scientists preserved the fact of nature that had been clarified and separated off by the error and connected this fact to other facts or data. Fleming saw that a mold, that he erroneously allowed to contaminate a Petri dish, had destroyed the bacteria in its immediate vicinity. He connected this observation with the idea of disease or illness and, reasoning that the contaminating mold would serve a beneficial effect as a treatment of illness, conceived the idea of an antibacterial agent.[22] Roentgen inadvertently left a photosensitive medium on a bench where he was doing experiments with cathode rays, and Pasteur's chickens erroneously got cholera.[23] Such events involving conversion of error must be distinguished from the broad range of purely accidental discoveries.

Pasteur suggested the point I am making here in his famous aphorism "chance favors the prepared mind." I have generally avoided the use of the word "chance" in my discussion so far because I believe "error" more adequately represents the *discrepancy between intent and execution* in the foregoing events. That there is a distinct phenomenal relationship between error and chance is indisputable; it is partly because of an essential phenomenal similarity that errors lead to truly new, creative events. Chance is critically related to creativity and the appearance of new entities. Mutations are chance events in the biological realm that introduce new qualities which are selected out and subsequently preserved. These are creative events in nature. So, too, chance in the realm of mental operations introduces some degree of new material that is selected out, preserved, and articulated into creations.[24]

THE PROCESS OF ARTICULATION OF ERROR IN PSYCHOTHERAPY

With regard to the creative process in psychotherapy, articulation of error involves transference and countertransference particularly. That transference and the interpersonal transaction of psychotherapy involve error and distortion are important intrinsic aspects of these phenomena. Because feelings are transferred from earlier persons and experiences onto the person of the therapist, they are essentially erroneous and are truly "wanderings." It is because such errors appear in the therapy that the therapist knows that transference exists.[25] And for the patient, one of the aspects of working-through and resolution of the transference is a recognition of his errors and distortions about the therapeutic situation and the therapist.

With regard to the actively creative feature of therapy, it is important to note that transference, and thereby transference error, is especially induced within the therapeutic situation. Numerous authors have pointed out that therapy affords, as Freud said, "especially favorable conditions" for the development of transference because of the structured aspects of the therapeutic situation, the therapist's empathic and interpretative interventions, as well as other factors.[26] Transference error is facilitated by the therapy and the therapist, not because of an interest in deceiving or confusing the patient, but because of the functional importance of error in therapeutic action. This action involves a creative articulation of transference errors and distortions.

Recognition of error by the patient is an early aspect of working-through and resolution of transference. This recognition may be clear and explicit, or it may only be diffusely sensed or felt. Most penetrating is the recognition of "wandering" involving deviations of feelings and beliefs from the current reality. When such deviations are recognized, they are not merely corrected but are then subjected to a creative process of articulation. I say "not merely corrected" in order to emphasize the distinction from trial and error thinking, as well as from a procedure of scientific induction. Patient and therapist do not engage in a predominantly intellectual discourse where errors about the latter are discovered and then systematically corrected or renounced. Some correction does occur, but other important steps are also undertaken, such as the tracing of the background of the error and its vicissitudes and permutations.

Regardless of the specific sequence and types of steps, and despite the direction of the process—I state this to avoid becoming too doctrinaire or prescriptive about technique—articulation of the transference error in which both separation and connection occur is an end therapeutic result. The patient is able to experience the therapist as separate from parents and other earlier persons but at the same time is able to connect and revalue real attributes from both past and present relationships of all types. Also, the patient is able to separate and connect internal and external reality, as well as conscious, preconscious, and unconscious ideas and experiences. To do this, he has had to separate and identify internal structures that have been renounced, projected, or disowned—and intrinsically incorporated into pathological thinking and behavior—and to connect these structures with a coherent sense of self. This consists of the sense of being a volitional integrated person, responsible for all aspects of one's thought and action. In articulating transference error, as with other articulation, the patient achieves separation between his past and present motives, views of others, and experiences; at the same time, he accepts connection, psychological legacy, and continuity between present and past.

A major point is that transference error is connected and incorporated rather than being obliterated in the articulation process. As Loewald graphically states: "Without such transference—of the intensity of the unconscious, of the infantile ways of experiencing life that have no language and little organization, but the indestructibility and power of the origins of life—to the preconscious and to present day life and contemporary objects—without such transference, or to the extent to which such transference miscarries, human life becomes sterile and an empty shell."[27] Interestingly, Loewald in another place describes transference neurosis as a creative repetition of disease, but he is there using the term "creative" in a limited meaning sense of produced in another, or a new, context. In the more extended sense of the term "creative" (N.B., *both* new and valuable) that I am using here, the creative process consists of the working-through of transference error.

Both therapists and patients can limit the therapeutic effectiveness of this creative working-through process because of an unwillingness to hazard error, as well as an intolerance when error appears. Patients are characteristically unwilling to experience transference error. From the first, they usually avoid, deny, and fight off involvements with the therapist that lead to full-blown development and recognition of transference feelings. Early transference errors and distortions are clung to as especially rigid resistances in order to avoid more extensive transference development. Partly this is because of fear of the impulses, structures, and affects involved in the transference illness itself, but partly—for patients of all types—there is a fear of risk, error, and new experience. On the therapist's side, there may be a fear of facilitating transference error and a tendency to correct disturbing transference errors as soon as they appear. Examples of this tendency are a therapist's denying or arguing with a patient's accusations about himself and, as a more subtle manifestation, prematurely asking for, or making, connections between a patient's current feelings about the therapist and feelings about persons in the patient's past. Another type of manifestation of intolerance of error is a protracted and overexhaustive error-eradicating search for all past roots of particular transference feelings.

Creative articulation of error in the therapeutic process involves the same approach to error as in other creative processes. Like the creative writer or artist, both therapist and patient need to be willing to take chances and commit errors in both the form and substance of their relationship. When errors occur, they need to recognize them and then to clarify them as much as possible. As a "wandering," an error provides the beginning of a separation which, through constant clarification, yields up some of its unconscious content and intent. Rather than exhaustive breakdown and analysis—using the term analysis in its precise meaning of systematic dissection—the error is connected, usually through interpretive interventions, to issues in the patient's current and past life. When the connections suggested are appropriate or correct, further meaningful separations occur and these can be further connected into articulated structures. When the connections suggested are inappropriate or wrong, therapist and patient then need to clarify and examine these as new errors, because they too may yield meaningful new separations. An overall result of this mutual and continuing process of separating and connecting is the creative integration of the patient's personality.

With regard to countertransference, the process of articulation of error operates in a somewhat different but related way. While countertransference surely involves error and distortion in a manner similar to transference, the therapist by and large articulates countertransference error privately without the patient's direct collaboration. There are significant exceptions to this that deserve attention in their own right, but first I would like to emphasize that the therapist's continual attention to countertransference—another cornerstone of psychotherapy—may appropriately involve both an inductive process involving recognition with correction of error and a creative articulation process in which countertransference errors are separated and connected. For example, a therapist may be troubled by growing aggressive feelings toward a patient and recognize that they are a response in part to the patient's masochistic stance. While he privately analyzes the roots of his own discomfort, he may also share his recognition explicitly with the patient in order to help loosen masochistic defenses and reduce the resistant stance. Here, the articulation process involves the simultaneous separating and connecting of the elements in both therapist's and patient's aggressive impulses.

Countertransference error cannot generally be managed privately when the therapist makes an overt mistake, either in the form of forgetting, distortion, and parapraxis, or else in the form of a technical therapeutic error. Such therapist mistakes almost inevitably do become a manifest issue in the therapy. Indeed, a technical point bearing emphasis is that overt therapist mistakes should properly become a manifest issue in the therapy. To some degree, this point follows the well-established therapeutic maxim of making all issues with emotional charge – always the case with therapist errors – a matter of "grist for the mill" in therapy. To go beyond mere acknowledgment of a therapist error, however – or else, to take the mill-grist metaphor narrowly, to go beyond a systematic and sometimes sterile grinding down – and attempt a creative articulation of the error, is a therapeutic challenge.

When the therapist makes an overt mistake or error, he is vividly provided with a clue to his own unconscious concerns and therefore to countertransference matters to be articulated in the therapy. This is so whether or not the patient openly notes the mistake because, almost invariably, it is registered, consciously or unconsciously. Overt disregard on the patient's part probably requires attention in its own right as a first step. When the patient does point out or otherwise openly responds to the therapist error, the articulation process can develop actively.

For example, a patient became interested in a psychiatry text in her therapist's bookshelf and asked if she could borrow it. The therapist, for various conscious reasons, decided to deviate from routine practice with this quite difficult patient and lent it to her. While he had considered this at the time to be a possible minor technical error, several sessions later he learned about a rather extensive mistake. His patient told him that she had found a passage in the book underlined with *her own name* pencilled by him in the margin. It was a passage about the dynamics of acting-out. Remembering that he had underlined that passage because he thought it applied particularly to that patient, he felt embarrassed and disturbed. Immediately he apologized to the patient and told her he had made a mistake, but she became hostile and derisive toward him for some time afterward.

Later, when he gave some extended consideration to the reason he had made this particular error, his associations led him to the realization that he had recently thought of giving that same patient a manual of sexual information because, though she was an adult, he felt that she had very little valid knowledge about sex. This realization led him to recognize some distinct feelings of sexual attraction to her. The patient seemed also to be struggling with sexual feelings toward him. Now, if this understanding of his feelings had been available to him at the time she challenged him with his mistake, could he have articulated the error? Could he indeed have articulated the error even later?

Merely acknowledging the error and apologizing served very little therapeutic purpose in this case, and it was an instance of pure correcting rather than articulation. Silence or focusing on the patient's hostile affect would probably have escalated the patient's hostility and alienation. Under certain circumstances—depending on the level and current state of treatment—the therapist could have acknowledged his error and, touching directly on his realization of his sexual attraction to the patient, he could have indicated that he was probably also responding to sexual feelings in her. This is in part an articulating type of response because it separates a salient factor in the error and connects it to the therapeutic interaction. In most cases, however, such specificity is threatening and counterproductive and the most appropriate articulating response would therefore be the following: "I think the reason I may have given you that particular book when you asked for it was that I somehow wanted to convey to you that you have been acting out some feelings that are bothersome to you." In response to this, the patient would presumably ask for, and would also provide, further clarification that would eventually articulate the sexual factors in the interaction.

In another instance, a hospitalized patient was informed by her therapist that Good Friday was a hospital holiday and that their therapy session that day would be cancelled. As it turned out, the hospital had never provided a Good Friday holiday, and in the next therapy session two days later, the patient angrily confronted the therapist with his mistake. She insisted that the mistake inconvenienced her terribly because she had decided to go to her grandmother's house for a visit on the Good Friday weekend and was now forced to change all her plans in order not to miss the reinstated therapy session. When the therapist hesitated before responding to her onslaught, she walked out of the therapy session in fury. Thinking about his mistake later, this therapist became aware that he had in fact wished to avoid seeing the patient because of material in her therapy sessions of the previous days. She had been talking about her father's successful suicide, and this had touched on the therapist's feelings about his own mother's suicide attempts many years before.

When the patient returned the next day for her regularly scheduled session, the therapist focused on his mistake and her response to it. He attempted to get her to clarify why his making a mistake was such an issue for her, and whether she felt that he must never err at all and therefore not be human. Also, he asked what it was that had made her furiously walk out of the previous session. She responded that she had left the session because he "just sat there and didn't do anything." Realizing that she was very likely referring to his lack of action about her weekend trip plans, the therapist said that he thought she had the topic of leaving on her mind and connected that idea with her leaving the session. The patient then indicated that leaving the hospital for the weekend trip to her grandmother's house was a problem and revealed her deep ambivalence about the trip. Talking of feelings of hatred for her grandmother and mother, she described current suicidal preoccupations of her own.

While there are numerous psychodynamic factors operating in this sequence of events, I want only to point out the matter of articulation. The therapist's rather simple and unelaborate response was a creative articulating one because it separated and connected salient issues in the error. Connecting the patient's leaving the office to the topic of leaving itself served to separate out the issue of her leaving the hospital at all. This in turn served to separate out the issue of death, a salient matter involved both in his mistake and the patient's furious response, and surely also in the symbolic meaning of Good Friday. For the patient, death and suicidal feelings were connected with feelings of hatred toward her mother. By recognizing his own countertransference concerns, the therapist was able to focus on his error without guilt and see its connection to her feelings about leaving on a trip. As with the artistic examples discussed earlier, such articulation does not involve obliteration or covering up of error, but instead letting it stand and using it in the overall effect.

Not all countertransference error derives from deep conflicts, nor is it negatively or regressively charged. Indeed, we now recognize that transference is properly distinguished from transference neurosis and that both transference and countertransference are to some degree a factor in the development of all adult relationships. Furthermore, the therapist monitors all his personal feelings in a broad way and uses them to facilitate therapy in an ongoing process of articulation that may or may not involve errors. When errors do occur, however, they always deserve special attention. Also, tapping the therapist's preconscious and unconscious contents, they may actually contain more positively charged growth-enhancing feelings than consciously correct therapeutic behavior.

For example: A 44-year-old borderline patient with obsessive-compulsive personality features alerted his therapist in the springtime that he was not looking forward to summer sessions because he disliked the somewhat noisy room air conditioner in the office. Accordingly, when summer came, the therapist adopted the routine of shutting off the air conditioner immediately prior to this patient's appointment time. Neither he nor the patient commented on this, but it was carried out through the early summer months. One day, three-quarters of the way through August, the therapist forgot, for the first time, to turn off the air conditioner prior to the session and, as soon as the patient entered, he commented on this, asking: "Do we have to have the air conditioner on?" At this, the therapist invited the patient to turn the machine off and then got up and walked to his office window and opened it. Angrily, the patient snapped: "Small things are important to me. You knew I didn't like the air conditioner and you seemed annoyed when you walked to your window and opened it."

Knowing that he actually had not felt annoyed when he went to open the window, the therapist quickly tried then to think of why he might have forgotten to turn off the air conditioner that day. He remembered a fleeting thought he had had when routinely turning off the air conditioner a few sessions earlier, consisting of a question to himself: "Why do I do this all the time? Shouldn't the patient really be doing this?" While separating out this thought, he made an articulating connection in his mind and realized that the patient had been taking more initiative in bringing up material in recent sessions. Taking initiative had long been one of the patient's major problems. So he said: "I think the reason I may have personally forgotten to turn off the air conditioner this time was that I was responding to your wish to take more initiative in here recently." Interestingly, the patient's first response was to misunderstand the therapist's comment completely. He thought the therapist had criticized him for not taking enough initiative in the sessions. But, after further clarification, and clearly following the therapist's example of openness, acknowledgment of his mistake and his humanness, and of this articulation of an error, the patient thought about his own misunderstanding and realized that it came from his concerns about not taking enough initiative. For this quite passive, perfectionistic patient with hypersensitivity tending toward paranoid obsessionality, this was a significant therapeutic opening up and advance.

Articulation of error may have its greatest therapeutic pertinence in the treatment of schizophrenia. Although the two patients I just described were not schizophrenic, a particular feature of the therapist's response with those patients has general application and importance in the psychotherapy of schizophrenia. This is the feature of connecting error directly or indirectly with humanness and being human. In schizophrenia, as in other types of narcissistic disorders, there invariably is a preoccupation with perfection[28] and, because of primitive fusions and projective identifications, there is an inability to accept any lack of perfection in the therapist. Moreover, disavowal of therapist error, together with disavowal of errors by, or in, the patient's self, serves to deny that both therapist and patient are human beings. It is a vicious circle involving omnipotent perfectionism along with the patient's feelings of being a nonhuman entity in the first place. And it is a circle that is in part broken by the therapist's active use of error.

The use of error in the therapy of schizophrenic patients seldom can consist only of acknowledging mistakes, because such patients can neither forgive nor forget nor learn from that which is not accepted. So important is this matter that there is a sense in which the psychotherapy of schizophrenia seems to move along, and to progress, by means of coping with and handling of error. It often appears as though the course of therapy consists of a series of encounters that sometimes go smoothly, but which are invariably disrupted or interrupted in some way by a therapist error. This error is almost always a very minuscule and hidden one—seldom of the proportions of an overt mistake about cancelling a session or even forgetting to do something—but it is experienced as devastating by the patient and leads to major disruption in the therapy. This often takes the form of patient withdrawal or regression and flagrant psychotic production. Weeks or months may go by while the disruption continues and the patient covertly indicates the nature of the therapist's mistake in seemingly chance or indirect comments or behavior. When the patient is at a relatively high level of integration, or when there is some degree of engagement and understanding in the therapy, the disruptive response may be more gradual and progressive. At first there may only be lateness at appointments, silence, or the missing of sessions. If such reactions are not clarified and the therapist's error is not somehow incorporated into the therapy, more disruption usually ensues.

Lest I be misunderstood on this matter, I mean to suggest neither that therapist and patient always discuss each error explicitly after a disruption occurs nor that the therapist learns the precise nature of each error he has committed. Sometimes a schizophrenic patient only reveals the nature of these errors weeks or months after a disruption has ceased, sometimes not until the termination phase of the therapy. What I mean is that the therapist recognizes that the patient's disruption is related to something either done or not done in the therapy and, when identifying an error, the therapist does not pull back either by simple apology or rapid correction but attempts both to separate and connect the error in an articulation process.

Errors in the psychotherapy of schizophrenia are by no means errors in ordinary interaction. These patients are so exquisitely tuned to rejection and so constantly suspicious of others' reactions that they ferret out and attack the slightest whisper of countertransference and, along with that, the slightest suggestion of the therapist's need. They cannot tolerate any lack of omniscience and consequent imperfection and humanity. For instance, take approval by the therapist in a therapy hour. Various types of patients with very low self-esteem are sometimes ambivalent and uncomfortable about a therapist's tacit or explicit approval of something they have done. With the schizophrenic patient, however, there may be regression or actual disruption of treatment after being complimented on work in an hour, on general progress, on a generous action, or even after the therapist appears merely to be gratified by some particular words or interactions. Because one cannot always anticipate this in advance, and because one cannot, and should not, monitor all positive reactions, therapists must—strange to say—commit errors of approval. In treating schizophrenia, by and large, one must be destined to err to such a degree that error itself becomes a major focus. For the therapist, examination of what appears as error allows for the close monitoring and use of countertransference issues and, on a reciprocal basis, insight into the nature of the patient's transference. For the patient, articulation of errors, instead of simple correction, teaches acknowledgment and acceptance of human imperfections.

This is not to say that therapists do not constantly learn from errors or actively correct their impact in the course of therapy. In recognizing and focusing on errors, both learning and correcting inevitably occur. But incorporating the model of the approach of creative thinkers, if one possesses requisite therapeutic skills, one should not at all be afraid of making errors and should allow oneself a freedom that incurs errors and mistakes. One incurs errors, and is ready to articulate them, and thereby incorporates into the therapy one's own and the patient's individuality, and the humanity of both.

CHAPTER IX

The Mutual Creative Process and Therapeutic Action

As a creative process, psychotherapy emphasizes worth, innovation, and volition for both therapist and patient. Both are engaged in enhancing the patient's self and social worth, ego growth and development. While growth is required in treatment to reverse developmental stasis, fixation, and impairment, the course of growth is never simply reparative or smooth. The patient goes beyond the correction of deficiency to develop new and better ways of understanding, behaving, and interacting with others. To facilitate these effects, highly developed and actively applied skills are required on the therapist's part and, for the patient, an active making of choices. Only through active participation and decision-making can creative effects take place. In this creative process of psychotherapy, the patient feels that he has had a major share in producing the results. He chooses new patterns of behavior just as the creative artist actively chooses to produce newly structured content and the creative scientist actively chooses new theoretical formulations.

I shall not discuss supportive or directive orientations in relation to the creative process because these have little to do with the model I have been presenting. All types of psychotherapy involve some degree of supportiveness and directiveness which, although potentially suppressive of active choice, may not in practice interfere. Overall goals, effects, and operations may stimulate active patient choice in a way that is not clearly stipulated in general descriptions of particular therapeutic techniques.

The therapeutic process begins, as we know, before the patient and therapist actually meet and before the initial appointment is made. It begins when, in the course of a patient's illness, a particular shift in a balance of forces occurs. At this point, illness has either become overbearing, or treatment of some type has become attractive and feasible, or both factors operate, and the patient makes a decision to seek help. Again, I will not go into instances of manifestly directed or forced therapy such as those resulting from psychotic breakdown and institutionalization, suicide attempt, antisocial acts and the like, because any of these may represent indirect requests or decisions for treatment. Although available evidence is, to some degree, retrospective, it seems highly likely that no therapy of psychiatric illness can succeed unless some shift by the patient toward actively overcoming the illness takes place.

At the point of shifting, however, a decision to enter into a creative process has not been made. Although some patients may be aware of the growth-enhancing effects of psychotherapy and know or believe that such growth is necessary to overcome their discomfort, most initially prefer not to change. Unlike other creative activities, where an artist or scientist is highly motivated to create something out of particular materials, a patient seeking help has selected the materials but not the process of creation. He has, at that point, only decided that the subject of therapy is primarily himself. Nevertheless, this shift does constitute a step toward entering into a creative process, and it is a palpable and risky one.

After the patient meets with the therapist, the conditions for improvement are set. Different therapists may offer interventions ranging from medication, hypnosis, and advice on the one end of the spectrum to formal psychoanalysis at the other. Or they may offer a number of types of combinations from throughout the range. Regardless of particular treatment content offered, instigation to enter into a creative process occurs when a structure involving a trial domain is presented as well. As described in Chapter II, if the therapist tells the patient that the treatment will involve meetings with definite time limits and regularity, offers confidentiality, and indicates that improvement will result from the sessions themselves rather than a change in the patient's environment, a potential trial domain of interpersonal interaction is set up. If, in subsequent behavior, the therapist continues to avoid interfering in the patient's (including family or group as the patient unit) environment, he will further extend the instigation to engage in a creative process, even if also giving medication or being directive.

This is not to say that such instigation is sufficient to motivate the patient toward a creative effect. Indicating to him that his problems derive from patterns of living, unconscious conflict, or life history experiences also enters in. Most patients resist such formulations, and although many psychiatrists today believe they are less pertinent than biological ones, they must be accepted to some degree by both patient and therapist in order for the creative process to begin. A specific agreement or verbal "therapeutic contract" about the nature and structure of the treatment can then be established. I must point out here, as I did earlier, that even if psychiatric illness were caused by biological factors alone there would still be psychological sequelae of having experienced the illness. New structures and attributes are needed both to overcome the experience of the illness and to cope with future stresses.

The early preparation for active engagement in a therapeutic creative process consists of helping a patient to see or experience connections between conflicts and maladaptive patterns and the symptoms and suffering for which he sought help. Much of the initial phase of psychotherapy is concerned with establishing this. Continuing on, sometimes over considerable periods of time, and requiring reinforcement at later phases as well, the understanding of connections is at no point a purely intellectual matter. The patient must find that talking with the therapist about factors in his life is itself relieving and beneficial.

Without this preparation, without what for the creative artist would be respect for and interest in the materials he uses, little creative activity on the patient's part would be possible. The motivation still, however, does not arise automatically after this preparation occurs. The stage is set, the trial domain is structured, and the patient as major participant is ready. However, it is the therapist's creative activity that effectively instigates the mutual creative process.

The therapist's absorption in and love for the material of psychotherapy, of which I spoke earlier (Chapter IV), antedate the patient's interest. This love and absorbed regard for what the patient brings pervade the entire therapeutic transaction and are major instigating factors. Through his interest in the patient's presentation—including the form and structure of the symptoms, the intricate workings of recurrent behavior patterns, factors of symbolization in both the illness and verbal and nonverbal productions in sessions, the give and take of the verbal interaction—the therapist also conveys interest in and respect for the patient himself. The therapist experiences the doing of therapy with another human being as an especially worthy endeavor, and the patient, partly as a result, feels himself a worthy participant. Therapists do not often speak or write about their love for and gratification in the material the patient brings; they more often talk only of feelings about the patient as a person. Although these feelings are distinctly interrelated, the creative therapist's love for the human materials of his work is the same as the artist's love and fascination for the words, pigments, and sounds that are used to produce literature, visual art, and music, and the creative scientist's fascination with the puzzles and mechanisms of his field. Without such involvement and absorption, the creative process could not take place. No one, I have found, creates without this.

Other motivations for creating, such as drives for mastery, growth, and understanding, operate for both therapist and patient. However, the patient's motivation to participate in therapeutic creation is primarily facilitated by the treatment interaction. Out of a developing sense of worth comes a feeling of ability to make changes and—although not explicitly formulated in these terms—to produce creative effects. Once the patient feels the possibility of inducing change and making active choices, the therapist's creative skill facilitates the process and helps determine the nature of the creative outcome. At that point, all the faculties and processes I have discussed in this book play a role in activating the mutual creative process. Focus on form and structure, use of homospatial and janusian processes, articulating error, and guiding the overall process of articulation all have a part in inducing and maintaining the creative engagement. All of these factors contribute to the ongoing production of new and valuable effects. The therapist's application of these creative functions is critically responsible for the course of the creative process and also serves as a model of creative action for the patient.

UNDERSTANDING IN THE THERAPEUTIC CREATIVE PROCESS

Enhancement of the therapist's understanding is a generative function of the focus on form and use of the homospatial and janusian processes. This understanding is a core facilitator of the creative process. Transmitted through the therapist's particular interventions, interpretations, and overall approach, it provides the springboard from which the patient develops insight, resolves conflict, makes choices, and develops new attributes and structures. Only if the patient feels understood in a meaningful way can he undertake the risk of engaging in a creative therapeutic process. Having risked a shift in the direction of overcoming illness at the start, he cannot and will not undertake the further risk of change and creation unless he feels it will be for his own sake. The therapist's transmitted understanding assures the patient that there are reasons to change and he, not the therapist or another person, will be the primary beneficiary. In particular, the therapist's transmitted understanding helps the patient to overcome, in each case, the self-defeating factors and resistances that interfere with his engaging in the therapeutic process.

Although there are numerous other means besides the homospatial and janusian processes for achieving understanding, these are creative ones. In the creation of empathy in the course of treatment, the homospatial process provides a specially important type of knowledge. Freud made a strong claim for empathic understanding when he stated that empathy was "the mechanism by means of which we are enabled to take up any attitude at all toward another mental life."[1] Because empathy in treatment provides pre-sentational or presented validity and other types of knowledge described in Chapter IV, it does, at a minimum, provide a special access to another's mental life that is probably not available by other means. So much reasona-bly successful psychotherapy is carried out without any particular creative functioning on the therapist's part that I would be subject to the charge of extravagance were I to make a stronger claim. In order to improve therapeu-tic practice above the reasonably successful, however, and attain more meaningful and useful understanding of a patient's mental life, creative modes of thought are necessary.

Interventions derived from empathic understanding bear the marks of their creative origins. Because these interventions develop from mental superimposition and a "feeling into" by the therapist, they are accompanied by warmth and genuineness. Creative thinking and activity in any field always involve giving to others, whether that effort results in gratifying artworks, useful scientific theories, or other products. Indeed, creative work cannot derive exclusively from narcissism because of the necessity for a highly developed giving factor. Especially operative in the achievement of empathic understanding, giving over of oneself and warmth emerge from the highly focused concentration on another person. Because only a genu-ine self representation is functional in this process, genuineness pervades the understanding and interventions derived. Emotional warmth also is genera-ted by the therapist's experiencing his self representation together with the other person in a complicated way that I cannot explain or dwell on here. Suffice it to say that the genuineness and warmth connected with the

therapist's empathic understanding and resulting interventions often provide the patient with support and stimulation to continue to pursue the
challenging creative therapeutic process.

Understanding derived from the janusian process consists of flashes of
insight or discovery and solutions to therapeutic dilemmas. Immediate and
comprehensive grasp of a patient's conflicts is a particular feature of such
understanding. There may be early rapid formulations of conflicts or later
realizations and breakthroughs. In both cases, the constructed simultaneous
antitheses pertaining to the conflict are developed and transformed into
extensive dynamic understanding. They then become the bases for interpretations and other interventions.

Such understanding is often described by a therapist as intuitive without
recognition of its generative function in an ongoing therapeutic creative
process. Janusian "intuitions" may serve to initiate the process, as in the case
described in Chapter V, or may facilitate creative movement at different
points along the way. In the latter instances, janusian formulations often
serve as factors in a process of creative problem-solving. A therapeutic
impasse is present, or a countertransference issue blocks the therapist's
recognition, or both, and the formulation of the simultaneous antithesis
provides a new approach or breakthrough. As in any creative process, this
understanding produces continued shifts, new elements and directions, and
further elaboration.

Interventions derived from understanding achieved through the janusian
process may also bear creative earmarks. Rapid achievement of comprehension may at times produce rapid interventions that speed up and facilitate
the treatment process. Creative therapists have, in other ways, designed
briefer therapy approaches in recent years, based on better understanding
and concise use of psychodynamics. Judicious application of the comprehensive grasp provided by the janusian process may facilitate the patient's
development of insight and also help to shorten therapy. Paradoxical interventions and irony are often used with just this purpose in mind.

Use of the janusian process by the therapist requires both flexibility of
thinking and a willingness to take both mental and emotional risks. Such
features of a creative orientation are often conveyed to a patient by the
nature of the therapist's understanding and interventions. They provide a
model for the patient's own creative work. However, directly indicating the
sudden or immediate nature of a particular illumination would not usually
be beneficial. Doubt and competition may be instilled rather than emula-
tion or insight. Doubt would result both from the implicit indication that
the therapist has been a good deal in the dark and stymied and from a

seeming emphasis on his own thinking. Competition would be induced by the sense of his showing off proficiency and skill.

Understanding is the primary creative effect resulting from the use of the homospatial and janusian processes. Although not the usual tangible effect found in other creative fields, it is appropriate to the task and goals of therapy. While it is not a final created product, understanding is a facilitator and waystation in the ongoing creative process. Thus, the homospatial and janusian processes function overall as they do in other fields; they are responsible for interim effects that are transformed, modified, and otherwise developed into final created products.

One reason that these processes are the same within different types of creative activities, with overlapping types of functions and similar sequences, is that they relate to universal features of cognitive and affective function. The same processes that provide understanding of intrapsychic and interpersonal phenomena in psychotherapy also lead to gratifying effects in artistic fields where these phenomena are developed and explored as well. Metaphor and conflict, for example, are of abiding interest in all the arts and their construction and display provoke understanding and enjoyment. In scientific fields, focus on opposites or metaphorical constructions and models derives from particular proclivities in human cognition. That these foci lead to successful creative results in the latter might be, on the one hand, because the natural world that is the subject of scientific contemplation is organized in terms of oppositional factors. Or else it might be based on related principles such as symmetry.[2] Also, the structure of metaphorical interactions might be the structure of nature. On the other hand, scientists might have primarily come to know the oppositional, symmetrical, and metaphorically describable aspects of an enormous variety of substances, organizations, and structures. Historian of science Andrew Pickering has stated, "it would be useful to replace the idea that scientists are passive *discoverers* of the . . . facts of nature with the alternate view that they *actively* construct their world."[3] The reason that these cognitive proclivities produce their effects is not known and possibly not knowable. That intrapsychic conflict pervades all human activities is known, however, and conflict of that type may play a role in promoting cognitive construction and manipulation of opposites.

Understanding derived from these processes in psychotherapy is transmitted to the patient in various ways. In psychoanalysis and psychodynamic psychotherapy, these interventions are frequently in the form of verbal interpretations; depending on the type of understanding achieved, other types of interventions, such as clarification, reconstruction, silence or non-intervention, and confrontation, may be used. The early grasp of conflict derived from the janusian process may, as suggested in Chapter V, be a basis for the use and development of interpretations throughout therapy. With respect to the homospatial process, empathic understanding achieved may be especially linked, as suggested by the writings of Kohut and his followers on empathy, to interventions leading to "transmuting internalizations."[4] In other types of psychotherapy, directive types of interventions may be derived from both processes. Regardless of type of intervention or of psychotherapy, however, the therapist's creative understanding helps to focus on critical issues and open up new areas for exploration. It facilitates the articulation process and the development of both insight and new personality attributes and structure.

Particular types of interventions are developed directly from the homospatial and janusian processes in conjunction with the therapist's understanding (from both creative and noncreative sources). These types—metaphorical, paradoxical, and ironic—also serve as interpretations or identifiers of conflicts. However, usually they do not involve literal propositional statements about conflict but consist of dramatic or enacted types of interpretations. Tending to be more affectively charged than literal interpretations, these interventions all stimulate patient response and engagement. Because they are products of creative homospatial and janusian processes, they initiate a particular course of innovative development that is taken up and continued by the patient. A metaphorical intervention, for instance, provides both affective acceptance and a new direction, and the patient begins to explore some of the embedded conceptual and affective implications. With paradoxical interventions and irony, compressed formulations are presented that instigate shifts and changes. The conflicts focused upon by all the interventions mentioned may be directly acted on or may become separated and clarified in a dialectical therapeutic process and resolved.

CREATION OF INSIGHT AND PERSONALITY ATTRIBUTES AND STRUCTURE

Two endpoints of the creative process in psychotherapy are the production of insight and of personality attributes and structure. Usually, and especially in what is called the expressive type of psychotherapy,[5] insight precedes the development of personality structure. This may not necessarily be the case in all types of psychotherapy, particularly if insight is narrowly defined as involving conceptual or intellectual comprehension. Patients frequently experience a largely affective, or at least nonconceptual, type of insight that instigates choice and positive change.

As I suggested in the previous two chapters, creation of both insight and personality attributes and structure results from an articulation function that operates throughout the course of therapy. In addition to this continuing articulation, with its separating and connecting in general, it is important to remember that both homospatial and janusian processes provide particular types of articulation. The homospatial process involves bringing together along with separation of multiple sensory images. Superimposition of mentally represented spatial entities maintains the separate identities of these entities while they come together and interact. Both particular elements and whole mental representations may interact while specific features continue to be discrete and identifiable. Following the formulation of a homospatial conception, continued articulation occurs and a new identity is produced.

In the janusian process, contradictory, mutually exclusive, opposite and antithetical propositions are brought together and also retain their separate identities. Whereas the homospatial process involves articulation of spatial entities, the janusian articulation is a temporal one. Multiple opposites or antitheses are conceived as operating separately while simultaneous in time; they are neither compromised nor absorbed into one another. Following the formulation of a janusian conception, continued articulation usually occurs. Often, the homospatial process articulates a janusian conception further. In the creation of metaphors, a janusian process may be modified and further articulated by a homospatial one. In this way, metaphors having simultaneously antithetical or paradoxical structures are produced.

Particular articulations constructed by the homospatial and janusian processes, whether in the form of understanding or interventions or both, are subjected to further articulation either by the therapist alone, by patient and therapist together, or by the patient alone. When the therapist continues on his own to articulate the understanding developed from the two processes, he achieves fuller and more integrated insight into the patient and sometimes into himself as well. Similarly, the patient on his own articulates his reactions and responses into integrated insights and new patterns of behavior. The primary mode of articulation in the therapeutic process involves both therapist and patient working together. In this way it goes beyond both homospatial and janusian processes and incorporates their effects.

Jointly, the therapist and patient develop the connections together with separations that constitute insight. In the overall articulation process, they connect experiences in the trial domain of therapy with behavior and experiences in the patient's current and past life and concomitantly clarify the separations. Resulting insights consist of affective and cognitive apprehension, precisely, of the relationships both between the world of current reality and the trial domain of therapy, and between past and present experiences and patterns of behavior. These relationships invariably involve concurrent connections and separations.

I must emphasize that, in this view of the matter, insight is created in the interaction between the therapist and patient. It does not consist of an exact replication in memory of actual events of childhood or even thoughts and feelings connected with them. On the basis of recent research on memory and development, there is reason to believe that all childhood events are construed in adulthood in accordance with the child's level of cognitive and affective development at the time they occurred.[6] At certain levels of development, for instance, only sensory and motor aspects of an event will be apprehended and experienced. This plays a role in the substance and structure of memories about infantile masturbation or primal scene experiences, for example, and the range of experiences involving love or loss as well. Reconstructions in adulthood of the relationships between childhood experiences and the present are further affected by the context in which they are developed. In therapy, they are necessarily influenced by factors and experiences in the interpersonal relationship. Reconstructions and other insights regarding the past are articulated by the patient and therapist working together and have new and created aspects.

Articulation of insight leads, in an intrinsic way, to articulation of personality attributes and structure. Also, the former in some measure requires the accompaniment of the latter. As the therapist asks the patient about connections and separations among different experiences, feelings, and actions, the patient begins to develop a similar orientation, both in therapy sessions and in everyday life. Whereas previously the patient acted on impulses without consideration, he begins to ask himself questions about how his impulses are connected with and separated from other feelings and experiences. Articulation of insight and of personality attributes and structure occurs concomitantly, each serving, to some degree, as a function of the other. Further action also is required. Based on insight, the patient actively tries out and adopts new outlooks and patterns.

Creation of insight, making of active choices, and creation of new personality attributes and structure are all necessary, because psychopathology cannot be simply removed or eradicated. The conflicts and maladaptive patterns that produce symptoms and psychological suffering have, almost invariably, been operating for a long enough period to affect growth and development as well as overall personality organization. These conflicts and patterns have therefore assumed functional importance in the patient's life and makeup. Both including and extending beyond the secondary gain of particular symptoms, conflicts and maladaptive patterns influence current adjustment as well as further growth and development. They help determine what and how a person learns, choice of friends and other affectionate ties, and the nature of skills. Defensive patterns of reaction formation and ego splitting, for instance, may play a role in the development of certain types of executive skills; defensive projection may enhance artistic interest and appreciation, and so on. In more extensive ways, schizoid patterns may dictate solitary work and recreational pursuits and hysterical ones facilitate development of role-playing skills. On the side of nonadaptive function, conflicts about one area may help to avoid or protect another difficulty. Conflicts and concerns about homosexuality, for example, may function as protection against psychotic decompensation. Conflicts about eating may justify serious social inadequacies or result in the poor development of social skills.

Alteration of maladaptive patterns and resolution of conflict, therefore, cannot alone result in improvement. New patterns and structures are needed that the patient never before experienced or used. These patterns must serve some of the functions of maladaptive ones and also be adaptive and reduce suffering. They are articulated from both the particular understanding developed in the therapeutic interaction and the direct experience of the interaction itself.

CREATIVITY IN PSYCHOTHERAPY

As I cautioned at the beginning of this book, all psychotherapeutic activity is not directly creative and creative therapists are not the only satisfactory ones. Use of ordinary logic, problem-solving, and trial and error learning characterizes a good deal of psychotherapeutic interaction. Even compliance and acceptance of the status quo are sometimes quite important. For the therapist, broad understanding of human motivation and behavior, as well as qualities ranging from complex abilities to postpone gratification to simple practicality, are necessary to carry treatment forward. Although these qualities may often be involved in creative actions, they are not creative in themselves.

As in any creative activity, much of psychotherapy is not directly oriented to creative effects. Composition of artworks involves a good deal of imitation and reproduction of past successful effects. Plots, designs, and musical forms need not be original; they may be reproduced, polished, and perfected to produce an aesthetic effect. One of the most creative figures in literary history, Shakespeare, took many of the plots of his plays from previous sources. Much of scientific activity involves reproduction, rigorous testing, and trial and error assessment. In psychotherapy, a large proportion of the interaction is designed to be supportive, reduce anxiety, facilitate an alliance, educate, solve concrete problems, apply general principles to particular cases, and allow for the development of understanding. Although these activities are often the background, or foundation, for creative work, they are not specifically creative. For many patients and for many types of problems, such activities are, however, often sufficient to promote improvement.

As I have suggested throughout, creative activity is necessary to move the practice of psychotherapy into more efficient and effective directions. Moreover, the capacity to engage in such creative activity does not appear to be inborn, for either therapists or patients. The processes I have discussed have all already been employed and further learning is feasible. Although all have operated in outstanding and often dazzling accomplishments in other creative fields, their increased application to psychotherapy will produce less tangible but no less important individual results.

It would, furthermore, be a mistake to assume that creativity in the therapist or in therapeutic activity is incompatible at any time with competent health care or with therapeutic effect. Stereotypes about creativity abound. Nonetheless, solidity, reliability, means-end thinking, and good reality-testing are all compatible with creativity and creative thinking, despite some popular and professional conceptions to the contrary. Creative therapists can, and routinely do, carry out the entire range of activities connected with effective treatment.

FORM AND CONTENT OF PSYCHOTHERAPY

The therapist's focus on form and structure and his use of the homospatial, janusian, and overall articulation processes are interrelated. Both the homospatial and janusian processes are form and structure oriented in that they primarily concern relationships among potentially unlimited components and types of content. The homospatial process concerns formal factors of spatial configuration and discreteness; in the janusian process, temporal configuration and the relationships of opposition or antithesis are formal matters. Also, articulation processes concern formal relationships of connection and separation, similarly among potentially unlimited content. Creative thinking and creative processes, then, are highly involved with considerations of form and structure.

Is content then a secondary matter in psychotherapeutic treatment? Such a rhetorical question must now be turned on its head because there is a sense in which content is all-important in therapy. I have not really ignored that point before this despite my emphasis on form because, as I said earlier, form and content are inextricably related and any formal process must both derive from and influence content. The janusian process, for instance, begins with the identification of salient opposites within the content of the patient's thoughts and productions. Also, this process pertains to psychological conflict, tendencies to conceptualize in opposites, and other factors in the makeup of human beings. The homospatial process pertains to psychological fusion and tendencies toward unification. Articulation involves form together with all psychological content, conscious and unconscious; it involves all sociological and biological substance as well.

One reason content is all-important in therapy is that the content of a human being's experience constitutes a good deal of what makes him a unique individual. Uniqueness in turn is a quintessential aspect of what constitutes a creation, because to be one of a kind is to be truly new with respect to the world of events and objects. One can be new in relation to a particular context, or in relation to what one was before, but something unique is new in relation to the known universe. Consequently, content of therapy and of a particular human being's experience is inextricably involved in the creative process.

Content of psychotherapy consists of all the narratives regarding the patient's current life and past experience that are woven by the patient together with the therapist. It ranges from the substance of his mental and emotional life to social and biologically instigated experiences. As the patient speaks of fantasies, feelings, thoughts, and dreams, the therapist may consider psychodynamic content, as well as symptoms, information processing, systems content, learned patterns of behavior, or cognitive and affective functions.

For the patient seeking therapy, the content at the beginning is quite concrete. Some of the frequent types of difficulties patients bring to therapy are as follows: inability to cope with loss and rejection, difficulties in marriage and intimate relationships, problems in choosing a life's commitment, extreme impulsiveness and rebelliousness as manifestations of personality disorder, inability to learn in school or perform well on the job, sexual problems, suicidal preoccupations, criminal and violent behavior, psychosomatic problems, eating disorders, addiction to alcohol and drugs, mood swings and depression, symptoms of anxiety disorders and psychosis.

Narratives that patient and therapist construct regarding the background, current condition, and potential future of these types of difficulties become part of the ongoing content of therapy. These narratives are not literary ones that unfold with beginning, middle, and end. They are articulated throughout the therapy in disorganized bits and pieces. Unlike literary narratives, they do not emerge from the interaction with built-in elements of suspense along the way. But suspense is engendered and felt by both patient and therapist; it is the suspense of discovery. This arises from a mutual conviction that more underlies the surface of a story than may be immediately revealed. When true narratives of the entire psychotherapy process are written or told, they must be told as narratives of discovery rather than as unfolding literary tales.

From the point of view of the creative process of psychotherapy, two factors of content are particularly related to the therapeutic effect. These are transference and dependency. With regard to transference content, I have already described the creative articulation of transference (Chapter VIII) and its therapeutic effect. Transference distortions are both separated and connected and thereby incorporated rather than being obliterated. By means of this articulation process, the patient is able to separate the therapist from parents and other influential individuals; at the same time, he actively accepts or chooses attributes of both past and present persons. The patient is able to separate past from present motives and experiences and also accept a continuity.

Excessive dependency is a feature of all the concrete content of initial patient difficulties I have listed. Intense reaction to loss and criticism is based on a person's strong need to have the support, recognition, and care of others rather than relying on oneself. Difficulties in marriage and other intimate relationships often derive from excessive dependency of one partner on another. Sexual problems involving inability to satisfy oneself or one's partner frequently result from enslavement to internalized prohibitions instilled by parents and others, or from attempting to conform to oversimplified and restrictive images about masculinity or femininity dictated by parents or society. There is excessive dependency in depressive illness with its catastrophic reaction to loss; also, compulsive rituals and phobias involve unconscious fears of experiencing drives, affects, or the implications of ideas that might alienate an internalized parent or a real spouse or friend. In such a ubiquitous feature of personality disorder as passive-aggressive obstructionism, the pouting resistant state is directly reminiscent of the resentful dependence of the three- or four-year-old on his parents. In addiction and alcoholism, the obvious dependency on a chemical always seems clearly derived from excessive dependency on people. And, running through all of the difficulties, poor self-images or low self-esteem ultimately seem to derive from feelings of being at the mercy of others, inability to be the master of oneself and one's fate, and troubles both in coping with one's environment and being effective in social relationships. Again, excessive dependency is an important enemy. Spoken of another way, regression and fixation are factors in symptom formation and illness.

Excessive dependency also is a feature of schizophrenic disorder. Although considered a thought disorder, one of the cardinal behavioral features of schizophrenia is a withdrawn demeanor and flat or inappropriate expression of affect or emotion. These patients appear to feel "dead" inside and sometimes say that. Although there are many reasons for this condition, it amounts functionally to being unable to experience or express one's feelings. One explanation is that schizophrenia involves a physiological interference with experiencing and expressing feelings or thinking connected with feelings. Or, there is another physiological mediating factor such as intensely high levels of anxiety that interferes with feeling expression. Other explanations have been that it results from double binding experiences,[7] attention disturbance, input disfunction,[8] or transmission of irrationality in upbringing and intercategorical fixation.[9] Although all of these factors may be critically involved, an essential and potentially remediable ingredient of the condition is the connection between fear of expressing or experiencing feelings and excessive dependency on others. If the schizophrenic individual were to express feelings of anger or love, he would take the risk of alienating or losing a person, or the internalized representation of a person, on whom he desperately depends. In referring to dependency in this condition, I mean to indicate the construction of the entire ego and self around the internalized representation of a parent or parents. If the representation is lost, the ego becomes obliterated.

ARTICULATION AND THE CREATION OF INDEPENDENCE AND INTEGRATION

One of the primary effects of the articulation process, including both janusian and homospatial processes and others yet undetermined, is the independence and integration of a final created product. In human beings, independence consists of being both separated and connected to other persons at once. No one stands completely isolated and alone; all must recognize responsibilities and connections with others in order to function independently within a social context. Independence from family does not involve total renunciation, at least not on a psychological level. In order to feel independent, one must accept and be comfortable with one's own attributes, many of which are shared with parents and other family members. One cannot renounce these shared connections without renouncing features of oneself. Similarly, independence within human history involves acceptance of both connection and separation with past social and cultural experience.

A criterial feature of artistic creation is that a completed artwork is an independent entity. It has both connections and separations with previous artworks produced throughout the course of history as well as with other artworks produced by the same artist. Because of the latter it bears the stamp of the artist's individuality, but stands as a separate entity in the corpus of his works. Also, artworks accorded high degrees of value or approval are usually integrated—in the sense I have discussed above—with coordination and interaction among their parts and a distinct identity to the whole. Neither lacking in discreteness nor submerged within the whole, these parts interact and contribute to overall function and organization. This integration is often likened to the living biological organism, and valued artworks are said to have organic unity. In the biological organism, discrete identifiable body parts, on a molar and molecular level, interact and contribute to the function of the body as a whole. In this way, an organism is a fully self-sufficient and independent entity.

In the other field of our interest, scientific creations may not always have the same degree of integration as valued artworks. However, they clearly are articulated and independent. For a scientific discovery or theory to be acknowledged and accepted it must connect, to some degree, with previous canons of knowledge, and to be recognized as a creation it must be clearly separated from those canons at the same time. Scientific creations are often designated with the name of the individual or group who developed them because of this factor of independence. Einstein's theory of relativity, Bohr's complementarity, Darwin's evolution, Fermi's slow neutrons, and Mendelian heredity are examples of creative work that is recognized as singular and independent despite the tendency in science for individual work to be absorbed, changed, and superseded.

In the creative process of psychotherapy, the patient's achievement of independence and integration is the final creative outcome. Although excessive dependency, as well as related factors of regression and fixation, may not be a sole or even major causative factor in all mental and emotional illness, it is invariably involved. The articulation process, which develops separation from the past together with continuity, and separateness from other individuals together with connectedness, counters excessive dependency and produces independence. With the achievement of valid independence, many, if not all, psychological symptoms are reduced in intensity or they disappear. Whether residual symptomatology and disability are due either to incompleteness of independence gained or to fixation of learned patterns of functioning, or whether there is persistence of other types of causes, cannot be determined with the present state of our knowledge.

The creative process of psychotherapy involves ego development and growth. Unlike other living organisms—although this difference cannot be ascertained with certainty—human beings do not seem to grow psychologically without active volition coming into play at some point. Perhaps difficulties with both growth and dependency in humans derive from the fact that we sustain and require a longer period of dependency on progenitors and others than most other organisms. Knowledge about this matter again is lacking, but not about the *course* of growth. Human mental and emotional growth does not occur in a smooth unfolding way. Spurts and deficits, pits and valleys appear throughout its course. Some of this erratic course is connected with and caused by psychological stress and difficulty. As a creative process involving choice and articulation that leads to independence and integration, psychotherapy does not smooth the course but produces spurts of growth and durable variations. While reversing some of the noxious effects of past interferences with growth, it reaches beyond itself into the future.

Notes

CHAPTER I (*pages 3–15*)

1. Albert Rothenberg, "The Iceman Changeth: Toward an Empirical Approach to Creativity," *Journal of the American Psychoanalytic Association*, 17(1969):549–607; "The Process of Janusian Thinking in Creativity," *Archives of General Psychiatry*, 24(1971):195–205; "Poetic Process and Psychotherapy," *Psychiatry*, 3(1972):238–254; "Word Association and Creativity," *Psychological Reports*, 33(1973):3–12; "Opposite Responding as a Measure of Creativity," *Psychological Reports*, 33(1973):15–18; "Homospatial Thinking in Creativity," *Archives of General Psychiatry*, 33(1979):17–26; *The Emerging Goddess: The Creative Process in Art, Science and Other Fields*, Chicago: University of Chicago Press, 1979; "Psychopathology and Creative Cognition. A Comparison of Hospitalized Patients, Nobel Laureates, and Controls," *Archives of General Psychiatry*, 40(1983):937–942; "Janusian Process and Scientific Creativity: The Case of Niels Bohr," *Contemporary Psychoanalysis*, 19(1983):101–119; "Artistic Creation as Stimulated by Superimposed Versus Combined-Composite Visual Images," *Journal of Personality and Social Psychology*, 50(1986):370–381. Albert Rothenberg and Robert S. Sobel, "Creation of Literary Metaphors as Stimulated by Superimposed Versus Separated Visual Images," *Journal of Mental Imagery*, 4(1980):77–91; "Effects of Shortened Exposure Time on the Creation of Literary Metaphors as Stimulated by Superimposed Versus Separated Visual Images," *Perceptual and Motor Skills*, 53(1981):1007–1009. Robert S. Sobel and Albert Rothenberg, "Artistic Creation as Stimulated by Superimposed Versus Separated Visual Images," *Journal of Personality and Social Psychology*, 39(1980):953–961.

2. Subsequent to participating in the research project, some subjects granted me permission to disclose their names in connection with *specific* material and reports. Those names appear throughout this book. In other instances, disclosure permission has not been granted and anonymity is maintained.

3. See Calvin S. Hall and Gardner Lindzey, *Theories of Personality*, New York: John Wiley and Sons, 1978, pp. 6–8, for a discussion of the difficulty in providing a general substantive definition of personality. The definition I shall follow here is that personality consists of the organization of an individual's patterns of action and behavior as well as all intrapsychic and interpersonal functions. In referring to personality attributes and structure, I mean to include both particular features and overall organization.

4. It is generally acknowledged that some degree of residual identification with the therapist persists and cannot be analyzed or worked through.

5. Rothenberg, "Homospatial Thinking"; *The Emerging Goddess*.

6. Ernst Kris, *Psychoanalytic Studies of Art*, New York: International Universities Press, 1952.

7. Alexander Grinstein, *Freud's Rules of Dream Interpretation*, New York: International Universities Press, 1983, p. 187.

8. Albert Rothenberg, "Translogical Secondary Process Cognition in Creativity," *Journal of Altered States of Consciousness*, 4(1978–9):171–187; *The Emerging Goddess*.

9. Author's name and citation withheld upon request.

10. Eleanor B. Pyle, "Fuller Albright's Inimitable Style," *Harvard Medical Alumni Bulletin*, 56(1982):46–51.

11. Rothenberg, "Superimposed versus Combined-Composite Visual Images"; and Sobel, *op. cit.*, 1980, 1981; Sobel and Rothenberg, 1980.

12. L. A. Holland, *Janus and the Bridge*, Rome: American Academy, 1961.

13. Rothenberg, *The Emerging Goddess*.

14. Emphasis added.

15. Albert Rothenberg, "Einstein, Bohr, and Creative Thinking in Science," *History of Science*, 25 (1987): 147–166.

16. Creativity ratings were based on questionnaire responses regarding strength of creative interests and previous awards and achievements. This questionnaire had been cross-validated with independent creativity ratings by teachers and peers in a separate study.

17. Rothenberg, "Word Association"; "Opposite Responding"; "Psychopathology and Creative Cognition." Results of comparisons of high creative and low creative business executives' responses by means of t-test as indicated here were not reported in the "Opposite Responding" article concerning those groups because these subjects were used only to devise a standardized method for scoring creative responding at that time.

CHAPTER II (*pages 16–37*)

1. From John Dollard and Frank Auld, Jr., *Scoring Human Motives*, New Haven: Yale University Press, 1959. References to patient's and therapist's tone of voice in the original transcript have been deleted in the quotation here. Other minor editorial changes have also been made for clarity.

2. *Ibid.*, p. 290.

3. For an interesting discussion of the psychological basis of form from a psychoanalytic point of view, see Gilbert J. Rose, *The Power of Form*, New York: International Universities Press, 1980. Rose's analysis pertains primarily to aesthetic form and does not include the focus on psychotherapy presented here.

4. *Webster's Third International New Dictionary*, Springfield, Mass.: G. & C. Merriam Co., 1965.

5. Walter Pater, *The Renaissance (1893)*, edited by Donald L. Hill, Berkeley: University of California Press, 1980, p. 106.

6. Richard Wilbur, "Running," *Walking to Sleep. New Poems and Translations*, New York: Harcourt, Brace and World, 1963, pp. 26–29.

7. A special word association task was constructed and administered to Mr. Wilbur in a separate procedure. To construct the task, all manuscript versions of the poem were analyzed by the investigator and words that had been either deleted or added during the course of composing the poem were compiled. Both types of words were randomly arrayed, along with unchanged "chaff" words from the poem as well as randomly chosen words from sources other than the poem, and constructed into a word association test protocol. In administering this test, the words on the protocol were each stated aloud and the subject was instructed to give the first word, image, or series of words that came to mind. Responses were tape recorded and speed of response separately measured. Both content and speed of response to all types of stimulus words were compared. This procedure is designated "The Poet's Own Poem (P.O.P.) Test," Research Scientist Career Development Award Application No. MH 23621, National Institute of Mental Health, Washington, D.C., 1969.

8. Dollard and Auld, *op. cit.*, pp. 226, 228.

9. *Ibid.*, pp. 228, 230.

10. *Ibid.*, pp. 250, 252.

11. *Ibid.*, pp. 284, 286, 288.

12. The patient did not commit suicide after this session but no final outcome is reported by Dollard and Auld.

13. Jacob A. Arlow, "Interpretation and Psychoanalytic Psychotherapy: A Clinical Illustration," in

Evelyne A. Schwaber (ed.), *The Transference in Psychotherapy: Clinical Management*, New York: International Universities Press, 1985, pp. 103–120.

14. The psychoanalytic injunction that a patient is to tell the analyst everything that comes to mind—without censorship or fear of retribution—within the period of the analytic hour, was first responsible for establishing this structural principle. Other therapies not explicitly using free association also provide a structured trial domain.

15. The requirements of third-party payment and, in the case of hospitalized patients, state and federal government regulations produce some therapist action on the patient's behalf in the form of filling out forms, sending reports, etc. However, these are not usually of a magnitude to affect the trial domain in a significant way. When such requirements do have a significant effect, they must be dealt with in the therapy or they will subvert treatment.

16. Paul Mies, *Beethoven's Sketches. An Analysis of His Style Based on a Study of His Sketch-Books*, translated by Doris L. MacKinnon, New York: Dover Publications, 1974, p. 69.

17. Leonard Meyer, *Emotion and Meaning in Music*, Chicago: University of Chicago Press, 1956; Gordon Epperson, *The Musical Symbol*, Ames: Iowa State University Press, 1967.

18. Leonard Bernstein, *The Unanswered Question*, Cambridge: Harvard University Press, 1976.

19. Cf. *ibid.*, p. 153; Bernstein states that formal transformations *are* meaning.

20. I am not here using the term "form" in visual art in the traditional sense of shape as opposed to color, but I include a focus on color relationships as a part of the primary concern with form.

21. Pamela Taylor (ed.), *The Notebooks of Leonardo da Vinci*, New York: New American Library, 1960, p. 57.

22. Popper and other philosophers of science relate elegance to simplicity, and they, in turn, consider simplicity to be a factor only in aiding testability of a theory. However, creative scientists use principles of elegance and simplicity in their thinking during the course of the creative process in order to *generate* the theories and discoveries themselves. See Karl Popper, *Conjectures and Refutations*, New York: Harper Torchbooks, 1965, pp. 61, 241; *The Logic of Scientific Discovery*, New York: Harper Torchbooks, 1968, pp. 136–145.

23. Henri Poincaré, *Science and Method*, Francis Maitland (trans.), New York: Dover Press, 1952, p. 59.

24. Gerald Holton, "On Trying to Understand Scientific Genius," *Thematic Origins of Scientific Thought. Kepler to Einstein*, Cambridge: Harvard University Press, 1973, pp. 362ff; A. F. Chalmers, "Curie's Principle," *British Journal for the Philosophy of Science*, 21(1970):133–148; M. N. McMorris, "Aesthetic Elements in Scientific Theories," *Main Currents*, 26(1970):82–96. A recent work on symmetry in physics gives many examples of the importance of this principle in having guided particular formulations and discoveries; it also describes the principle of symmetry in the fundamental workings of the Universe. See A. Zee, *Fearful Symmetry*, New York: Macmillan, 1986.

25. Gerald Holton, *The Advancement of Science and Its Burdens*, Cambridge: Cambridge University Press, 1986, pp. 86–87.

26. Pierre Curie (1894), quoted in Chalmers, *op. cit.*, p. 133.

27. *Ibid.*

28. McMorris, *op. cit.*, p. 88.

29. Howard E. Gruber, "Darwin's 'Tree of Nature' and Other Images of Wide Scope," in Judith Wechsler (ed.), *On Aesthetics in Science*, Cambridge: M.I.T. Press, 1978, pp. 121–140.

30. *Ibid.*, p. 127.

CHAPTER III (pages 38–55)

1. Virgil Aldrich, "Visual Metaphor," *Journal of Aesthetic Education*, 2(1968):73–86.

2. Bernstein, *op. cit.*

3. Rothenberg, *The Emerging Goddess*, pp. 304–306.

4. Arthur Koestler, *The Act of Creation*, New York: Macmillan, 1964.

5. Max Black, *Models and Metaphors*, Ithaca: Cornell University Press, 1962; Monroe Beardsley, "The Metaphorical Twist," *Philosophy and Phenomenological Research*, 22(1962):293–307; C. C. Anderson, "The Psychology of Metaphor," *Journal of Genetic Psychology*, 105(1964):53–73; Harold Voth, "The Analysis of Metaphor," *Journal of the American Psychoanalytic Association*, 18(1970):599–621; Benjamin

B. Rubenstein, "On Metaphor and Related Phenomena," *Psychoanalysis and Contemporary Science*, 1(1972):70–108; Robert Rogers, *Metaphor: A Psychoanalytic View*, Berkeley: University of California Press, 1978; Sheldon Sacks, *On Metaphor*, Chicago: University of Chicago Press, 1979; David S. Miall (ed.), *Metaphor: Problems and Perspectives*, Sussex: The Harvester Press, 1982.

6. For the purposes of this discussion, I have simplified the original metaphorical phrase, "How long can my hands be a bandage to his hurt?" Sylvia Plath, "Three Women," *Winter Trees*, London: Faber and Faber, 1971, p. 50.

7. Integration involves discrete identifiable elements interacting and contributing to the function and structure of the whole. See an experimental assessment of differences between combinatory and integrating phenomena in Rothenberg, "Superimposed Versus Combined-Composite Visual Images," and also see further discussion of integration here in Chapters VII and IX.

8. I am indebted to T. Schuyler for this example.

9. Now that I have drawn direct attention to them, we may begin to think about such things but that is because I am reviving a meaningful context. See Rothenberg, *The Emerging Goddess*, for further discussion of metaphors as unities.

10. This example was provided to me by Dr. Eric Plakun.

11. I have elsewhere discussed these homologies between the structure of art products and of unconscious structures (Rothenberg, *The Emerging Goddess*). Homospatial process and other types of creative cognition function as "mirror images of dreaming," and they are homologous—but obverse—to primary process and dream structures. Consequently, because art structures and contents are derived from mirror image of dreaming creative processes that are homologous with unconscious primary process and dream elements, art resonates with unconscious structures and contents.

12. I am not referring to psychological or psychoanalytic studies of metaphor or to studies of patients' use of metaphor, topics on which much has been written. Patient metaphors, i.e., nonpoetic figures of speech, may often derive primarily from primary process operations. See Howard R. Pollio, Jack M. Barlow, Harold J. Fine, and Marilyn R. Pollio, *Psychology and the Poetics of Growth: Figurative Language in Psychology, Psychotherapy, and Education*, Hillsdale, N.J.: Erlbaum, 1977; Harold J. Fine, Howard R. Pollio, and Charles H. Simpkinson, "Figurative Language, Metaphor, and Psychotherapy," *Psychotherapy: Theory, Research and Practice*, 10(1973):87–91; Ella F. Sharpe, "Psycho-Physical Problems Revealed in Language: An Examination of Metaphor," *International Journal of Psycho-Analysis*, 21(1940):201–213; Jitka Lindén, "Insight Through Metaphor in Psychotherapy and Creativity," *Psychoanalysis and Contemporary Thought*, 8(1985):375–406; Jacob A. Arlow, "Metaphor and the Psychoanalytic Situation," *Psychoanalytic Quarterly*, 48(1979):363–385.

13. William H. Sledge, "The Therapist's Use of Metaphor," *International Journal of Psychoanalytic Psychotherapy*, 6(1977):113–130.

14. Elaine Caruth and Robert Eckstein, "Interpretation Within the Metaphor: Further Considerations," *Journal of the Academy of Child Psychiatry*, 5(1966):35–45, p. 36; see also Robert Eckstein and Judith Wallerstein, "Choice of Interpretation in the Treatment of Borderline and Psychotic Children," *Bulletin of the Menninger Clinic*, 2(1956):199–207.

15. Norman Reider, "Metaphor as Interpretation," *International Journal of Psycho-Analysis*, 53(1972):463–469.

16. Sam Glucksberg, "Metaphors in Conversation: How Are They Understood? Why Are They Used?" *Metaphor and Symbolic Activity*, in press; Sam Glucksberg, Patricia Gildea, and Howard Bookin, "On Understanding Nonliteral Speech: Can People Ignore Metaphors?" *Journal of Verbal Learning and Verbal Behavior*, 21(1982):85–98.

17. A similar metaphor has also been used creatively in the context of individual therapy. See Albert Rothenberg, "Creativity and Psychotherapy," *Psychoanalysis and Contemporary Thought*, 7(1984):233–268, pp. 245–246.

18. Stephen R. Lankton and Carol H. Lankton, *The Answer Within: A Clinical Framework of Ericksonian Hypnotherapy*, New York: Brunner/Mazel, 1983.

19. *Ibid.*, p. 112ff.

20. *Ibid.*, p. 116.

21. Philip Barker, *Using Metaphors in Psychotherapy*, New York: Brunner/Mazel, 1985.

22. John P. Muller, "Sense of Competence and Self-Desensitization," Ph.D. dissertation, Harvard University, 1971, pp. 102–103.

23. I am indebted to Dr. Stanley Jackson for this example.

24. Figurative expressions may represent primary process condensations, but created or poetic

metaphors are not condensations; they are purposely and deliberately constructed, linguistically economical expressions with multiple conscious and unconscious referents. See Rothenberg, *The Emerging Goddess*.

CHAPTER IV (*pages 56–77*)

1. Sigmund Freud, "Delusions and Dreams in Jensen's Gradiva" (1907), *Standard Edition*, 9:7–93, New York: W. W. Norton, 1959, p. 8.

2. Theodor Lipps, "Empathy, Inner Imitation and Sense-Feelings" (1903), in Melvin Rader (ed.), *A Modern Book of Aesthetics*, New York: Holt, Rinehart and Winston, 1965, pp. 374–382; *Ästhetik: Psychologie des Schönen und der Kunst*, Hamburg and Leipzig: L. Voss, 1903–1906; "Empathy and Aesthetic Pleasure" (1905), in Karl Aschenbrenner and Arnold Isenberg, *Aesthetic Theories: Studies in the Philosophy of Art*, Englewood Cliffs, N.J.: Prentice-Hall, Inc., 1965, pp. 403–412; "Das Wissen von Fremden Ichen," *Psychologische Untersuchungen*, 1(1907):694–722.

3. Mark Kanzer, "Freud, Theodore Lipps, and 'Scientific Psychology,'" *Psychoanalytic Quarterly*, 50(1981):393–410.

4. Edward B. Titchener, *Lectures on the Experimental Psychology of the Thought Processes*, New York: Macmillan, 1909, p. 21.

5. Vernon Lee (Violet Paget), *The Beautiful*, Cambridge: Cambridge University Press, 1913.

6. *Ibid.*, p. 61.

7. Karl Groos, *The Play of Man*, London: William Heinemann, 1901.

8. Wilhelm Worringer, *Abstraktion und Einfühlung*, München: R. Piper Verlag, 1948.

9. Lois B. Murphy, *Social Behavior and Child Personality: An Exploratory Study of Some Roots of Sympathy*, New York: Columbia University Press, 1937; Carl R. Rogers, *Client-Centered Therapy*, Boston: Houghton Mifflin, 1951; Robert L. Katz, *Empathy*, Glencoe: Free Press, 1963; Norma D. Feshbach and Kiki Roe, "Empathy in Six- and Seven-Year-Olds," *Child Development*, 39(1968):133–145; Ezra Stotland, "Exploratory Investigations of Empathy," in Leonard Berkowitz (ed.), *Advances in Experimental Social Psychology*, New York: Academic Press, 1969, pp. 271–314; Ezra Stotland, Stanley E. Sherman and Kelly G. Shaver, *Empathy and Birth Order*, Lincoln: University of Nebraska Press, 1971; Henry M. Bachrach, "Empathy," *Archives of General Psychiatry*, 33(1976):35–38; Paul H. Mussen and Nancy Eisenberg-Berg, *Roots of Caring, Sharing and Helping*, San Francisco: W. H. Freeman, 1977.

10. Robert Fliess, "The Metapsychology of the Analyst," *Psychoanalytic Quarterly*, 11(1942):211–227; Ralph R. Greenson, "Empathy and Its Vicissitudes," *International Journal of Psycho-Analysis*, 41(1960):418–424; Antonio J. Ferreira, "Empathy and the Bridge Function of the Ego," *Journal of the American Psychoanalytic Association*, 9(1961):91–105; Roy Schafer, "Generative Empathy in the Treatment Situation," *Psychoanalytic Quarterly*, 28(1959):342–373, and "The Psychoanalyst's Empathic Activity," *The Analytic Attitude*, New York: Basic Books, 1983, pp. 34–57; David Beres and Jacob A. Arlow, "Fantasy and Identification in Empathy," *Psychoanalytic Quarterly*, 43(1974):26–50.

11. Rogers, *op. cit.*; also see Carl R. Rogers and Rosalind F. Dymond (eds.), *Psychotherapy and Personality Change: Coordinated Studies in the Client-Centered Approach*, Chicago: University of Chicago Press, 1954.

12. Heinz Kohut, "Introspection, Empathy, and Psychoanalysis," *Journal of the American Psychoanalytic Association*, 7(1959):459–483; "Forms and Transformations of Narcissism," *Journal of the American Psychoanalytic Association*, 14(1966):261–266; *The Analysis of the Self*, New York: International Universities Press, 1971; *The Restoration of the Self*, New York: International Universities Press, 1977; "Introspection, Empathy, and the Semi-Circle of Health," *International Journal of Psycho-Analysis*, 63(1982): 395–407.

13. Paul H. Ornstein, "Remarks on the Central Position of Empathy in Psychoanalysis," *Bulletin of the Association of Psychoanalytic Medicine*, 18(1979):95–108.

14. See, for an exposition of this aspect of Kohut's approach: Steven T. Levy, "Empathy and Psychoanalytic Technique," *Journal of the American Psychoanalytic Association*, 33(1985):353–378.

15. Compare, for example, some recent efforts at considering empathy in the artistic context without attention to earlier formulations in aesthetics: Jerome D. Oremland, "Empathy and Its Relation to the Appreciation of Art," and Mary Gedo, "Looking at Art from the Empathic Viewpoint," in Joseph

D. Lichtenberg, Melvin Bornstein, and Donald Silver (eds.), *Empathy I*, New York: International Universities Press, 1984, pp. 239–266 and 267–300 respectively.

16. See also, for a similar comparison, Stanley L. Olinick, "A Critique of Empathy and Sympathy," in Joseph D. Lichtenberg *et al., op. cit.*, pp. 137–166.

17. These connections to some extent derivable from Lipps's and Lee's theories of empathy and aesthetic pleasure, and shall be spelled out in future communications.

18. Kohut, *op. cit.*, 1982.

19. Beres and Arlow, *op. cit.*

20. Sigmund Freud, "Group Psychology and the Analysis of the Ego" (1921), *Standard Edition*, 18:69–143, New York: W. W. Norton, 1955, p. 110.

21. Both Schafer and Wolf have pointed out that their experience of empathy in the treatment context differs from that in their everyday life with friends, etc. See Schafer, *op. cit.*, 1983, and Ernest S. Wolf, "Empathy and Countertransference," in Arnold Goldberg (ed.), *The Future of Psychoanalysis*, New York: International Universities Press, 1983, p. 319.

22. Maurice Merleau-Ponty, *The Phenomenology of Perception*, translated by C. S. Smith, London: Routledge and Kegan Paul, 1962, pp. 243ff.

23. See also Alfred Margulies, "Toward Empathy: The Uses of Wonder," *American Journal of Psychiatry*, 141(1984):1025–1033. This author also emphasizes active will in empathy and relates empathy to creative activity. His view of creativity is based on Keats's "negative capability," a very broad construct but not incompatible with the processes and dynamisms presented here.

24. Schafer, *op. cit.*, 1959, p. 360.

25. G. Herbert Mead, *Mind, Self and Society*, Chicago: University of Chicago Press, 1934.

26. See Leston Havens, "Explorations in the Uses of Language in Psychotherapy. Simple Empathic Statements," *Journal of Abnormal Psychology*, 87(1978):336–345; "Explorations in the Uses of Language in Psychotherapy. Complex Empathic Statements," *Psychiatry*, 42(1979):40–48.

27. Stotland, *op. cit.*

28. Freud, *op. cit.*, 1921, p. 110.

29. Otto Fenichel, "Identification" (1926), *Collected Papers of Otto Fenichel, Volume I*, New York: W. W. Norton, 1953, pp. 97–112.

30. Schafer, *op. cit.*, 1959, p. 357; Fliess, *op. cit.*; Beres and Arlow, *op. cit.* See also the earlier formulation of transient identification by David Beres, "The Role of Empathy in Psychotherapy and Psychoanalysis," *Journal of the Hillside Hospital*, 17(1968):362–369.

31. Greenson, *op. cit.*; Theodore Shapiro, "The Development and Distortions of Empathy," *Psychoanalytic Quarterly*, 43(1974):4–25; Dan H. Buie, "Empathy: Its Nature and Limitations," *Journal of the American Psychoanalytic Association*, 29(1981):281–307; Michael F. Basch, "Empathic Understanding: A Review of the Concept and Some Theoretical Considerations," *Journal of the American Psychoanalytic Association*, 31(1983):101–126.

32. W. W. Meissner, "Notes on Identification. III. The Concept of Identification," *Psychoanalytic Quarterly*, 41(1972):224–260.

33. Shapiro, *op. cit.*

34. Annie Reich, "Empathy and Countertransference" (1966), in *Annie Reich: Psychoanalytic Contributions*, New York: International Universities Press, 1973, pp. 344–360.

35. Roy Schafer, "Identification: A Comprehensive and Flexible Definition," *Aspects of Internalization*, New York: International Universities Press, 1968, pp. 140–180.

36. See Michael H. Tansey and Walter F. Burke, "Projective Identification and the Empathic Process," *Contemporary Psychoanalysis*, 21(1985):42–69.

37. Schafer, *op. cit.*, 1959; Beres and Arlow, *op. cit.*

38. Beres and Arlow, *op. cit.*

39. See, for a discussion of the creation of insight in relation to the therapeutic action of psychoanalysis: Hans Loewald, "On the Therapeutic Action of Psychoanalysis," *Papers on Psychoanalysis*, New Haven: Yale University Press, 1980, pp. 221–256.

40. For similar conceptions of the therapist's model of the patient, see Schafer, *op. cit.*, 1959; Greenson, *op. cit.*; Daniel P. Schwartz, "Loving Action and the Shape of the Object," in David B. Feinsilver (ed.), *Towards a Comprehensive Model for Schizophrenic Disorders*, Hillsdale, N.J.: The Analytic Press, 1986, pp. 323–344.

41. Langer's original term referred to the presentational form of symbols, but it is readily applied to knowledge. See Susan Langer, *Philosophy in a New Key*, Cambridge: Harvard University Press, 1942.

42. Richard Wilbur, "Love Calls Us to the Things of this World," *The Poems of Richard Wilbur*, New York: Harcourt, Brace and World, 1963, p. 65.

43. For a similar epistemological perspective, see Arnold Goldberg, "On the Scientific Status of Empathy," *Annual of Psychoanalysis*, 11(1983):155–169; Timothy Binkley, "On the Truth and Probity of Metaphor," *Journal of Aesthetics and Art Criticism*, 33(1974):171–180.

44. Rothenberg, *The Emerging Goddess*; "Janusian Process and Scientific Creativity."

45. A seemingly paradoxical feature of the creative process is the arousal of anxiety. Creative persons deliberately engage and re-engage in thinking and activity that instigates anxiety. The motivation for this courting of anxiety in the creative process is both the achievement of some degree of insight and the pleasure generated by anxiety arousal and subsequent anxiety reduction. See Rothenberg, *The Emerging Goddess*.

46. *Ibid.*, pp. 15–99.

47. Beres and Arlow, *op. cit.*

48. Dean P. Eyre, "Identification and Empathy," *International Review of Psycho-Analysis*, 5(1978):351–359; Stephen L. Post, "Origins, Elements and Functions of Therapeutic Empathy," *International Journal of Psycho-Analysis*, 61(1980):277–293; Bennett Simon, "Confluence of Visual Image Between Patient and Analyst: Communication of Failed Communication," *Psychoanalytic Inquiry*, 1(1981):471–488; Ping-Nie Pao, "Therapeutic Empathy and the Treatment of Schizophrenics," *Psychoanalytic Inquiry*, 3(1983):145–167.

49. Simon, *op. cit.*, quotations in this example are all from p. 473.

50. Joseph D. Lichtenberg, "The Empathic Mode of Perception and Alternate Vantage Points for Psychoanalytic Work," *Psychoanalytic Inquiry*, 1(1981):329–355.

51. Evelyne A. Schwaber, "Empathy: A Mode of Analytic Listening," *Psychoanalytic Inquiry*, 1(1981):357–392.

52. Greenson, *op. cit.*, p. 421, emphasis added.

53. Despite Greenson's use of the linguistic construction "as if I were the patient," the context makes clear that full mental superimposition, rather than substitution, occurred.

54. Beres and Arlow, *op. cit.*

55. Monroe Beardsley, "On the Creation of Art," *Journal of Aesthetics and Art Criticism*, 23(1965):291–304.

56. In his personal description of the process of creating the general theory of relativity, Einstein referred to his initial feelings in the following way: "The thought that one is dealing here with two fundamentally different cases [the Faraday and Maxwell-Lorentz theories] was, for me, unbearable [war mir unerträglich]." See Rothenberg, *The Emerging Goddess*, p. 112; Albert Rothenberg, "Einstein's Creative Thinking and the General Theory of Relativity: A Documented Report," *American Journal of Psychiatry*, 136(1979):38–43.

57. See discussion of investigator interference effects in Rothenberg, *The Emerging Goddess*, p. 392, n.2, and description of mirror image effects in Chapter 3, pp. 53–81. See also discussion in Rothenberg, "Janusian Process and Scientific Creativity," pp. 116–117.

58. See note 45 above.

59. See Rothenberg, *The Emerging Goddess*, and Albert Rothenberg, "Creativity, Articulation and Psychotherapy," *Journal of the American Academy of Psychoanalysis*, 11(1983):55–85.

CHAPTER V (*pages 78–101*)

1. Arthur Miller, personal correspondence, September 27, 1976.

2. Rothenberg, *op. cit.*, 1969.

3. For descriptions and analyses of these experiences, see Rothenberg, *The Emerging Goddess*, pp. 100–124, 138–206; "Janusian Process and Scientific Creativity."

4. Theodore Reik, *Surprise and the Psychoanalyst*, New York: E. P. Dutton and Co., 1937, pp. 80–84.

5. *Ibid.*, p. 80.

6. *Ibid.*

7. *Ibid.*, p. 81.

8. *Ibid.*, p. 84.

9. *Ibid.*, p. 82, emphasis added.

10. Reik believed that his own intuition was the result of unconscious processes. Although unconscious processes surely play some role, his actual description indicates an active conscious formulation. Creative people frequently do not pay careful attention to their mental state and the structure of their thinking. Moreover, janusian formulations are surprising and therefore may seem to arise from a source extrinsic to consciousness.

11. Sigmund Freud, *Interpretation of Dreams* (1900), *Standard Edition*, 4, New York: W. W. Norton, 1953, dedication page.

12. Sigmund Freud, letter to Fliess, April 12, 1896, in Marie Bonaparte, Anna Freud, and Ernst Kris (eds.), *The Origins of Psychoanalysis*, New York: Basic Books, 1954, p. 172.

13. Freud, *op. cit.*, 1900, p. 133.

14. Sigmund Freud, *The Psychopathology of Everyday Life* (1901), *Standard Edition*, 6:1–279, New York: W. W. Norton, 1960.

15. Brian Bird, "Notes on Transference: Universal Phenomenon and Hardest Part of Analysis," *Journal of the American Psychoanalytic Association*, 20(1972):267–301, p. 269.

16. Sigmund Freud, "On the History of the Psycho-analytic Movement" (1914), *Standard Edition*, 14:7–71, New York: W. W. Norton, 1957, p. 12.

17. Sigmund Freud, "The Psychotherapy of Hysteria," in Josef Breuer and Sigmund Freud, *Studies in Hysteria* (1893–5), *Standard Edition*, 2:255–305, New York: W. W. Norton, 1955, p. 302.

18. Sigmund Freud, "Fragment of Analysis of a Case of Hysteria" (1905), *Standard Edition*, 7:7–122, New York: W. W. Norton, 1953, p. 117.

19. Sigmund Freud, "Introductory Lectures on Psychoanalysis. (Part III)" (1917), *Standard Edition*, 16:243–463, New York: W. W. Norton, 1963, p. 444.

20. See Merton Gill's creative extension of these early issues pertaining to transference in: *Analysis of Transference. Volume I*, New York: International Universities Press, 1982.

21. In Chapter IV here, and in Rothenberg, *The Emerging Goddess*, I have discussed the mirror reversal relationship between the janusian process and equivalence of opposites in the unconscious.

22. Sigmund Freud, *Jokes and Their Relationship to the Unconscious* (1905), *Standard Edition*, 8:9–238, New York: W. W. Norton, 1960, p. 205. Emphasis added. Acknowledgment to Joanna Fanos for her aid in identifying this passage.

23. Sigmund Freud, "Three Essays on Sexuality" (1905), *Standard Edition*, 8:135–243, New York: W. W. Norton, 1953, pp. 159–160.

24. Sigmund Freud, "Notes Upon a Case of Obsessional Neurosis" (1909), *Standard Edition*, 10:155–249, New York: W. W. Norton, 1955, p. 192.

25. Sigmund Freud, "The Uncanny" (1919), *Standard Edition*, 17:219–252, New York: W. W. Norton, 1955.

26. *Ibid.*, pp. 220, 224, 226.

27. *Ibid.*, p. 245.

28. The distinction between dialectical reasoning and the janusian process is demonstrated and discussed at length in relation to Bohr's formulation of the theory of complementarity in Rothenberg, "Janusian Process and Scientific Creativity."

29. Sigmund Freud, "A Case of Successful Treatment by Hypnotism With Some Remarks on the Origin of Hysterical Symptoms Through 'Counterwill'" (1892–93), *Standard Edition*, 1:117–128, New York: W. W. Norton, 1966.

30. Harold P. Blum, "The Curative and Creative Aspects of Insight," *Journal of the American Psychoanalytic Association Supplement*, 27(1979):41–69, p. 62.

31. Freud, *op. cit.*, 1892–93, p. 119.

32. *Ibid.*

33. *Ibid.*

34. *Ibid.*, p. 120.

35. Blum, *op. cit.*, p. 64.

36. *Ibid.*, p. 65.

37. This step, of course, required him to recognize that the problem was in fact psychological and that itself was a portion of his recognition of salient features.

38. Arlow, *op. cit.* Quotations in this paragraph are taken from pages 104–105.

39. Arlow's description makes the so-called intuition sound like a flash of insight.

40. *Ibid.*, p. 117.

41. *Ibid.*

42. Phyllis Greenacre, "On Reconstruction," *Journal of the American Psychoanalytic Association*, 23(1975):693–712, p. 697.

43. The use of the word "cognitive" here is quite restrictive; intuitive processes are also cognitive, for example.

44. Rothenberg, *The Emerging Goddess*, pp. 207–251.

45. Acknowledgment to Dr. Jonathan Aronoff for this case material.

46. Roy Schafer, *Language and Insight*, New Haven: Yale University Press, 1978, p. 100.

47. Georg W. F. Hegel, *Hegel's Logic: Being Part One of the Encyclopedia of Philosophical Sciences* (1830), William Wallace (trans.), London: Oxford University Press, 1975.

48. For interesting extensions and further formulations regarding conflict and working-through, see Anton O. Kris, "Resistance in Convergent and in Divergent Conflicts," *Psychoanalytic Quarterly*, 54(1985):537–568, and Leo Rangell, "Structural Problems in Intrapsychic Conflict," *Psychoanalytic Study of the Child*, 18(1963):103–138; Kris introduces a distinction between convergent and divergent conflict and Rangell discusses topological conflict. Neither of these extensions contradicts the description of clinical recognition of conflict I have presented here but point to potential enriching developments regarding further understanding of the janusian process.

49. Rothenberg, *op. cit.*; 1971, *The Emerging Goddess*, pp. 58ff.

50. In the mirror reversal operation, the janusian process serves as a template to equivalence of opposites in the unconscious. Defensive negation is one of the mechanisms through which this template functions.

CHAPTER VI *(pages 102–126)*

1. *Webster's, op. cit.*

2. Zeno's paradox (discussed by Plato and Parmenides) and Russell's and Cantor's paradoxes have been important milestones in the development of modern philosophical perspectives.

3. August Aichhorn, *Wayward Youth*, London: Imago Publishing Co., 1951, pp. 139–142.

4. Gregory Bateson, Don D. Jackson, Jay Haley, and John H. Weakland, "Toward a Theory of Schizophrenia," *Behavioral Science*, 1(1956):251–264.

5. Jay Haley, "Development of a Theory: A History of a Research Project," in Carlos E. Sluzki and Donald C. Ransom (eds.), *Double Bind: The Foundation of the Communicational Approach to the Family*, New York: Grune and Stratton, 1976, pp. 59–104.

6. Viktor E. Frankl, "Paradoxical Intention: A Logotherapeutic Technique," *American Journal of Psychotherapy*, 14(1960):520–535.

7. Mara Selvini-Palazzoli, Luigi Boscolo, Gianfranco Cecchin, Giuliana Prata, *Paradox and Counterparadox: A New Model in the Therapy of the Family in Schizophrenic Transaction*, Elisabeth V. Burt (trans.), New York: Jason Aronson, 1978.

8. Jay Haley, "Whither Family Therapy?" *Family Process*, 1(1962):69–100; *Problem-Solving Therapy*, San Francisco: Jossey-Bass Publishers, 1976; *Leaving Home: The Therapy of Disturbed Young People*, New York: McGraw-Hill Book Co., 1980; Paul Watzlawick, John H. Weakland, Richard Fisch, *Change: Principles of Problem Formation and Problem Resolution*, New York: W. W. Norton, 1974; Gerald R. Weeks and Luciano L'Abate, "A Compilation of Paradoxical Methods," *American Journal of Family Therapy*, 7(1979):61–76; Peggy Papp, "The Greek Chorus and Other Techniques of Paradoxical Therapy," *Family Process*, 19(1980):45–57; Cloë Madanes, "Protection, Paradox, and Pretending," *Family Process*, 19(1980):73–85; Michael Rohrbaugh, Howard Tennen, Samuel Press, Larry White, "Compliance, Defiance, and Therapeutic Paradox," *American Journal of Orthopsychiatry*, 51(1981):454–467.

9. Papp, *op. cit.*

10. Jay Haley, *Ordeal Therapy*, San Francisco: Jossey-Bass Publishers, 1984.

11. Rohrbaugh *et al.*, *op. cit.*, p. 456.

12. Haley, *op. cit.*, 1980, pp. 244–253.

13. Lyman C. Wynne, "Paradoxical Interventions. Leverage for Change in Individual and Family Systems," in John S. Strauss, Malcolm Bowers, T. Wayne Downey, Stephen Fleck, Stanley Jackson, Ira Levine (eds.), *The Psychotherapy of Schizophrenia*, New York: Plenum, 1980, pp. 191–202.

14. *Ibid.*, pp. 199–200.

15. *Ibid.*, p. 200.

16. *Ibid.*, p. 201.

17. John R. Jordan, "Paradox and Polarity: The Tao of Family Therapy," *Family Process*, 24(1985): 165–174.

18. Robert L. Rosenbaum, "Paradox as Epistemological Jump," *Family Process*, 21(1982):85–90.

19. M. Duncan Stanton, "Fusion, Compression, Diversion, and the Workings of Paradox: A Theory of Therapeutic/Systemic Change," *Family Process*, 23(1984):135–167.

20. Carlos E. Sluzki and Eliseo Verón, "The Double Bind as a Universal Pathogenic Situation," *Family Process*, 10(1971):397–410.

21. John Schwartzman, "Creativity, Pathology and Family Structure: A Cybernetic Metaphor," *Family Process*, 21(1982):113–127.

22. Vernon E. Cronen, Kenneth M. Johnson, and John W. Lannaman, "Paradoxes, Double Binds, and Reflexive Loops: An Alternative Theoretical Perspective," *Family Process*, 21(1982):91–112.

23. Jeffrey L. Bogdan, "Paradoxical Communication as Interpersonal Influence," *Family Process*, 21(1982):443–452.

24. Haley, *op. cit.*, 1976; Rohrbaugh, *op. cit.*; Bogdan, *op. cit.*

25. Rosenbaum, *op. cit.*, p. 88.

26. See Haley, *op. cit.*, 1984, for systematic use of aversive procedures and for descriptions of Erickson's use of this type of intervention. For an earlier description of Erickson's approach, including aversive procedures, see: Jay Haley, *Uncommon Therapy. The Psychiatric Techniques of Milton H. Erickson, M.D.*, New York: W. W. Norton, 1973.

27. Albert Rothenberg, "Eating Disorder as a Modern Obsessive-Compulsive Syndrome," *Psychiatry*, 49(1986):45–53.

28. Lynn Hoffman, *Foundations of Family Therapy*, New York: Basic Books, Inc., 1981, pp. 232–235.

29. Haley, *op. cit.*, 1973, p. 18.

30. *Ibid.*, pp. 17–40.

31. Watzlawick *et al.*, *op. cit.*, p. ix.

32. Sidney Rosen, "The Psychotherapeutic and Hypnotherapeutic Approaches of Milton H. Erickson, M.D.," *The American Journal of Psychoanalysis*, 44(1984):133–145.

33. Milton H. Erickson, Ernest L. Rossi, Sheila I. Rossi, *Hypnotic Realities. The Induction of Clinical Hypnosis and Forms of Indirect Suggestion*, New York: Irvington Publishers, 1976, pp. 6–9.

34. *Ibid.*, p. 72.

35. *Ibid.*; Lankton and Lankton, *op. cit.*

36. Jay Haley (ed.), *Advanced Techniques of Hypnosis and Therapy. Selected Papers of Milton H. Erickson, M.D.*, New York: Grune and Stratton, 1967, p. 128.

37. Milton H. Erickson and Ernest L. Rossi, "Two Level Communication and the Microdynamics of Trance and Suggestion," *American Journal of Clinical Hypnosis*, 18(1976):153–171, p. 160.

38. Alan Leveton, "Between: A Study Showing the Relationships Between Erickson, Winnicott, and Bachelard," in J. Zeig (ed.), *Ericksonian Psychotherapy. Volume II: Clinical Applications*, New York: Brunner/Mazel, 1985, pp. 515–553.

39. This case was reported by Erickson to Haley and described by the latter in Haley, *op. cit.*, 1973, pp. 86–88.

40. Hoffman, *op. cit.*, pp. 233–234.

41. Hoffman, *op. cit.*, points out that the suggestions to the patient to visit both his paternal and maternal grandparents played a role by focusing on a conflict of loyalties the patient may have been experiencing. This supposition is completely in accord with the point I am making here but I have omitted the material regarding the grandparents to avoid unnecessary detail and complexity.

42. The term "action-embedded," as well as other terms applied here to interpretations such as "enacted" or "dramatic" are not formal ones but they are consistent with the concept of "presented knowledge" explained in Chapter IV.

43. Milton H. Erickson and Ernest L. Rossi, *Hypnotherapy. An Exploratory Casebook*, New York: Irvington Publishers, 1979, pp. 102–123, especially pp. 106–107. This case is also reported and discussed in Lankton and Lankton, *op. cit.*, pp. 69–72.

44. Erickson and Rossi, *op. cit.*, 1979, p. 109.

45. Haley, *op. cit.*, 1973, p. 158.

46. Personal communication, Alan and Eva Leveton.

47. See Martin H. Stein, "Irony in Psychoanalysis," *Journal of the American Psychoanalytic Association*, 33(1985):35–57; see also discussion of the ironic vision in Roy Schafer, "The Psychoanalytic Vision of Reality," *International Journal of Psycho-Analysis*, 51(1970):279–297.

48. *Webster's, op. cit.*

49. Wayne C. Booth, *A Rhetoric of Irony*, Chicago: University of Chicago Press, 1974; J. A. K. Thomson, *Irony, An Historical Introduction*, Cambridge: Harvard University Press, 1927; Søren Kierkegaard, *The Concept of Irony: With Constant Reference to Socrates*, M. Lee Capel (trans.), Bloomington: Indiana University Press, 1968.

50. Freud, *op. cit.*, 1905.

51. Personal acknowledgment to Dr. Jules V. Coleman for stimulating my early interest in this topic.

52. See especially: Lawrence S. Kubie, "The Destructive Potential of Humor in Psychotherapy," *American Journal of Psychiatry*, 127(1971):37–42; "Letters to the Editor," by Henry J. Friedman, Richard Schaengold, Morton S. Rapp, Robert Silbert, Richard A. Kunin, Jules V. Coleman, Norman R. Schakne, Francis H. Hoffman, Leon Salzman, and "Reply," by Lawrence Kubie, *American Journal of Psychiatry*, 128(1971):118–121; Warren S. Poland, "The Place of Humor in Psychotherapy," *American Journal of Psychiatry*, 128(1971):635–637; John L. Schimel, "The Function of Wit and Humor in Psychoanalysis," *Journal of the American Academy of Psychoanalysis*, 6(1978):369–379. Kubie takes a broadly negative position about the use of humor in psychotherapy and this is countered to some degree by the other authors listed.

See also, for different types of positions about humor in psychotherapy, the following: Martin Grotjahn, *Beyond Laughter*, New York: Blakiston Division, McGraw-Hill Book Co., 1957; Gilbert J. Rose, "*King Lear* and the Use of Humor in Treatment," *Journal of the American Psychoanalytic Association*, 17(1969):927–940; Eliyahu Rosenheim, "Humor in Psychotherapy," *American Journal of Psychotherapy*, 28(1974):584–591; Irene Bloomfield, "Humor in Psychotherapy and Analysis," *International Journal of Social Psychiatry*, 26(1980):135–141; Steven Sands, "The Use of Humor in Psychotherapy," *Psychoanalytic Review*, 71(1984):441–460.

53. Freud, *op. cit.*, 1905.

54. Stein, *op. cit.*, pp. 48–49.

55. Schafer, *op. cit.*, 1970, p. 294.

CHAPTER VII (*pages 127–148*)

1. See Rothenberg, *op. cit.*, 1969. The term "articulation" was not used in this article to describe the process, as the concept had not at that time been formulated. See also Chapter VIII here.

2. Herman Melville, *Moby Dick*, New York: Random House, 1930, pp. 1–2.

3. The poem is protected by copyright; quotations from the poem and manuscripts are used with permission. Author's name withheld upon request.

4. Italics added.

5. Italics added.

6. Emphasis added. Italics for the word "mind" added in the following paragraph.

7. John Hersey, *Too Far to Walk*, New York: Alfred A. Knopf, 1966.

8. Arousal and anxiety evoked by artistic works are contributory factors in aesthetic appeal. See, for findings regarding arousal in aesthetics, David E. Berlyne, *Aesthetics and Psychobiology*, New York: Appleton-Century-Crofts, 1971. It is, however, the modulation of anxiety and the struggle for psychological freedom from the past and from the effects of repressed unconscious elements that constitute a major aspect of positive aesthetic experience. I discuss these issues at length in Rothenberg, *The Emerging Goddess*.

9. Italics added in the quotations from the manuscript versions.

10. Hersey, *op. cit.*, pp. 211–212.

11. Of course, we cannot rule out transference feelings to me, but these are also incorporated in the articulation process.

12. Kris, *op. cit.*

13. For discussion of the role of inspiration in creativity, its history as a construct, and evidence regarding its defensive and revelatory functions, see Albert Rothenberg, "Poetic Process and Psychotherapy," *Psychiatry*, 3(1972):238–254.

14. David Beres, "Communication in Psychoanalysis and in the Creative Process: A Parallel," *Journal of the American Psychoanalytic Association*, 5(1957):408–423.

15. Rothenberg, *The Emerging Goddess*; Rothenberg and Sobel, *op. cit.*, 1980, and *op. cit.*, 1981; Sobel and Rothenberg, *op. cit.*, 1980.

16. Jacques Lacan, "The Function and Field of Speech and Language in Psychoanalysis," *Ecrits: A Selection*, translated by A. Sheridan, New York: W. W. Norton, 1977, pp. 30–113; for a good presentation of Lacan's concepts, see also John P. Muller and William J. Richardson, *Lacan and Language: A Reader's Guide to the Ecrits*, New York: International Universities Press, 1982.

17. Marshall Edelson, *Language and Interpretation in Psychoanalysis*, New Haven: Yale University Press, 1975.

18. Victor H. Rosen, "Sign Phenomena and Their Relationship to Unconscious Meaning," *International Journal of Psycho-Analysis*, 50(1969):197–207; "The Nature of Verbal Interventions in Psychoanalysis," *Psychoanalysis and Contemporary Science*, 3(1974):189–209.

19. Charles Rycroft, *Imagination and Reality*, New York: International Universities Press, 1968.

20. Loewald, *op. cit.*, pp. 242–243.

21. Articulation has particular effect upon ego boundaries, as boundaries of any type involve both separation and connection of adjoining areas or factors.

22. Sigmund Freud, *op. cit.*, 1900, p. 103. Emphasis added.

CHAPTER VIII (*pages 149–168*)

1. Hermann Paul, *Prinzipien der Sprachgeschichte*, Halle a.d.s.: Niemeyer, 1880.

2. Georg von der Gabelentz, *Die Sprachwissenschaft: Ihre dufgaben Methoden, und Bisherigen Ergebnisse*, Leipzig: T. O. Weigel, 1891.

3. Otto Jespersen, *Progress in Language with Special References to English*, London: S. Sonnenschein, 1894.

4. B. Delbrück, "Amnestische Aphasie," *Sitzungsberichte der Janaischen Gesellschaft für Medizin und Naturwissenschaft*, 10(1887):91.

5. Rudolf Meringer, *Aus dem Leben der Sprache*, Berlin: V. Behr, 1908; Rudolf Meringer and C. Mayer, *Versprechen und Verlesen, Eine Psychologisch-linguistische Studie*, Stuttgart: Göschense Verlagsbuchhandlung, 1895.

6. Sigmund Freud, *op. cit.*, 1901.

7. See Andrew W. Ellis, "On the Freudian Theory of Speech Errors," in Victoria A. Fromkin (ed.), *Errors in Linguistic Performance*, New York: Academic Press, 1980, pp. 123–132; Michael T. Motley, "Verification of 'Freudian Slips' and Semantic Prearticulatory Editing Via Laboratory-Induced Spoonerisms," in Fromkin, *op. cit.*, pp. 133–148.

8. See discussion of the rationale for extending error analysis to the study of literary revision in Rothenberg, *op. cit.*, 1969. With their very high level of skill, literary creators commit errors consisting of discrepancies between intent and execution in the revision process.

9. See discussion of the mirror reversal process leading to unearthing of unconscious contents by both homospatial and janusian processes in Chapters IV and V here and also in Rothenberg, *The Emerging Goddess*.

10. Kris, *op. cit.*

11. Sigmund Freud, "The Subleties of a Faulty Action" (1935), *Standard Edition*, 22:233–235, New York: W. W. Norton, 1964, p. 234.

12. Freud cited this passage as an example of creative writers' understanding of parapraxes. See Sigmund Freud, "Introductory Lectures on Psychoanalysis (Parts I and II)," (1916–1917), *Standard Edition*, 15:15–239, New York: W. W. Norton, 1963, p. 38.

13. Hersey, *op. cit.*

14. Cf. *ibid.*, pp. 107–108, in final version.

15. Italics indicating changes in this section are added.

16. Kris, *op. cit.*

17. See Rothenberg, *op. cit.*, 1969. The quotations from the O'Neill manuscripts used here all appear in that article. They are from manuscripts at the Yale University Beineke Library American Literature Collection.

18. "More Stately Mansions," written by Eugene O'Neill in 1938 (New Haven: Yale University Press, 1964). "The Iceman Cometh" was written in 1940.

19. Italics added in the quotations following.

20. The Bahle study is extensively reported in Camille Jacobs, "Psychology of Music: Some European Studies," *Acta Psychologica*, 17(1960):273–297; see p. 278.

21. Walter R. Reitman, *Cognition and Thought*, New York: John Wiley and Sons, 1966, p. 177.

22. Fleming described this as follows: "While working with staphylococcus variants, culture plates were set aside on the laboratory bench and examined from time to time. In the examination these plates were *necessarily exposed to the air* and they became contaminated with various micro-organisms. It was noticed that around a large colony of a contaminating mould the staphylococcus colonies became transparent and were obviously undergoing lysis." Alexander Fleming, "On the Antibacterial Action of Cultures of a *Penicillium*, With Special Reference to Their Use in the Isolation of B. Influenzae," *British Journal of Experimental Pathology*, 10(1929):226–236, p. 226, emphasis added.

23. For Pasteur's story, see Rene Dubos, *Pasteur and Modern Science*, Garden City, N.Y.: Doubleday, 1960, pp. 113–114; for Roentgen, see J. R. Baker, *The Scientific Life*, London: George Allen and Unwin Ltd., 1942.

24. For a similar formulation of the creative role of chance and error in evolution, see Lewis Thomas, "The Wonderful Mistake," *The Medusa and the Snail. More Notes of a Biology Watcher*, New York: Viking Press, 1979, pp. 27–30.

25. See Gill, *op. cit.*, for a somewhat different perspective on transference.

26. Sigmund Freud, "Remembering, Repeating, and Working Through" (1914), *Standard Edition*, 12:146–156, New York: W. W. Norton, 1958, p. 154. See, for a good review and for references to the psychoanalytic literature on the nature of transference, E. M. Weinshel, "The Transference Neurosis: A Survey of the Literature," *Journal of the American Psychoanalytic Association*, 19(1971):67–88; see also Arlow, *op. cit.*, p. 110, who dissents regarding the instigation of transference by the analytic situation.

27. Loewald, *op. cit.*, p. 250.

28. Arnold Rothstein, *The Narcissistic Pursuit of Perfection*, New York: International Universities Press, 1980.

CHAPTER IX *(pages 169–185)*

1. Freud, *op. cit.*, 1921, p. 110. Also see above, Chapter IV.

2. See Zee, *op. cit.*, for presentation of extensive data and a theory of symmetry as fundamental in the laws of nature and the structure of the Universe.

3. Quoted in Holton, *op. cit.*, 1986, p. 236.

4. Heinz Kohut, *op. cit.*, 1971, pp. 49ff.; Robert D. Stolorow, "Self Psychology—A Structural Psychology," in Joseph D. Lichtenberg and Samuel Kaplan (eds.), *Reflections on Self Psychology*, Hillsdale, N.J.: The Analytic Press, 1983, pp. 281–296.

5. Robert S. Wallerstein, *Forty-Two Lives in Treatment*, New York: The Guilford Press, 1986, pp. 373–388.

6. Jean G. Schimek, "A Critical Re-examination of Freud's Concept of Unconscious Mental Representation," *International Review of Psycho-Analysis*, 2(1975):171–187.

7. Bateson, *et al.*, *op. cit.*

8. P. H. Venables, "Input Dysfunction in Schizophrenia," in Brendan A. Maher (ed.), *Progress in Experimental Personality Research. Vol. 1*, New York: Academic Press, 1964, pp. 1–47.

9. Theodore Lidz, *The Origin and Treatment of Schizophrenic Disorders*, New York: Basic Books, 1973.

Name Index

Subject Index